Modernity

at Large

PUBLIC WORLDS

Dilip Gaonkar and Benjamin Lee

Series Editors

VOLUME 1

Arjun Appadurai, *Modernity at Large: Cultural Dimensions of Globalization*

ARJUN APPADURAI

Modernity

at Large

Cultural Dimensions

of Globalization

PUBLIC WORLDS, VOLUME 1

UNIVERSITY OF MINNESOTA PRESS

MINNEAPOLIS   LONDON

The Public Worlds series is a product of Public Works Publications, which includes Public Planet Books and the journal *Public Culture.*

Chapter 2 is reprinted in revised form from *Public Culture* 2.2 (1990): 1–24. Copyright 1990 Center for Transnational Cultural Studies. Chapter 3 is reprinted in revised form from *Recapturing Anthropology: Working in the Present,* ed. Richard G. Fox. School of American Research Advanced Seminar Series, 191–210. Copyright 1991 School of American Research Press, Santa Fe, New Mexico. Chapter 4 is reprinted in revised form from *Stanford Literature Review* 10.1–2 (1993): 11–23. Copyright 1993 Arjun Appadurai. Chapter 5 is reprinted in revised form from *Consuming Modernity: Public Culture in a South Asian World,* ed. Carol A. Breckenridge (Minneapolis: University of Minnesota Press, 1995), 23–48. Copyright 1995 the Regents of the University of Minnesota. Chapter 6 is reprinted in revised form from *Orientalism and the Postcolonial Predicament: Perspectives on South Asia,* ed. Carol A. Breckenridge and Peter van der Veer (Philadelphia: University of Pennsylvania Press, 1993), 314–39. Copyright 1993 University of Pennsylvania Press. Chapter 8 is reprinted in revised form from *Public Culture* 5.3 (1993): 411–29. Copyright 1993 by The University of Chicago. Chapter 9 is reprinted in revised form from *Counterworks: Managing the Diversity of Knowledge,* ed. Richard Fardon (London and New York: Routledge, 1995). Copyright 1995 Arjun Appadurai.

Published by the University of Minnesota Press
111 Third Avenue South, Suite 290, Minneapolis, MN 55401-2520
http://www.upress.umn.edu
Printed in the United States of America on acid-free paper

Ninth printing 2010

Library of Congress Cataloging-in-Publication Data

Appadurai, Arjun, 1949–
    Modernity at large : cultural dimensions of globalization / Arjun Appadurai.
        p.   cm. — (Public worlds ; v. 1)
    Includes bibliographical references and index.
    ISBN 0-8166-2792-4
    ISBN 0-8166-2793-2 (pbk.)
    1. Culture. 2. Civilization, Modern—1950–   3. Ethnicity.   4. Mass
media—Social aspects.   I. Title.   II. Series.
HM101.A644   1996
306—dc20   96-9276

≈

For my son Alok,

My home in the world

Contents

Acknowledgments

This book was written over a period of six years, and during that time I have benefited from contact with many persons and institutions. The idea for the book took shape during 1989–90, when I was a MacArthur Fellow at the Institute for Advanced Study in Princeton. Parts of it were written while I was at the University of Pennsylvania, as codirector of the Center for Transnational Cultural Studies. It was completed at the University of Chicago, where I have enjoyed a great range of cross-disciplinary conversations at the Chicago Humanities Institute, and where I have benefited from the energies of the Globalization Project. Also, in Chicago during this period, conversations and debates at the Center for Transcultural Studies (previously the Center for Psycho-Social Studies) provided national and international perspectives that were invaluable.

The following individuals have given me valuable criticisms and suggestions in regard to various parts and versions of the chapters in this book: Lila Abu-Lughod, Shahid Amin, Talal Asad, Fredrik Barth, Sanjiv Baruah, Lauren Berlant, John Brewer, Partha Chatterjee, Fernando Coronil, Valentine Daniel, Micaela di Leonardo, Nicholas Dirks, Virginia Dominguez, Richard Fardon, Michael Fischer, Richard Fox, Sandria Freitag, Susan Gal, Clifford Geertz, Peter Geschiere, Michael Geyer, Akhil Gupta, Michael Hanchard, Miriam Hansen, Marilyn Ivy, Orvar Lofgren,

David Ludden, John MacAloon, Achille Mbembe, Ashis Nandy, Gyanendra Pandey, Peter Pels, Roy Porter, Moishe Postone, Paul Rabinow, Bruce Robbins, Roger Rouse, Marshall Sahlins, Lee Schlesinger, Terry Smith, Stanley J. Tambiah, Charles Taylor, Michel-Rolph Trouillot, Greg Urban, Ashutosh Varshney, Toby Volkman, Myron Weiner, and Geoffrey White. To those I have inadvertently overlooked, my sincere apologies.

A few persons deserve special mention for their more general and generous support. My teacher, friend, and colleague Bernard S. Cohn started me on a journey involving anthropology and history in 1970 and has been a steadfast source of ideas, friendship, and critical realism ever since. Nancy Farriss kept me always alert to the challenges of historical comparison and to the meanings of fidelity to the archive. Ulf Hannerz has been my partner in the study of things global since 1984, when we spent a year together at the Center for Advanced Study in the Behavioral Sciences (Palo Alto). Peter van der Veer, in both Philadelphia and Amsterdam, has been a steadfast source of friendship, wit, and engaged debate. John and Jean Comaroff, through both their scholarship and their stimulating presence in the department of anthropology at the University of Chicago, contributed in many ways to the shaping of this book. Sherry Ortner encouraged the project from the start and provided one of two careful, suggestive readings of the manuscript for the University of Minnesota Press. I am grateful to the second, anonymous reader as well. Dilip Gaonkar and Benjamin Lee (coeditors of the series in which this book appears) have been friends, colleagues, and interlocutors in more ways that I can easily describe. Homi Bhabha, Jacqueline Bhabha, Dipesh Chakrabarty, Steven Collins, Prasenjit Duara, and Sheldon Pollock provided a community of ideas which, even as it forms, has helped me complete this book and imagine many futures.

Lisa Freeman, the director of the University of Minnesota Press, and Janaki Bakhle (previously at the Press) stayed with me, combining patience and prodding, critical suggestions and editorial wisdom.

Many students, both at the University of Pennsylvania and the University of Chicago, have been a source of inspiration and energy. I must make special mention of those whose work has enriched the ideas contained in this book: Brian Axel, William Bissell, Caroline Cleaves, Nicholas De Genova, Victoria Farmer, Gautam Ghosh, Manu Goswami, Mark Liechty, Anne Lorimer, Caitrin Lynch, Jacqui McGibbon, Vyjayanthi Rao, Frank Romagosa, Philip Scher, Awadendhra Sharan, Sarah Strauss, Rachel Tolen, Amy Trubek, and Miklos Voros. Eve Darian-Smith, Ritty Lukose, and Janelle Taylor deserve special mention for both their intellectual contributions to this book and for their practical assistance. Caitrin Lynch did a splendid job on the index. Others who have helped in the complex process of producing this text include Namita Gupta Wiggers and Lisa McNair.

My family has lived with this book, always generously and sometimes without knowing it. My wife and colleague, Carol A. Breckenridge, is present in some way on every page: this book is one more document of our life adventure. My son Alok, to whom the book is dedicated, has grown to adulthood with it. His talent for love and his passion for life have been a steady reminder that books are not the world: they are about it.

1

Here and Now

Modernity belongs to that small family of theories that both declares and desires universal applicability for itself. What is new about modernity (or about the idea that its newness is a new kind of newness) follows from this duality. Whatever else the project of the Enlightenment may have created, it aspired to create persons who would, after the fact, have wished to have become modern. This self-fulfilling and self-justifying idea has provoked many criticisms and much resistance, in both theory and everyday life.

In my own early life in Bombay, the experience of modernity was notably synaesthetic and largely pretheoretical. I saw and smelled modernity reading *Life* and American college catalogs at the United States Information Service library, seeing B-grade films (and some A-grade ones) from Hollywood at the Eros Theatre, five hundred yards from my apartment building. I begged my brother at Stanford (in the early 1960s) to bring me back blue jeans and smelled America in his Right Guard when he returned. I gradually lost the England that I had earlier imbibed in my Victorian schoolbooks, in rumors of Rhodes scholars from my college, and in Billy Bunter and Biggles books devoured indiscriminately with books by Richmal Crompton and Enid Blyton. Franny and Zooey, Holden Caulfield, and Rabbit Angstrom slowly eroded that part of me that had been, until then, forever England. Such are the little defeats that explain how England lost the Empire in postcolonial Bombay.

I did not know then that I was drifting from one sort of postcolonial subjectivity (Anglophone diction, fantasies of debates in the Oxford Union, borrowed peeks at *Encounter*, a patrician interest in the humanities) to another: the harsher, sexier, more addictive New World of Humphrey Bogart reruns, Harold Robbins, *Time*, and social science, American-style. By the time I launched myself into the pleasures of cosmopolitanism in Elphinstone College, I was equipped with the Right Stuff—an Anglophone education, an upper-class Bombay address (although a middle-class family income), social connections to the big men and women of the college, a famous (now deceased) brother as an alumnus, a sister with beautiful girl-friends already in the college. But the American bug had bit me. I found myself launched on the journey that took me to Brandeis University (in 1967, when students were an unsettling ethnic category in the United States) and then on to the University of Chicago. In 1970, I was still drifting toward a rendezvous with American social science, area studies, and that triumphal form of modernization theory that was still a secure article of Americanism in a bipolar world.

The chapters that follow can be seen as an effort to make sense of a journey that began with modernity as embodied sensation in the movies in Bombay and ended face-to-face with modernity-as-theory in my social science classes at the University of Chicago in the early 1970s. In these chapters, I have sought to thematize certain cultural facts and use them to open up the relationship between modernization as fact and as theory.[1] This reversal of the process through which I experienced the modern might account for what might otherwise seem like an arbitrary disciplinary privileging of the cultural, a mere professional anthropological bias.

The Global Now

All major social forces have precursors, precedents, analogs, and sources in the past. It is these deep and multiple genealogies (see chap. 3) that have frustrated the aspirations of modernizers in very different societies to synchronize their historical watches. This book, too, argues for a general rupture in the tenor of intersocietal relations in the past few decades. This view of change—indeed, of rupture—needs to be explicated and distinguished from some earlier theories of radical transformation.

One of the most problematic legacies of grand Western social science

(Auguste Comte, Karl Marx, Ferdinand Toennies, Max Weber, Émile Durkheim) is that it has steadily reinforced the sense of some single moment—call it the modern moment—that by its appearance creates a dramatic and unprecedented break between past and present. Reincarnated as the break between tradition and modernity and typologized as the difference between ostensibly traditional and modern societies, this view has been shown repeatedly to distort the meanings of change and the politics of pastness. Yet the world in which we now live—in which modernity is decisively at large, irregularly self-conscious, and unevenly experienced—surely does involve a general break with all sorts of pasts. What sort of break is this, if it is not the one identified by modernization theory (and criticized in chap. 7)?

Implicit in this book is a theory of rupture that takes media and migration as its two major, and interconnected, diacritics and explores their joint effect on the *work of the imagination* as a constitutive feature of modern subjectivity. The first step in this argument is that electronic media decisively change the wider field of mass media and other traditional media. This is not a monocausal fetishization of the electronic. Such media transform the field of mass mediation because they offer new resources and new disciplines for the construction of imagined selves and imagined worlds. This is a relational argument. Electronic media mark and reconstitute a much wider field, in which print mediation and other forms of oral, visual, and auditory mediation might continue to be important. Through such effects as the telescoping of news into audio-video bytes, through the tension between the public spaces of cinema and the more exclusive spaces of video watching, through the immediacy of their absorption into public discourse, and through their tendency to be associated with glamour, cosmopolitanism, and the new, electronic media (whether associated with the news, politics, family life, or spectacular entertainment) tend to interrogate, subvert, and transform other contextual literacies. In the chapters that follow, I track some ways in which electronic mediation transforms preexisting worlds of communication and conduct.

Electronic media give a new twist to the environment within which the modern and the global often appear as flip sides of the same coin. Always carrying the sense of distance between viewer and event, these media nevertheless compel the transformation of everyday discourse. At the same time, they are resources for experiments with self-making in all sorts of societies, for all sorts of persons. They allow scripts for possible lives to be imbricated with the glamour of film stars and fantastic film plots and yet also to be tied to the plausibility of news shows, documentaries, and other black-and-white forms of telemediation and printed text. Because of the sheer multiplicity of the forms in which they appear (cinema, television, computers, and telephones) and because of the rapid way in which they move through daily life routines, electronic media provide resources for self-imagining as an everyday social project.

As with mediation, so with motion. The story of mass migrations (voluntary and forced) is hardly a new feature of human history. But when it is juxtaposed with the rapid flow of mass-mediated images, scripts, and sensations, we have a new order of instability in the production of modern subjectivities. As Turkish guest workers in Germany watch Turkish films in their German flats, as Koreans in Philadelphia watch the 1988 Olympics in Seoul through satellite feeds from Korea, and as Pakistani cabdrivers in Chicago listen to cassettes of sermons recorded in mosques in Pakistan or Iran, we see moving images meet deterritorialized viewers. These create diasporic public spheres, phenomena that confound theories that depend on the continued salience of the nation-state as the key arbiter of important social changes.

Thus, to put it summarily, electronic mediation and mass migration mark the world of the present not as technically new forces but as ones that seem to impel (and sometimes compel) the work of the imagination. Together, they create specific irregularities because both viewers and images are in simultaneous circulation. Neither images nor viewers fit into circuits or audiences that are easily bound within local, national, or regional spaces. Of course, many viewers may not themselves migrate. And many mass-mediated events are highly local in scope, as with cable television in some parts of the United States. But few important films, news broadcasts, or television spectacles are entirely unaffected by other media events that come from further afield. And few persons in the world today do not have a friend, relative, or coworker who is not on the road to somewhere else or already coming back home, bearing stories and possibilities. In this sense, both persons and images often meet unpredictably, outside the certainties of home and the cordon sanitaire of local and national media effects. This mobile and unforeseeable relationship between mass-mediated events and migratory audiences defines the core of the link between globalization and the modern. In the chapters that follow, I show that the work of the imagination, viewed in this context, is neither purely emancipatory nor entirely disciplined but is a space of contestation in which individuals and groups seek to annex the global into their own practices of the modern.

The Work of the Imagination

Ever since Durkheim, and the work of the *Anneés Sociologiques* group, anthropologists have learned to regard collective representations as social facts—that is, to see them as transcending individual volition, as weighted with the force of social morality, and as objective social realities. What I wish to suggest is that there has been a shift in recent decades, building on technological changes over the past century or so, in which the imagination has become a collective, social fact. This development, in turn, is the basis of the plurality of imagined worlds.

On the face of it, it seems absurd to suggest that there is anything new about the role of the imagination in the contemporary world. After all, we are now accustomed to thinking about all societies as having produced their versions of art, myth, and legend, expressions that implied the potential evanescence of ordinary social life. In these expressions, all societies showed that they could both transcend and reframe ordinary social life by recourse to mythologics of various kinds in which social life was imaginatively deformed. In dreams, finally, individuals even in the most simple societies have found the space to refigure their social lives, live out proscribed emotional states and sensations, and see things that have then spilled over into their sense of ordinary life. All these expressions, further, have been the basis of a complex dialogue between the imagination and ritual in many human societies, through which the force of ordinary social norms was somehow deepened, through inversion, irony, or the performative intensity and the collaborative work demanded by many kinds of ritual. All this is the surest sort of knowledge bequeathed to us by the best of canonical anthropology over the past century.

In suggesting that the imagination in the postelectronic world plays a newly significant role, I rest my case on three distinctions. First, the imagination has broken out of the special expressive space of art, myth, and ritual and has now become a part of the quotidian mental work of ordinary people in many societies. It has entered the logic of ordinary life from which it had largely been successfully sequestered. Of course, this has precedents in the great revolutions, cargo cults, and messianic movements of other times, in which forceful leaders implanted their visions into social life, thus creating powerful movements for social change. Now, however, it is no longer a matter of specially endowed (charismatic) individuals, injecting the imagination where it does not belong. Ordinary people have begun to deploy their imaginations in the practice of their everyday lives. This fact is exemplified in the mutual contextualizing of motion and mediation.

More people than ever before seem to imagine routinely the possibility that they or their children will live and work in places other than where they were born: this is the wellspring of the increased rates of migration at every level of social, national, and global life. Others are dragged into new settings, as the refugee camps of Thailand, Ethiopia, Tamil Nadu, and Palestine remind us. For these people, they move and must drag their imagination for new ways of living along with them. And then there are those who move in search of work, wealth, and opportunity often because their current circumstances are intolerable. Slightly transforming and extending Albert Hirschman's important terms *loyalty* and *exit*, we may speak of diasporas of hope, diasporas of terror, and diasporas of despair. But in every case, these diasporas bring the force of the imagination, as both memory and desire, into the lives of many ordinary people, into mythographies different from the disciplines of myth and ritual of the classic sort. The key difference here is that these new mythographies are charters for new social projects, and not just a counterpoint to the certainties of daily life. They move the glacial force of the habitus into the quickened beat of improvisation for large groups of people. Here the images, scripts, models, and narratives that come through mass mediation (in its realistic and fictional modes) make the difference between migration today and in the past. Those who wish to move, those who have moved, those who wish to return, and those who choose to stay rarely formulate their plans outside the sphere of radio and television, cassettes and videos, newsprint and telephone. For migrants, both the politics of adaptation to new environments and the stimulus to move or return are deeply affected by a mass-mediated imaginary that frequently transcends national space.

The second distinction is between imagination and fantasy. There is a large and respectable body of writing, notably by the critics of mass culture of the Frankfurt School and anticipated in the work of Max Weber, that views the modern world as growing into an iron cage and predicts that the imagination will be stunted by the forces of commoditization, industrial capitalism, and the generalized regimentation and secularization of the world. The modernization theorists of the past three decades (from Weber by way of Talcott Parsons and Edward Shils to Daniel Lerner, Alex Inkeles, and many others) largely accepted the view of the modern world as a space of shrinking religiosity (and greater scientism), less play (and increasingly regimented leisure), and inhibited spontaneity at every level. There are many strands in this view, strands that link theorists as different as Norbert Elias and Robert Bell, but there is something fundamentally wrong with it. The error works on two levels. First, it is based on a premature requiem for the death of religion and the victory of science. There is vast evidence in new religiosities of every sort that religion is not only not dead but that it may be more consequential than ever in today's highly mobile and interconnected global politics. On another level, it is wrong to assume that the electronic media are the opium of the masses. This view, which is only beginning to be corrected, is based on the notion that the mechanical arts of reproduction largely reprimed ordinary people for industrial work. It is far too simple.

There is growing evidence that the consumption of the mass media throughout the world often provokes resistance, irony, selectivity, and, in general, *agency*. Terrorists modeling themselves on Rambo-like figures (who have themselves generated a host of non-Western counterparts); housewives reading romances and soap operas as part of their efforts to construct their own lives; Muslim family gatherings listening to speeches by Islamic leaders on cassette tapes; domestic servants in South India taking packaged tours to Kashmir: these are all examples of the active way in which media are appropriated by people throughout the world. T-shirts, billboards, and graffiti as well as rap music, street dancing, and slum housing all show that the images of the media are quickly moved into local repertoires of irony, anger, humor, and resistance.

Nor is this just a matter of Third World people reacting to American media, but it is equally true of people throughout the world reacting to their own national, electronic media. On these grounds alone, the theory of media as the opium of the people needs to be looked at with great skepticism. This is not to suggest that consumers are *free* agents, living happily in a world of safe malls, free lunches, and quick fixes. As I suggest in chapter 4, consumption in the contemporary world is often a form of drudgery, part of the capitalist civilizing process. Nevertheless, where there is consumption there is pleasure, and where there is pleasure there is agency. Freedom, on the other hand, is a rather more elusive commodity.

Further, the idea of fantasy carries with it the inescapable connotation of thought divorced from projects and actions, and it also has a private, even individualistic sound about it. The imagination, on the other hand, has a projective sense about it, the sense of being a prelude to some sort of expression, whether aesthetic or otherwise. Fantasy can dissipate (because its logic is so often autotelic), but the imagination, especially when collective, can become the fuel for action. It is the imagination, in its collective forms, that creates ideas of neighborhood and nationhood, of moral economies and unjust rule, of higher wages and foreign labor prospects. The imagination is today a staging ground for action, and not only for escape.

The third distinction is between the individual and collective senses of the imagination. It is important to stress here that I am speaking of the imagination now as a property of collectives, and not merely as a faculty of the gifted individual (its tacit sense since the flowering of European Romanticism). Part of what the mass media make possible, because of the conditions of collective reading, criticism, and pleasure, is what I have elsewhere called a "community of sentiment" (Appadurai 1990), a group that begins to imagine and feel things together. As Benedict Anderson (1983) has shown so well, print capitalism can be one important way in which groups who have never been in face-to-face contact can begin to think of themselves as Indonesian or Indian or Malaysian. But other forms of electronic capitalism can have similar, and even more powerful effects, for they do not work only at the level of the nation-state. Collective experiences of the mass media, especially film and video, can create sodalities of worship and charisma, such as those that formed regionally around the Indian female deity Santoshi Ma in the seventies and eighties and transnationally around Ayatollah Khomeini in roughly the same period. Similar sodalities can form around sport and internationalism, as the transnational effects of the Olympics so clearly show. Tenements and buildings house video clubs in places like Kathmandu and Bombay. Fan clubs and political followings emerge from small-town media cultures, as in South India.

These sodalities resemble what Diana Crane (1972) has called "invisible colleges" in reference to the world of science, but they are more volatile, less professionalized, less subject to collectively shared criteria of pleasure, taste, or mutual relevance. They are communities in themselves but always potentially communities for themselves capable, of moving from shared imagination to collective action. Most important, as I will argue in the conclusion to this chapter, these sodalities are often transnational, even postnational, and they frequently operate beyond the boundaries of the nation. These mass-mediated sodalities have the additional complexity that, in them, diverse local experiences of taste, pleasure, and politics can crisscross with one another, thus creating the possibility of convergences in translocal social action that would otherwise be hard to imagine.

No single episode captures these realities better than the now mind-numbing Salman Rushdie affair, involving a banned book, a religiously mandated death sentence, and an author committed to personal voice and aesthetic freedom. *The Satanic Verses* provoked Muslims (and others) across the world to debate the politics of reading, the cultural relevance of censorship, the dignity of religion, and the freedom of some groups to judge authors without independent knowledge of the text. The Rushdie affair is about a text-in-motion, whose commoditized trajectory brought it outside the safe haven of Western norms about artistic freedom and aesthetic rights into the space of religious rage and the authority of religious scholars in their own transnational spheres. Here, the transnational worlds of liberal aesthetics and radical Islam met head-on, in the very different settings of Bradford and Karachi, New York and New Delhi. In this episode, we can also see how global processes involving mobile texts and migrant audiences create implosive events that fold global pressures into small, already politicized arenas (see chap. 7), producing locality (chap. 9) in new, globalized ways.

This theory of a break—or rupture—with its strong emphasis on electronic mediation and mass migration, is necessarily a theory of the recent past (or the extended present) because it is only in the past two decades or so that media and migration have become so massively globalized, that is to say, active across large and irregular transnational terrains. Why do I consider this theory to be anything more than an update of older social theories of the ruptures of modernization? First, mine is not a teleological theory, with a recipe for how modernization will universally yield rationality, punctuality, democracy, the free market, and a higher gross national product. Second, the pivot of my theory is not any large-scale project of social engineering (whether organized by states, international agencies, or other technocratic elites) but is the everyday cultural practice through which the work of the imagination is transformed. Third, my approach leaves entirely open the question of where the experiments with modernity that electronic mediation enables might lead in terms of nationalism, violence, and social justice. Put another way, I am more deeply ambivalent about prognosis than any variant of classical modernization theory of which I am aware. Fourth, and most important, my approach to the break caused by the joint force of electronic mediation and mass migration is explicitly transnational—even postnational—as I suggest in the last part of this book. As such, it moves away dramatically from the architecture of classical modernization theory, which one might call fundamentally realist insofar as it assumes the salience, both methodological and ethical, of the nation-state.

We cannot simplify matters by imagining that the global is to space what the modern is to time. For many societies, modernity is an elsewhere, just as the global is a temporal wave that must be encountered in *their* present. Globalization has shrunk the distance between elites, shifted key relations between producers and consumers, broken many links between labor and family life, obscured the lines between temporary locales and imaginary national attachments. Modernity now seems more practical and less pedagogic, more experiential and less disciplinary than in the fifties and sixties, when it was mostly experienced (especially for those outside the national elite) through the propaganda apparatuses of the newly independent nation-states and their great leaders, like Jawaharlal Nehru, Gamal Abdel Nasser, Kwame Nkrumah, and Sukarno. The megarhetoric of developmental modernization (economic growth, high technology, agribusiness, schooling, militarization) in many countries is still with us. But it is often punctuated, interrogated, and domesticated by the micronarratives of film, television, music, and other expressive forms, which allow modernity to be rewritten more as vernacular globalization and less as a concession to large-scale national and international policies. As I suggested earlier, there was something of this experiential quality for those (such as myself) born into the ruling classes of the new nations in the fifties and sixties, but for many working people and the poor, this experiential engagement with modernity is a relatively recent fact.

These subversive micronarratives also fuel oppositional movements, ranging from the Shining Path in Peru to Habitat for Humanity, from green movements in Europe to Tamil nationalism in Sri Lanka, from Islamic groups in Egypt to breakaway nationalist guerrillas in Chechnya. In these movements, some of which are repressive and violent while others are democratic and peaceful, we can see that electronic mass mediation and transnational mobilization have broken the monopoly of autonomous nation-states over the project of modernization. The transformation of everyday subjectivities through electronic mediation and the work of the imagination is not only a cultural fact. It is deeply connected to politics, through the new ways in which individual attachments, interests, and aspirations increasingly crosscut those of the nation-state.

The diasporic public spheres that such encounters create are no longer small, marginal, or exceptional. They are part of the cultural dynamic of urban life in most countries and continents, in which migration and mass mediation coconstitute a new sense of the global as modern and the modern as global. Mira Nair's film *Mississippi Masala*, for example, is an epic of diaspora and race redoubled, exploring how Indians transformed and displaced by race relations in Uganda deal with the intricacies of race in the American South, all the time retaining their sense of Indianness-in-motion. The viewing of cricket matches between India and Pakistan by migrants in the Gulf states from these countries (see chap. 5) is about the peculiarities of diasporic nationalism in an emergent Indian Ocean politics. The intense battles over the English language and about immigrant rights now heating up (again) in the United States are not just one more variant on the politics of pluralism: they are about the capability of American politics to contain the diasporic politics of Mexicans in Southern California, Haitians in Miami, Colombians in New York, and Koreans in Los Angeles. Indeed, as I will propose in my concluding observations, it is the widespread appearance of various kinds of diasporic public spheres that constitute one special diacritic of the global modern.

So much for the global now. There is a here to these chapters as well. They are written in part out of an encounter between my postwar Anglophone upbringing and my encounter with the American social-science story of modernization as the theory of the true, the good, and the inevitable. They are also written from a professional perspective shaped substantially by two American research formations within which I have had the bulk of my training and in which I have spent much of my life as an academic: these are anthropology and area studies. Although this is a book about globalization, it is marked and constrained by the contests of the past two decades within both these American academic formations. Thus its epistemological anxieties are decidedly local, even if locality is no longer what it used to be (chap. 9).

The Eye of Anthropology

Anthropology is my archive of lived actualities, found in all sorts of ethnographies about peoples who have lived very different sorts of lives from my own, today and in the past. The archive of anthropology is a shadow presence in all the chapters that follow. That is not because it is inherently better than some other disciplinary archive. Indeed, critiques of this archive have been trenchant and untiring in the past fifteen years. But it is the one I best know how to read. As an archive, it also has the advantage of reminding one that every similarity hides more than one difference, and that similarities and differences conceal one another indefinitely, so that the last turtle is always a matter of methodological convenience or stamina. This archive, and the sensibility that it produces in the professional anthropologist, predisposes me strongly toward the idea that globalization is not the story of cultural homogenization. This latter argument is the very least that I would want the reader to take away from this book. But anthropology brings with it a professional tendency to privilege the cultural as the key diacritic in many practices (that to others might appear simply human, or stupid, or calculating, or patriotic, or something else). Because this book claims to be about the *cultural* dimensions of globalization, let me spell out the special force that this adjective carries in my usage.

I find myself frequently troubled by the word *culture* as a noun but centrally attached to the adjectival form of the word, that is, *cultural*. When I reflect on why this is so, I realize that much of the problem with the noun form has to do with its implication that culture is some kind of object, thing, or substance, whether physical or metaphysical. This substantialization seems to bring culture back into the discursive space of race, the very idea it was originally designed to combat. Implying a mental substance, the noun *culture* appears to privilege the sort of sharing, agreeing, and bounding that fly in the face of the facts of unequal knowledge and the differential prestige of lifestyles, and to discourage attention to the worldviews and agency of those who are marginalized or dominated. Viewed as a physical substance, culture begins to smack of any variety of biologisms, including race, which we have certainly outgrown as scientific categories. Alfred Kroeber's term *superorganic* nicely captures both sides of this substantialism, something with which I am not in sympathy. The efforts of the past few decades, notably in American anthropology, to escape this trap by looking at culture largely as a linguistic form (understood mainly in Saussurean structuralist terms) only partly avoids the dangers of such substantialism.

If *culture* as a noun seems to carry associations with some sort of substance in ways that appear to conceal more than they reveal, *cultural* the adjective moves one into a realm of differences, contrasts, and comparisons that is more helpful. This adjectival sense of culture, which builds on the context-sensitive, contrast-centered heart of Saussurean linguistics, seems to me one of the virtues of structuralism that we have tended to forget in our haste to attack it for its ahistorical, formal, binary, mentalist, and textualist associations.

The most valuable feature of the concept of culture is the concept of difference, a contrastive rather than a substantive property of certain things. Although the term *difference* has now taken on a vast set of associations (principally because of the special use of the term by Jacques Derrida and his followers), its main virtue is that it is a useful heuristic that can highlight points of similarity and contrast between all sorts of categories: classes, genders, roles, groups, and nations. When we therefore point to a practice, a distinction, a conception, an object, or an ideology as having a cultural dimension (notice the adjectival use), we stress the idea of situated difference, that is, difference in relation to something local, embodied, and significant. This point can be summarized in the following form: culture is not usefully regarded as a substance but is better regarded as a dimension of phenomena, a dimension that attends to situated and embodied difference. Stressing the dimensionality of culture rather than its substantiality permits our thinking of culture less as a property of individuals and groups and more as a heuristic device that we can use to talk about difference.

But there are many kinds of differences in the world and only some of these are cultural. And here I bring in a second component of my proposal about the adjectival form of the word *culture*. I suggest that we regard as cultural only those differences that either express, or set the groundwork for, the mobilization of group identities. This qualification provides a brute principle of selection that focuses us on a variety of differences having to do with group identity, both within and outside any particular social group. In putting the mobilization of group identities at the heart of the adjective *cultural*, I have in fact made a move that looks, at first glance, retrogressive, as it appears that I am beginning to bring the word *culture* uncomfortably close to the idea of ethnicity. And that gets me into some new problems that need to be unraveled.

Before I try to do the unraveling, which will allow me to move toward the idea of culturalism, let me review where we have been. Resisting ideas of culture that tempt us to think of actual social groups as cultures, I have also resisted the noun form *culture* and suggested an adjectival approach to culture, which stresses its contextual, heuristic, and comparative dimensions and orients us to the idea of culture as difference, especially difference in the realm of group identity. I have therefore suggested that culture is a pervasive dimension of human discourse that exploits difference to generate diverse conceptions of group identity.

Having veered so close to the idea of ethnicity—the idea of naturalized group identity—it is important to be clear about the relation between culture and group identity that I seek to articulate. Culture, unmarked, can continue to be used to refer to the plethora of differences that characterize the world today, differences at various levels, with various valences, and with greater and lesser degrees of social consequence. I propose, however, that we restrict the term *culture* as a marked term to the subset of these differences that has been mobilized to articulate the boundary of difference. As a boundary-maintenance question, culture then becomes a matter of group identity as constituted by some differences among others.

But is this not a way of simply equating ethnicity and culture? Yes and no. Yes, because in this usage *culture* would not stress simply the possession of certain attributes (material, linguistic, or territorial) but the consciousness of these attributes and their naturalization as essential to group identity (see chap. 7). That is, rather than falling prey to the assumption, at least as old as Weber, that ethnicity rests on some sort of extension of the primordial idea of kinship (which is in turn biological and genealogical), the idea of ethnicity I propose takes the conscious and imaginative construction and mobilization of differences as its core. Culture 1, constituting a virtually open-ended archive of differences is consciously shaped into Culture 2, that subset of these differences that constitutes the diacritics of group identity.

But this process of mobilizing certain differences and linking them to group identity is also unlike ethnicity, at least in an older understanding, because it does not depend on the extension of primordial sentiments to larger and larger units in some sort of unidirectional process, nor does it make the mistake of supposing that larger social units simply draw on the sentiments of family and kinship to give emotional force to large-scale group identities. Thus, in chapter 5 I show that far from drawing on the existing repertoire of emotions and moving them into a larger arena, Indian cricket is a large-scale form that comes to be inscribed on the body through a variety of practices of increasingly smaller scale. This logic is just the reverse of the old primordialist (or extensionist) idea of ethnic identity.

The idea of culture as involving the naturalized organization of certain differences in the interests of group identity, through and in the historical process, and through and in the tensions between agents and structures, comes closer to what has been called the instrumental conception of ethnicity, as opposed to the primordial one. I have two qualifications about this convergence, qualifications that lead to my discussion of culturalism. One is that the ends to which instrumental conceptions of ethnic identity are formed may themselves be counterstructural responses to existing valorizations of difference: they may thus be value-rational rather than instrumental-rational, in Weber's sense. They may have a purely identity-oriented instrumentality rather than an instrumentality that, as is so often implied, is extracultural (economic or political or emotional). Put another way, the mobilization of markers of group difference may itself be part of a contestation of values *about* difference, as distinct from the consequences of difference for wealth, security, or power. My second qualification about most instrumental accounts is that they do not explain the process by which certain criteria of difference, mobilized for group identity (in turn instrumental to other goals) are (re)inscribed into bodily subjects, thus to be experienced as both natural and profoundly incendiary at the same time.

We have now moved one step further, from culture as substance to culture as the dimension of difference, to culture as group identity based on difference, to culture as the process of naturalizing a subset of differences that have been mobilized to articulate group identity. We are at this point in a position to move to the question of culturalism.

We rarely encounter the word *culturalism* by itself: it is usually hitched as a noun to certain prefixes like *bi, multi,* and *inter,* to name the most prominent. But it may be useful to begin to use *culturalism* to designate a feature of movements involving identities consciously in the making. These movements, whether in the United States or elsewhere, are usually directed at modern nation-states, which distribute various entitlements, sometimes including life and death, in accordance with classifications and policies regarding group identity. Throughout the world, faced with the activities of states that are concerned with encompassing their ethnic diversities into fixed and closed sets of cultural categories to which individuals are often assigned forcibly, many groups are consciously mobilizing themselves according to identitarian criteria. Culturalism, put simply, is identity politics mobilized at the level of the nation-state.

This sort of culturalism is my principal focus in chapter 7, where I mount a sustained critique of the primordialist view of the ethnic violence of the past decade. What appears to be a worldwide rebirth of ethnic nationalisms and separatisms is not really what journalists and pundits all too frequently refer to as "tribalism," implying old histories, local rivalries, and deep hatreds. Rather, the ethnic violence we see in many places is part of a wider transformation that is suggested by the term *culturalism.* Culturalism, as I have already suggested, is the conscious mobilization of cultural differences in the service of a larger national or transnational politics. It is frequently associated with extraterritorial histories and memories, sometimes with refugee status and exile, and almost always with struggles for stronger recognition from existing nation-states or from various transnational bodies.

Culturalist movements (for they are almost always efforts to mobilize) are the most general form of the work of the imagination and draw frequently on the fact or possibility of migration or secession. Most important, they are self-conscious about identity, culture, and heritage, all of which tend to be part of the deliberate vocabulary of culturalist movements as they struggle with states and other culturalist focuses and groups. It is this deliberate, strategic, and populist mobilization of cultural material that justifies calling such movements culturalist, though they may vary in many ways. Culturalist movements, whether they involve African-Americans, Pakistanis in Britain, Algerians in France, native Hawaiians, Sikhs, or French speakers in Canada, tend to be counternational and metacultural. In the broadest sense, as I shall suggest in the last part of this book, culturalism is the form that cultural differences tend to take in the era of mass mediation, migration, and globalization.

How Areas Get Studied

The anthropological stress on the cultural, which is the main inflection I wish to give to the debate on globalization, is in my case further sustained by my training and practice as a scholar of area studies, specifically of South Asian studies in the United States. There has not yet been a sustained critical analysis of the link, in the United States, between the emergence of the idea of culture areas in anthropology between the World Wars and the full-fledged formation after World War II of area studies as the major way to look at the strategically significant parts of the developing world. Yet there is little doubt that both perspectives incline one to a particular sort of map in which groups and their ways of life are marked by differences of culture, and in the area-studies formation these differences slide into a topography of national cultural differences. Thus geographical divisions, cultural differences, and national boundaries tended to become isomorphic, and there grew a strong tendency to refract world processes through this sort of national-cultural map of the world. Area studies adds to this spatial imaginary a strong, if sometimes tacit, sense of the strategic importance of information gained in this perspective. This is the reason for the often noted links between the Cold War, government funding, and university expansion in the organization of area-studies centers after World War II. Nevertheless, area studies has provided the major counterpoint to the delusions of the view from nowhere that underwrites much canonical social science. It is this aspect of my training that compelled me to situate my genealogy of the global present in the area I know best: India.

There is a special anxiety that now surrounds the structures and ideologies of area studies in the United States. Recognizing that area studies is somehow deeply tied up with a strategizing world picture driven by U.S. foreign-policy needs between 1945 and 1989, leading figures in the world of universities, foundations, think tanks, and even the government have made it clear that the old way of doing area studies does not make sense in the world after 1989. Thus left-wing critics of area studies, much influenced by the important work of Edward Said on orientalism, have been joined by free-marketeers and advocates of liberalization, who are impatient with what they deride as the narrowness and history fetish of area-studies experts. Area-studies scholars are widely criticized as obstacles to the study of everything from comparison and contemporaneity to civil society and free markets. Of course, no critique that is so sweeping and so sudden could be entirely fair, and the odd mix of its critics suggests that area-studies scholarship might be taking the rap for a wider failure in the U.S. academy to deliver a broader and more prescient picture of the world after 1989.

The area-studies tradition is a double-edged sword. In a society notoriously devoted to exceptionalism, and to endless preoccupation with "America," this tradition has been a tiny refuge for the serious study of foreign languages, alternative worldviews, and large-scale perspectives on sociocultural change outside Europe and the United States. Bedeviled by a certain tendency toward philology (in the narrow, lexical sense) and a certain overidentification with the regions of its specialization, area studies has nonetheless been one of the few serious counterweights to the tireless tendency to marginalize huge parts of the world in the American academy and in American society more generally. Yet the area-studies tradition has probably grown too comfortable with its own maps of the world, too secure in its own expert practices, and too insensitive to transnational processes both today and in the past. So criticism and reform are certainly in order, but how can area studies help to improve the way that world pictures are generated in the United States?

From the perspective advanced here and in the rest of this book, area studies is a salutary reminder that globalization is itself a deeply historical, uneven, and even *localizing* process. Globalization does not necessarily or even frequently imply homogenization or Americanization, and to the extent that different societies appropriate the materials of modernity differently, there is still ample room for the deep study of specific geographies, histories, and languages. What I discuss in chapters 3 and 4 as the relationship between history and genealogy is impossible to engage without a strong sense of the actualities of the *longue durée*, which always produce specific geographies, both real and imagined. If the genealogy of cultural forms is about their circulation across regions, the history of these forms is about their ongoing domestication into local practice. The very interaction of historical and genealogical forms is uneven, diverse, and contingent. In this sense, history, the ruthless discipline of context (in E. P. Thompson's colorful phrase), is everything. But this recognition is not a warrant for knee-jerk localism of the sort sometimes associated with area studies. In any case, area studies is a specific Western technique of research and can hardly pretend to be a simple mirror of the civilizational Other. What does need to be recognized, if the area-studies tradition is to be revitalized, is that locality itself is a historical product and that the histories through which localities emerge are eventually subject to the dynamics of the global. This argument, which culminates in a reminder that there is nothing mere about the local, is the burden of the final chapter of this book.

This mixed review of area studies, a tradition in which I have been immersed for the past twenty-five years, underlies the presence at the center of this book of two chapters about India. These chapters, on the census and on cricket, are a counterpoint to those that might otherwise seem, well, too global. But I hasten to plead that India—in this book—is not to be read as a mere case, example, or instance of something larger than itself. It is, rather a *site* for the examination of how locality emerges in a globalizing world, of how colonial processes underwrite contemporary politics, of how history and genealogy inflect one another, and of how global facts take local form.[2] In this sense these chapters—and the frequent invocations of India throughout the book—are not about India (taken as a natural fact) but about the processes through which contemporary India has emerged. I am aware of the irony (even the contradiction) in having a nation-state be the anchoring referent of a book devoted to globalization and animated by a sense of the end of the era of the nation-state. But here my expertise and my limitations are two sides of the same coin, and I urge the reader to see India as an optic, and not as a reified social fact or a crude nationalist reflex.

I make this detour in recognition of the fact that any book about globalization is a mild exercise in megalomania, especially when it is produced in the relatively privileged circumstances of the American research university. It seems important to identify the knowledge forms through which any such megalomania comes to articulate itself. In my case, these forms—anthropology and area studies—predispose me by habit to the fixing of practices, spaces, and countries into a map of static differences. This is, counterintuitively, a danger even in a book such as this, which is consciously shaped by a concern with diaspora, deterritorialization, and the irregularity of the ties between nations, ideologies, and social movements.

Social Science after Patriotism

The final part of the here and now is a fact about the modern world that has exercised some of the best contemporary thinkers in the social and human sciences: it is the issue of the nation-state, its history, its current crisis, its prospects. I did not begin to write this book with the crisis of the nation-state as my principal concern. But in the six years over which its chapters were written, I have come to be convinced that the nation-state, as a complex modern political form, is on its last legs. The evidence is by no means clear, and the returns are hardly all in. I am aware that all nation-states are not the same in respect to the national imaginary, the apparatuses of the state, or the sturdiness of the hyphen between them. Yet there is some justification for what might sometimes seem like a reified view of *the* nation-state in this book. Nation-states, for all their important differences (and only a fool would conflate Sri Lanka with Great Britain), make sense only as parts of a system. This system (even when seen as a system of differences) appears poorly equipped to deal with the interlinked diasporas of people and images that mark the here and now. Nation-states, as units in a complex interactive system, are not very likely to be the long-term arbiters of the relationship between globality and modernity. That is why, in my title, I imply that modernity is at large.

The idea that some nation-states are in crisis is a staple of the field of comparative politics and was in some sense the justification for much of modernization theory, especially in the sixties. The idea that some states are weak, sick, corrupt, or soft has been around for several decades (remember Gunnar Myrdahl?). More recently, it has become widely acceptable to see nationalism as a disease, especially when it is somebody else's nationalism. The idea that all nation-states are to some extent bedeviled by globalized movements of arms, moneys, diseases, and ideologies is also hardly news in the era of the multinational corporation. But the idea that the very system of nation-states is in jeopardy is hardly popular. In this book, my persistent focus on the hyphen that links nation to state is part of an evolving argument that the very epoch of the nation-state is near its end. This view, which lies somewhere between a diagnosis and a prognosis, between an intuition and an argument, needs to be spelled out.

First, I need to distinguish between the ethical and the analytic components of my argument. On the ethical front, I am increasingly inclined to see most modern governmental apparatuses as inclined to self-perpetuation, bloat, violence, and corruption. Here, I am in mixed company, from the left and from the right. The ethical question I am often faced with is, if the nation-state disappears, what mechanism will assure the protection of minorities, the minimal distribution of democratic rights, and the reasonable possibility of the growth of civil society? My answer is that I do not know, but this admission is hardly an ethical recommendation for a system that seems plagued by endemic disease. As to alternative social forms and possibilities, there are actually existing social forms and arrangements that might contain the seeds of more dispersed and diverse forms of transnational allegiance and affiliation. This is part of the argument of chapter 8, although I readily admit that the road from various transnational movements to sustainable forms of transnational governance is hardly clear. I prefer, however, the exercise of looking for—indeed, imagining—these alternative possibilities to the strategy of defining some nation-states as healthier than others and then suggesting various mechanisms of ideology transfer. This latter strategy replays modernization-cum-development policy all over again, with the same triumphalist underpinnings and the same unhealthy prospects.

If the ethical front of my argument is necessarily fuzzy, the analytic front is somewhat sharper. Even a cursory inspection of the relationships within and among the more than 150 nation-states that are now members of the United Nations shows that border wars, culture wars, runaway inflation, massive immigrant populations, or serious flights of capital threaten sovereignty in many of them. Even where state sovereignty is apparently intact, state legitimacy is frequently insecure. Even in nation-states as apparently secure as the United States, Japan, and Germany, debates about race and rights, membership and loyalty, citizenship and authority are no longer culturally peripheral. While one argument for the longevity of the nation-state form is based on these apparently secure and legitimate instances, the other argument is an inverse one and bases itself on the new ethnonationalisms of the world, notably those of Eastern Europe. Bosnia-Herzegovina is almost always pointed to in the United States as *the* principal symptom of the fact that nationalism is alive and sick, while the rich democracies are simultaneously invoked to show that the nation-state is alive and well.

Given the frequency with which Eastern Europe is used to show that tribalism is deeply human, that other people's nationalism is tribalism writ large, and that territorial sovereignty is still the major goal of many large ethnic groups, let me propose an alternative interpretation. In my judgment, Eastern Europe has been singularly distorted in popular arguments about nationalism in the press and in the academy in the United States. Rather than being the modal instance of the complexities of all contemporary ethnonationalisms, Eastern Europe, and its Serbian face in particular, has been used as a demonstration of the continued vigor of nationalisms in which land, language, religion, history, and blood are congruent, a textbook case of what nationalism is all about. Of course, what is fascinating about Eastern Europe is that some of its own right-wing ideologues have convinced the liberal Western press that nationalism *is* a politics of primordia, whereas the real question is how it has been made to *appear* that way. This certainly makes Eastern Europe a fascinating and urgent case from many points of view, including the fact that we need to be skeptical when experts claim to have encountered ideal types in actual cases.

In most cases of counternationalism, secession, supranationalism, or ethnic revival on a large scale, the common thread is self-determination rather than territorial sovereignty as such. Even in those cases where territory seems to be a fundamental issue, such as in Palestine, it could be argued that debates about land and territory are in fact functional spin-offs of arguments that are substantially about power, justice, and self-determination. In a world of people on the move, of global commoditization and states incapable of delivering basic rights even to their majority ethnic populations (see chap. 2), territorial sovereignty is an increasingly difficult justification for those nation-states that are increasingly dependent on foreign labor, expertise, arms, or soldiers. For counternationalist movements, territorial sovereignty is a plausible idiom for their aspirations, but it should not be mistaken for their founding logic or their ultimate concern. To do so is to commit what I would call the Bosnia Fallacy, an error that involves (a) misunderstanding Eastern European ethnic battles as tribalist and primordial, an error in which the *New York Times* is the leader, and (b) compounding the mistake by taking the Eastern European case to be the modal case of all emergent nationalisms. To move away from the Bosnia Fallacy requires two difficult concessions: first, that the political systems of the wealthy northern nations may themselves be in crisis, and second, that the emergent nationalisms of many parts of the world may be founded on patriotisms that are not either exclusively or fundamentally territorial. Arguments for making these concessions animate many of the chapters in this book. In making them, I have not always found it easy to maintain the distinction between the analytic and the ethical perspectives on the future of the nation-state, although I have tried to do so.

As the nation-state enters a terminal crisis (if my prognostications prove to be correct), we can certainly expect that the materials for a postnational imaginary must be around us already. Here, I think we need to pay special attention to the relation between mass mediation and migration, the two facts that underpin my sense of the cultural politics of the global modern. In particular, we need to look closely at the variety of what have emerged as *diasporic public spheres*. Benedict Anderson did us a service in identifying the way in which certain forms of mass mediation, notably those involving newspapers, novels, and other print media, played a key role in imagining the nation and in facilitating the spread of this form to the colonial world in Asia and elsewhere. My general argument is that there is a similar link to be found between the work of the imagination and the emergence of a postnational political world. Without the benefit of hindsight (which we do have with respect to the global journey of the idea of the nation), it is hard to make a clear case for the role of the imagination in a postnational order. But as mass mediation becomes increasingly dominated by electronic media (and thus delinked from the capacity to read and write), and as such media increasingly link producers and audiences across national boundaries, and as these audiences themselves start new conversations between those who move and those who stay, we find a growing number of diasporic public spheres.

These diasporic spheres are frequently tied up with students and other intellectuals engaging in long-distance nationalism (as with activists from the People's Republic of China). The establishment of black majority rule in South Africa opens up new kinds of discourse of racial democracy in Africa as well as in the United States and the Caribbean. The Islamic world is the most familiar example of a whole range of debates and projects that have little to do with national boundaries. Religions that were in the past resolutely national now pursue global missions and diasporic clienteles with vigor: the global Hinduism of the past decade is the single best example of this process. Activist movements involved with the environment, women's issues, and human rights generally have created a sphere of transnational discourse, frequently resting on the moral authority of refugees, exiles, and other displaced persons. Major transnational separatist movements like the Sikhs, the Kurds, and the Sri Lankan Tamils conduct their self-imagining in sites throughout the world, where they have enough members to allow for the emergence of multiple nodes in a larger diasporic public sphere.

The wave of debates about multiculturalism that has spread through the United States and Europe is surely testimony to the incapacity of states to prevent their minority populations from linking themselves to wider constituencies of religious or ethnic affiliation. These examples, and others, suggest that the era in which we could assume that viable public spheres were typically, exclusively, or necessarily national could be at an end.

Diasporic public spheres, diverse among themselves, are the crucibles of a postnational political order. The engines of their discourse are mass media (both interactive and expressive) and the movement of refugees, activists, students, and laborers. It may well be that the emergent postnational order proves not to be a system of homogeneous units (as with the current system of nation-states) but a system based on relations between heterogeneous units (some social movements, some interest groups, some professional bodies, some nongovernmental organizations, some armed constabularies, some judicial bodies). The challenge for this emergent order will be whether such heterogeneity is consistent with some minimal conventions of norm and value, which do not require a strict adherence to the liberal social contract of the modern West. This fateful question will be answered not by academic fiat but by the negotiations (both civil and violent) between the worlds imagined by these different interests and movements. In the short run, as we can see already, it is likely to be a world of increased incivility and violence. In the longer run, free of the constraints of the nation form, we may find that cultural freedom and sustainable justice in the world do not presuppose the uniform and general existence of the nation-state. This unsettling possibility could be the most exciting dividend of living in modernity at large.

PART I

Global

Flows

2

Disjuncture and Difference in the

Global Cultural Economy

It takes only the merest acquaintance with the facts of the modern world to note that it is now an interactive system in a sense that is strikingly new. Historians and sociologists, especially those concerned with translocal processes (Hodgson 1974) and the world systems associated with capitalism (Abu-Lughod 1989; Braudel 1981–84; Curtin 1984; Wallerstein 1974; Wolf 1982), have long been aware that the world has been a congeries of large-scale interactions for many centuries. Yet today's world involves interactions of a new order and intensity. Cultural transactions between social groups in the past have generally been restricted, sometimes by the facts of geography and ecology, and at other times by active resistance to interactions with the Other (as in China for much of its history and in Japan before the Meiji Restoration). Where there have been sustained cultural transactions across large parts of the globe, they have usually involved the long-distance journey of commodities (and of the merchants most concerned with them) and of travelers and explorers of every type (Helms 1988; Schafer 1963). The two main forces for sustained cultural interaction before this century have been warfare (and the large-scale political systems sometimes generated by it) and religions of conversion, which have sometimes, as in the case of Islam, taken warfare as one of the legitimate instruments of their expansion. Thus, between travelers and merchants, pilgrims and conquerors, the world has seen much long-distance (and long-term) cultural traffic. This much seems self-evident.

But few will deny that given the problems of time, distance, and limited technologies for the command of resources across vast spaces, cultural dealings between socially and spatially separated groups have, until the past few centuries, been bridged at great cost and sustained over time only with great effort. The forces of cultural gravity seemed always to pull away from the formation of large-scale ecumenes, whether religious, commercial, or political, toward smaller-scale accretions of intimacy and interest.

Sometime in the past few centuries, the nature of this gravitational field seems to have changed. Partly because of the spirit of the expansion of Western maritime interests after 1500, and partly because of the relatively autonomous developments of large and aggressive social formations in the Americas (such as the Aztecs and the Incas), in Eurasia (such as the Mongols and their descendants, the Mughals and Ottomans), in island Southeast Asia (such as the Buginese), and in the kingdoms of precolonial Africa (such as Dahomey), an overlapping set of ecumenes began to emerge, in which congeries of money, commerce, conquest, and migration began to create durable cross-societal bonds. This process was accelerated by the technology transfers and innovations of the late eighteenth and nineteenth centuries (e.g., Bayly 1989), which created complex colonial orders centered on European capitals and spread throughout the non-European world. This intricate and overlapping set of Eurocolonial worlds (first Spanish and Portuguese, later principally English, French, and Dutch) set the basis for a permanent traffic in ideas of peoplehood and selfhood, which created the imagined communities (Anderson 1983) of recent nationalisms throughout the world.

With what Benedict Anderson has called "print capitalism," a new power was unleashed in the world, the power of mass literacy and its attendant large-scale production of projects of ethnic affinity that were remarkably free of the need for face-to-face communication or even of indirect communication between persons and groups. The act of reading things together set the stage for movements based on a paradox—the paradox of constructed primordialism. There is, of course, a great deal else that is involved in the story of colonialism and its dialectically generated nationalisms (Chatterjee 1986), but the issue of constructed ethnicities is surely a crucial strand in this tale.

But the revolution of print capitalism and the cultural affinities and dialogues unleashed by it were only modest precursors to the world we live in now. For in the past century, there has been a technological explosion, largely in the domain of transportation and information, that makes the interactions of a print-dominated world seem as hard-won and as easily erased as the print revolution made earlier forms of cultural traffic appear. For with the advent of the steamship, the automobile, the airplane, the camera, the computer, and the telephone, we have entered into an altogether new condition of neighborliness, even with those most distant from ourselves. Marshall McLuhan, among others, sought to theorize about this world as a "global village," but theories such as McLuhan's appear to have overestimated the communitarian implications of the new media order (McLuhan and Powers 1989). We are now aware that with media, each time we are tempted to speak of the global village, we must be reminded that media create communities with "no sense of place" (Meyrowitz 1985). The world we live in now seems rhizomic (Deleuze and Guattari 1987), even schizophrenic, calling for theories of rootlessness, alienation, and psychological distance between individuals and groups on the one hand, and fantasies (or nightmares) of electronic propinquity on the other. Here, we are close to the central problematic of cultural processes in today's world.

Thus, the curiosity that recently drove Pico Iyer to Asia (1988) is in some ways the product of a confusion between some ineffable McDonaldization of the world and the much subtler play of indigenous trajectories of desire and fear with global flows of people and things. Indeed, Iyer's own impressions are testimony to the fact that, if *a* global cultural system is emerging, it is filled with ironies and resistances, sometimes camouflaged as passivity and a bottomless appetite in the Asian world for things Western.

Iyer's own account of the uncanny Philippine affinity for American popular music is rich testimony to the global culture of the hyperreal, for somehow Philippine renditions of American popular songs are both more widespread in the Philippines, and more disturbingly faithful to their originals, than they are in the United States today. An entire nation seems to have learned to mimic Kenny Rogers and the Lennon sisters, like a vast Asian Motown chorus. But *Americanization* is certainly a pallid term to apply to such a situation, for not only are there more Filipinos singing perfect renditions of some American songs (often from the American past) than there are Americans doing so, there is also, of course, the fact that the rest of their lives is not in complete synchrony with the referential world that first gave birth to these songs.

In a further globalizing twist on what Fredric Jameson has recently called "nostalgia for the present" (1989), these Filipinos look back to a world they have never lost. This is one of the central ironies of the politics of global cultural flows, especially in the arena of entertainment and leisure. It plays havoc with the hegemony of Eurochronology. American nostalgia feeds on Filipino desire represented as a hypercompetent reproduction. Here, we have nostalgia without memory. The paradox, of course, has its explanations, and they are historical; unpacked, they lay bare the story of the American missionization and political rape of the Philippines, one result of which has been the creation of a nation of make-believe Americans, who tolerated for so long a leading lady who played the piano while the slums of Manila expanded and decayed. Perhaps the most radical postmodernists would argue that this is hardly surprising because in the peculiar chronicities of late capitalism, pastiche and nostalgia are central modes of image production and reception. Americans themselves are hardly in the present anymore as they stumble into the megatechnologies of the twenty-first century garbed in the film-noir scenarios of sixties' chills, fifties' diners, forties' clothing, thirties' houses, twenties' dances, and so on ad infinitum.

As far as the United States is concerned, one might suggest that the issue is no longer one of nostalgia but of a social *imaginaire* built largely around reruns. Jameson was bold to link the politics of nostalgia to the postmodern commodity sensibility, and surely he was right (1983). The drug wars in Colombia recapitulate the tropical sweat of Vietnam, with Ollie North and his succession of masks—Jimmy Stewart concealing John Wayne concealing Spiro Agnew and all of them transmogrifying into Sylvester Stallone, who wins in Afghanistan—thus simultaneously fulfilling the secret American envy of Soviet imperialism and the rerun (this time with a happy ending) of the Vietnam War. The Rolling Stones, approaching their fifties, gyrate before eighteen-year-olds who do not appear to need the machinery of nostalgia to be sold on their parents' heroes. Paul McCartney is selling the Beatles to a new audience by hitching his oblique nostalgia to their desire for the new that smacks of the old. *Dragnet* is back in nineties' drag, and so is *Adam-12*, not to speak of *Batman* and *Mission Impossible*, all dressed up technologically but remarkably faithful to the atmospherics of their originals.

The past is now not a land to return to in a simple politics of memory. It has become a synchronic warehouse of cultural scenarios, a kind of temporal central casting, to which recourse can be taken as appropriate, depending on the movie to be made, the scene to be enacted, the hostages to be rescued. All this is par for the course, if you follow Jean Baudrillard or

Jean-François Lyotard into a world of signs wholly unmoored from their social signifiers (all the world's a Disneyland). But I would like to suggest that the apparent increasing substitutability of whole periods and postures for one another, in the cultural styles of advanced capitalism, is tied to larger global forces, which have done much to show Americans that the past is usually another country. If your present is their future (as in much modernization theory and in many self-satisfied tourist fantasies), and their future is your past (as in the case of the Filipino virtuosos of American popular music), then your own past can be made to appear as simply a normalized modality of your present. Thus, although some anthropologists may continue to relegate their Others to temporal spaces that they do not themselves occupy (Fabian 1983), postindustrial cultural productions have entered a postnostalgic phase.

The crucial point, however, is that the United States is no longer the puppeteer of a world system of images but is only one node of a complex transnational construction of imaginary landscapes. The world we live in today is characterized by a new role for the imagination in social life. To grasp this new role, we need to bring together the old idea of images, especially mechanically produced images (in the Frankfurt School sense); the idea of the imagined community (in Anderson's sense); and the French idea of the imaginary (*imaginaire*) as a constructed landscape of collective aspirations, which is no more and no less real than the collective representations of Émile Durkheim, now mediated through the complex prism of modern media.

The image, the imagined, the imaginary—these are all terms that direct us to something critical and new in global cultural processes: *the imagination as a social practice.* No longer mere fantasy (opium for the masses whose real work is elsewhere), no longer simple escape (from a world defined principally by more concrete purposes and structures), no longer elite pastime (thus not relevant to the lives of ordinary people), and no longer mere contemplation (irrelevant for new forms of desire and subjectivity), the imagination has become an organized field of social practices, a form of work (in the sense of both labor and culturally organized practice), and a form of negotiation between sites of agency (individuals) and globally defined fields of possibility. This unleashing of the imagination links the play of pastiche (in some settings) to the terror and coercion of states and their competitors. The imagination is now central to all forms of agency, is itself a social fact, and is the key component of the new global order. But to make this claim meaningful, we must address some other issues.

Homogenization and Heterogenization

The central problem of today's global interactions is the tension between cultural homogenization and cultural heterogenization. A vast array of empirical facts could be brought to bear on the side of the homogenization argument, and much of it has come from the left end of the spectrum of media studies (Hamelink 1983; Mattelart 1983; Schiller 1976), and some from other perspectives (Gans 1985; Iyer 1988). Most often, the homogenization argument subspeciates into either an argument about Americanization or an argument about commoditization, and very often the two arguments are closely linked. What these arguments fail to consider is that at least as rapidly as forces from various metropolises are brought into new societies they tend to become indigenized in one or another way: this is true of music and housing styles as much as it is true of science and terrorism, spectacles and constitutions. The dynamics of such indigenization have just begun to be explored systemically (Barber 1987; Feld 1988; Hannerz 1987, 1989; Ivy 1988; Nicoll 1989; Yoshimoto 1989), and much more needs to be done. But it is worth noticing that for the people of Irian Jaya, Indonesianization may be more worrisome than Americanization, as Japanization may be for Koreans, Indianization for Sri Lankans, Vietnamization for the Cambodians, and Russianization for the people of Soviet Armenia and the Baltic republics. Such a list of alternative fears to Americanization could be greatly expanded, but it is not a shapeless inventory: for polities of smaller scale, there is always a fear of cultural absorption by polities of larger scale, especially those that are nearby. One man's imagined community is another man's political prison.

This scalar dynamic, which has widespread global manifestations, is also tied to the relationship between nations and states, to which I shall return later. For the moment let us note that the simplification of these many forces (and fears) of homogenization can also be exploited by nation-states in relation to their own minorities, by posing global commoditization (or capitalism, or some other such external enemy) as more real than the threat of its own hegemonic strategies.

The new global cultural economy has to be seen as a complex, overlapping, disjunctive order that cannot any longer be understood in terms of existing center-periphery models (even those that might account for multiple centers and peripheries). Nor is it susceptible to simple models of push and pull (in terms of migration theory), or of surpluses and deficits (as in traditional models of balance of trade), or of consumers and producers (as in most neo-Marxist theories of development). Even the most complex and flexible theories of global development that have come out of the Marxist tradition (Amin 1980; Mandel 1978; Wallerstein 1974; Wolf 1982) are inadequately quirky and have failed to come to terms with what Scott Lash and John Urry have called disorganized capitalism (1987). The complexity of the current global economy has to do with certain fundamental disjunctures between economy, culture, and politics that we have only begun to theorize.[1]

I propose that an elementary framework for exploring such disjunctures is to look at the relationship among five dimensions of global cultural flows that can be termed (a) *ethnoscapes*, (b) *mediascapes*, (c) *technoscapes*, (d) *financescapes*, and (e) *ideoscapes*.[2] The suffix *-scape* allows us to point to the fluid, irregular shapes of these landscapes, shapes that characterize international capital as deeply as they do international clothing styles. These terms with the common suffix *-scape* also indicate that these are not objectively given relations that look the same from every angle of vision but, rather, that they are deeply perspectival constructs, inflected by the historical, linguistic, and political situatedness of different sorts of actors: nation-states, multinationals, diasporic communities, as well as subnational groupings and movements (whether religious, political, or economic), and even intimate face-to-face groups, such as villages, neighborhoods, and families. Indeed, the individual actor is the last locus of this perspectival set of landscapes, for these landscapes are eventually navigated by agents who both experience and constitute larger formations, in part from their own sense of what these landscapes offer.

These landscapes thus are the building blocks of what (extending Benedict Anderson) I would like to call *imagined worlds*, that is, the multiple worlds that are constituted by the historically situated imaginations of persons and groups spread around the globe (chap. 1). An important fact of the world we live in today is that many persons on the globe live in such imagined worlds (and not just in imagined communities) and thus are able to contest and sometimes even subvert the imagined worlds of the official mind and of the entrepreneurial mentality that surround them.

By *ethnoscape*, I mean the landscape of persons who constitute the shifting world in which we live: tourists, immigrants, refugees, exiles, guest workers, and other moving groups and individuals constitute an essential feature of the world and appear to affect the politics of (and between) nations to a hitherto unprecedented degree. This is not to say that there are no relatively stable communities and networks of kinship, friendship, work, and leisure, as well as of birth, residence, and other filial forms. But it is to say that the warp of these stabilities is everywhere shot through with the woof of human motion, as more persons and groups deal with the realities of having to move or the fantasies of wanting to move. What is more, both these realities and fantasies now function on larger scales, as men and women from villages in India think not just of moving to Poona or Madras but of moving to Dubai and Houston, and refugees from Sri Lanka find themselves in South India as well as in Switzerland, just as the Hmong are driven to London as well as to Philadelphia. And as international capital shifts its needs, as production and technology generate different needs, as nation-states shift their policies on refugee populations, these moving groups can never afford to let their imaginations rest too long, even if they wish to.

By *technoscape*, I mean the global configuration, also ever fluid, of technology and the fact that technology, both high and low, both mechanical and informational, now moves at high speeds across various kinds of previously impervious boundaries. Many countries now are the roots of multinational enterprise: a huge steel complex in Libya may involve interests from India, China, Russia, and Japan, providing different components of new technological configurations. The odd distribution of technologies, and thus the peculiarities of these technoscapes, are increasingly driven not by any obvious economies of scale, of political control, or of market rationality but by increasingly complex relationships among money flows, political possibilities, and the availability of both un- and highly skilled labor. So, while India exports waiters and chauffeurs to Dubai and Sharjah, it also exports software engineers to the United States—indentured briefly to Tata-Burroughs or the World Bank, then laundered through the State Department to become wealthy resident aliens, who are in turn objects of seductive messages to invest their money and know-how in federal and state projects in India.

The global economy can still be described in terms of traditional indicators (as the World Bank continues to do) and studied in terms of traditional comparisons (as in Project Link at the University of Pennsylvania), but the complicated technoscapes (and the shifting ethnoscapes) that underlie these indicators and comparisons are further out of the reach of the queen of social sciences than ever before. How is one to make a meaningful comparison of wages in Japan and the United States or of real-estate costs in New York and Tokyo, without taking sophisticated account of the very complex fiscal and investment flows that link the two economies through a global grid of currency speculation and capital transfer?

Thus it is useful to speak as well of *financescapes*, as the disposition of global capital is now a more mysterious, rapid, and difficult landscape to follow than ever before, as currency markets, national stock exchanges, and commodity speculations move megamonies through national turnstiles at blinding speed, with vast, absolute implications for small differences in percentage points and time units. But the critical point is that the global relationship among ethnoscapes, technoscapes, and financescapes is deeply disjunctive and profoundly unpredictable because each of these landscapes is subject to its own constraints and incentives (some political, some informational, and some technoenvironmental), at the same time as each acts as a constraint and a parameter for movements in the others. Thus, even an elementary model of global political economy must take into account the deeply disjunctive relationships among human movement, technological flow, and financial transfers.

Further refracting these disjunctures (which hardly form a simple, mechanical global infrastructure in any case) are what I call *mediascapes* and *ideoscapes*, which are closely related landscapes of images. *Mediascapes* refer both to the distribution of the electronic capabilities to produce and disseminate information (newspapers, magazines, television stations, and film-production studios), which are now available to a growing number of private and public interests throughout the world, and to the images of the world created by these media. These images involve many complicated inflections, depending on their mode (documentary or entertainment), their hardware (electronic or preelectronic), their audiences (local, national, or transnational), and the interests of those who own and control them. What is most important about these mediascapes is that they provide (especially in their television, film, and cassette forms) large and complex repertoires of images, narratives, and ethnoscapes to viewers throughout the world, in which the world of commodities and the world of news and politics are profoundly mixed. What this means is that many audiences around the world experience the media themselves as a complicated and interconnected repertoire of print, celluloid, electronic screens, and billboards. The lines between the realistic and the fictional landscapes they see are blurred, so that the farther away these audiences are from the direct experiences of metropolitan life, the more likely they are to construct imagined worlds that are chimerical, aesthetic, even fantastic objects, particularly if assessed by the criteria of some other perspective, some other imagined world.

Mediascapes, whether produced by private or state interests, tend to be image-centered, narrative-based accounts of strips of reality, and what they offer to those who experience and transform them is a series of elements (such as characters, plots, and textual forms) out of which scripts can be formed of imagined lives, their own as well as those of others living in other places. These scripts can and do get disaggregated into complex sets of metaphors by which people live (Lakoff and Johnson 1980) as they help to constitute narratives of the Other and protonarratives of possible lives, fantasies that could become prolegomena to the desire for acquisition and movement.

Ideoscapes are also concatenations of images, but they are often directly political and frequently have to do with the ideologies of states and the counterideologies of movements explicitly oriented to capturing state power or a piece of it. These ideoscapes are composed of elements of the Enlightenment worldview, which consists of a chain of ideas, terms, and images, including *freedom, welfare, rights, sovereignty, representation,* and the master term *democracy.* The master narrative of the Enlightenment (and its many variants in Britain, France, and the United States) was constructed with a certain internal logic and presupposed a certain relationship between reading, representation, and the public sphere. (For the dynamics of this process in the early history of the United States, see Warner 1990.) But the diaspora of these terms and images across the world, especially since the nineteenth century, has loosened the internal coherence that held them together in a Euro-American master narrative and provided instead a loosely structured synopticon of politics, in which different nation-states, as part of their evolution, have organized their political cultures around different keywords (e.g., Williams 1976).

As a result of the differential diaspora of these keywords, the political narratives that govern communication between elites and followers in different parts of the world involve problems of both a semantic and pragmatic nature: semantic to the extent that words (and their lexical equivalents) require careful translation from context to context in their global movements, and pragmatic to the extent that the use of these words by political actors and their audiences may be subject to very different sets of contextual conventions that mediate their translation into public politics. Such conventions are not only matters of the nature of political rhetoric: for example, what does the aging Chinese leadership mean when it refers to the dangers of hooliganism? What does the South Korean leadership mean when it speaks of discipline as the key to democratic industrial growth?

These conventions also involve the far more subtle question of what sets of communicative genres are valued in what way (newspapers versus cinema, for example) and what sorts of pragmatic genre conventions govern the collective readings of different kinds of text. So, while an Indian audience may be attentive to the resonances of a political speech in terms of some keywords and phrases reminiscent of Hindi cinema, a Korean audience may respond to the subtle codings of Buddhist or neo-Confucian rhetoric encoded in a political document. The very relationship of reading to hearing and seeing may vary in important ways that determine the morphology of these different ideoscapes as they shape themselves in different national and transnational contexts. This globally variable synaesthesia has hardly even been noted, but it demands urgent analysis. Thus *democracy* has clearly become a master term, with powerful echoes from Haiti and Poland to the former Soviet Union and China, but it sits at the center of a variety of ideoscapes, composed of distinctive pragmatic configurations of rough translations of other central terms from the vocabulary of the Enlightenment. This creates ever new terminological kaleidoscopes, as states (and the groups that seek to capture them) seek to pacify populations whose own ethnoscapes are in motion and whose mediascapes may create severe problems for the ideoscapes with which they are presented. The fluidity of ideoscapes is complicated in particular by the growing diasporas (both voluntary and involuntary) of intellectuals who continuously inject new meaning-streams into the discourse of democracy in different parts of the world.

This extended terminological discussion of the five terms I have coined sets the basis for a tentative formulation about the conditions under which current global flows occur: they occur in and through the growing disjunctures among ethnoscapes, technoscapes, financescapes, mediascapes, and ideoscapes. This formulation, the core of my model of global cultural flow, needs some explanation. First, people, machinery, money, images, and ideas now follow increasingly nonisomorphic paths; of course, at all periods in human history, there have been some disjunctures in the flows of these things, but the sheer speed, scale, and volume of each of these flows are now so great that the disjunctures have become central to the politics of global culture. The Japanese are notoriously hospitable to ideas and are stereotyped as inclined to export (all) and import (some) goods, but they are also notoriously closed to immigration, like the Swiss, the Swedes, and the Saudis. Yet the Swiss and the Saudis accept populations of guest workers, thus creating labor diasporas of Turks, Italians, and other circum-Mediterranean groups. Some such guest-worker groups maintain continuous contact with their home nations, like the Turks, but others, like high-level South Asian migrants, tend to desire lives in their new homes, raising anew the problem of reproduction in a deterritorialized context.

Deterritorialization, in general, is one of the central forces of the modern world because it brings laboring populations into the lower-class sectors and spaces of relatively wealthy societies, while sometimes creating exaggerated and intensified senses of criticism or attachment to politics in the home state. Deterritorialization, whether of Hindus, Sikhs, Palestinians, or Ukrainians, is now at the core of a variety of global fundamentalisms, including Islamic and Hindu fundamentalism. In the Hindu case, for example, it is clear that the overseas movement of Indians has been exploited by a variety of interests both within and outside India to create a complicated network of finances and religious identifications, by which the problem of cultural reproduction for Hindus abroad has become tied to the politics of Hindu fundamentalism at home.

At the same time, deterritorialization creates new markets for film companies, art impresarios, and travel agencies, which thrive on the need of the deterritorialized population for contact with its homeland. Naturally, these invented homelands, which constitute the mediascapes of deterritorialized groups, can often become sufficiently fantastic and one-sided that they provide the material for new ideoscapes in which ethnic conflicts can begin to erupt. The creation of Khalistan, an invented homeland of the deterritorialized Sikh population of England, Canada, and the United States, is one example of the bloody potential in such mediascapes as they interact with the internal colonialisms of the nation-state (e.g., Hechter 1975). The West Bank, Namibia, and Eritrea are other theaters for the enactment of the bloody negotiation between existing nation-states and various deterritorialized groupings.

It is in the fertile ground of deterritorialization, in which money, commodities, and persons are involved in ceaselessly chasing each other around the world, that the mediascapes and ideoscapes of the modern world find their fractured and fragmented counterpart. For the ideas and images produced by mass media often are only partial guides to the goods and experiences that deterritorialized populations transfer to one another. In Mira Nair's brilliant film *India Cabaret*, we see the multiple loops of this fractured deterritorialization as young women, barely competent in Bombay's metropolitan glitz, come to seek their fortunes as cabaret dancers and prostitutes in Bombay, entertaining men in clubs with dance formats derived wholly from the prurient dance sequences of Hindi films. These scenes in turn cater to ideas about Western and foreign women and their looseness, while they provide tawdry career alibis for these women. Some of these women come from Kerala, where cabaret clubs and the pornographic film industry have blossomed, partly in response to the purses and tastes of Keralites returned from the Middle East, where their diasporic lives away from women distort their very sense of what the relations between men and women might be. These tragedies of displacement could certainly be replayed in a more detailed analysis of the relations between the Japanese and German sex tours to Thailand and the tragedies of the sex trade in Bangkok, and in other similar loops that tie together fantasies about the Other, the conveniences and seductions of travel, the economics of global trade, and the brutal mobility fantasies that dominate gender politics in many parts of Asia and the world at large.

While far more could be said about the cultural politics of deterritorialization and the larger sociology of displacement that it expresses, it is appropriate at this juncture to bring in the role of the nation-state in the disjunctive global economy of culture today. The relationship between states and nations is everywhere an embattled one. It is possible to say that in many societies the nation and the state have become one another's projects. That is, while nations (or more properly groups with ideas about nationhood) seek to capture or co-opt states and state power, states simultaneously seek to capture and monopolize ideas about nationhood (Baruah 1986; Chatterjee 1986; Nandy 1989a). In general, separatist transnational movements, including those that have included terror in their methods, exemplify nations in search of states. Sikhs, Tamil Sri Lankans, Basques, Moros, Quebecois—each of these represents imagined communities that seek to create states of their own or carve pieces out of existing states. States, on the other hand, are everywhere seeking to monopolize the moral resources of community, either by flatly claiming perfect coevality between nation and state, or by systematically museumizing and representing all the groups within them in a variety of heritage politics that seems remarkably uniform throughout the world (Handler 1988; Herzfeld 1982; McQueen 1988).

Here, national and international mediascapes are exploited by nation-states to pacify separatists or even the potential fissiparousness of all ideas of difference. Typically, contemporary nation-states do this by exercising taxonomic control over difference, by creating various kinds of international spectacle to domesticate difference, and by seducing small groups with the fantasy of self-display on some sort of global or cosmopolitan stage. One important new feature of global cultural politics, tied to the disjunctive relationships among the various landscapes discussed earlier, is that state and nation are at each other's throats, and the hyphen that links them is now less an icon of conjuncture than an index of disjuncture. This disjunctive relationship between nation and state has two levels: at the level of any given nation-state, it means that there is a battle of the imagination, with state and nation seeking to cannibalize one another. Here is the seedbed of brutal separatisms—majoritarianisms that seem to have appeared from nowhere and microidentities that have become political projects within the nation-state. At another level, this disjunctive relationship is deeply entangled with the global disjunctures discussed throughout this chapter: ideas of nationhood appear to be steadily increasing in scale and regularly crossing existing state boundaries, sometimes, as with the Kurds, because previous identities stretched across vast national spaces or, as with the Tamils in Sri Lanka, the dormant threads of a transnational diaspora have been activated to ignite the micropolitics of a nation-state.

In discussing the cultural politics that have subverted the hyphen that links the nation to the state, it is especially important not to forget the mooring of such politics in the irregularities that now characterize disorganized capital (Kothari 1989c; Lash and Urry 1987). Because labor, finance, and technology are now so widely separated, the volatilities that underlie movements for nationhood (as large as transnational Islam on the one hand, or as small as the movement of the Gurkhas for a separate state in Northeast India) grind against the vulnerabilities that characterize the relationships between states. States find themselves pressed to stay open by the forces of media, technology, and travel that have fueled consumerism throughout the world and have increased the craving, even in the non-Western world, for new commodities and spectacles. On the other hand, these very cravings can become caught up in new ethnoscapes, mediascapes, and, eventually, ideoscapes, such as democracy in China, that the state cannot tolerate as threats to its own control over ideas of nationhood and peoplehood. States throughout the world are under siege, especially where contests over the ideoscapes of democracy are fierce and fundamental, and where there are radical disjunctures between ideoscapes and technoscapes (as in the case of very small countries that lack contemporary technologies of production and information); or between ideoscapes and financescapes (as in countries such as Mexico or Brazil, where international lending influences national politics to a very large degree); or between ideoscapes and ethnoscapes (as in Beirut, where diasporic, local, and translocal filiations are suicidally at battle); or between ideoscapes and mediascapes (as in many countries in the Middle East and Asia) where the lifestyles represented on both national and international TV and cinema completely overwhelm and undermine the rhetoric of national politics. In the Indian case, the myth of the law-breaking hero has emerged to mediate this naked struggle between the pieties and realities of Indian politics, which has grown increasingly brutalized and corrupt (Vachani 1989).

The transnational movement of the martial arts, particularly through Asia, as mediated by the Hollywood and Hong Kong film industries (Zarilli 1995) is a rich illustration of the ways in which long-standing martial arts traditions, reformulated to meet the fantasies of contemporary (sometimes lumpen) youth populations, create new cultures of masculinity and violence, which are in turn the fuel for increased violence in national and international politics. Such violence is in turn the spur to an increasingly rapid and amoral arms trade that penetrates the entire world. The worldwide spread of the AK-47 and the Uzi, in films, in corporate and state security, in terror, and in police and military activity, is a reminder that apparently simple technical uniformities often conceal an increasingly complex set of loops, linking images of violence to aspirations for community in some imagined world.

Returning then to the ethnoscapes with which I began, the central paradox of ethnic politics in today's world is that primordia (whether of language or skin color or neighborhood or kinship) have become globalized. That is, sentiments, whose greatest force is in their ability to ignite intimacy into a political state and turn locality into a staging ground for identity, have become spread over vast and irregular spaces as groups move yet stay linked to one another through sophisticated media capabilities. This is not to deny that such primordia are often the product of invented traditions (Hobsbawm and Ranger 1983) or retrospective affiliations, but to emphasize that because of the disjunctive and unstable interplay of commerce, media, national policies, and consumer fantasies, ethnicity, once a genie contained in the bottle of some sort of locality (however large), has now become a global force, forever slipping in and through the cracks between states and borders.

But the relationship between the cultural and economic levels of this new set of global disjunctures is not a simple one-way street in which the terms of global cultural politics are set wholly by, or confined wholly within, the vicissitudes of international flows of technology, labor, and finance, demanding only a modest modification of existing neo-Marxist models of uneven development and state formation. There is a deeper change, itself driven by the disjunctures among all the landscapes I have discussed and constituted by their continuously fluid and uncertain interplay, that concerns the relationship between production and consumption in today's global economy. Here, I begin with Marx's famous (and often mined) view of the fetishism of the commodity and suggest that this fetishism has been replaced in the world at large (now seeing the world as one large, interactive system, composed of many complex subsystems) by two mutually supportive descendants, the first of which I call production fetishism and the second, the fetishism of the consumer.

By *production fetishism* I mean an illusion created by contemporary transnational production loci that masks translocal capital, transnational earning flows, global management, and often faraway workers (engaged in various kinds of high-tech putting-out operations) in the idiom and spectacle of local (sometimes even worker) control, national productivity, and territorial sovereignty. To the extent that various kinds of free-trade zones have become the models for production at large, especially of high-tech commodities, production has itself become a fetish, obscuring not social relations as such but the relations of production, which are increasingly transnational. The locality (both in the sense of the local factory or site of production and in the extended sense of the nation-state) becomes a fetish that disguises the globally dispersed forces that actually drive the production process. This generates alienation (in Marx's sense) twice intensified, for its social sense is now compounded by a complicated spatial dynamic that is increasingly global.

As for the *fetishism of the consumer*, I mean to indicate here that the consumer has been transformed through commodity flows (and the mediascapes, especially of advertising, that accompany them) into a sign, both in Baudrillard's sense of a simulacrum that only asymptotically approaches the form of a real social agent, and in the sense of a mask for the real seat of agency, which is not the consumer but the producer and the many forces that constitute production. Global advertising is the key technology for the worldwide dissemination of a plethora of creative and culturally well-chosen ideas of consumer agency. These images of agency are increasingly distortions of a world of merchandising so subtle that the consumer is consistently helped to believe that he or she is an actor, where in fact he or she is at best a chooser.

The globalization of culture is not the same as its homogenization, but globalization involves the use of a variety of instruments of homogenization (armaments, advertising techniques, language hegemonies, and clothing styles) that are absorbed into local political and cultural economies, only to be repatriated as heterogeneous dialogues of national sovereignty, free enterprise, and fundamentalism in which the state plays an increasingly delicate role: too much openness to global flows, and the nation-state is threatened by revolt, as in the China syndrome; too little, and the state exits the international stage, as Burma, Albania, and North Korea in various ways have done. In general, the state has become the arbitrageur of this *repatriation of difference* (in the form of goods, signs, slogans, and styles). But this repatriation or export of the designs and commodities of difference continuously exacerbates the internal politics of majoritarianism and homogenization, which is most frequently played out in debates over heritage.

Thus the central feature of global culture today is the politics of the mutual effort of sameness and difference to cannibalize one another and thereby proclaim their successful hijacking of the twin Enlightenment ideas of the triumphantly universal and the resiliently particular. This mutual cannibalization shows its ugly face in riots, refugee flows, state-sponsored torture, and ethnocide (with or without state support). Its brighter side is in the expansion of many individual horizons of hope and fantasy, in the global spread of oral rehydration therapy and other low-tech instruments of well-being, in the susceptibility even of South Africa to the force of global opinion, in the inability of the Polish state to repress its own working classes, and in the growth of a wide range of progressive, transnational alliances. Examples of both sorts could be multiplied. The critical point is that both sides of the coin of global cultural process today are products of the infinitely varied mutual contest of sameness and difference on a stage characterized by radical disjunctures between different sorts of global flows and the uncertain landscapes created in and through these disjunctures.

The Work of Reproduction in an Age of Mechanical Art

I have inverted the key terms of the title of Walter Benjamin's famous essay (1969) to return this rather high-flying discussion to a more manageable level. There is a classic human problem that will not disappear however much global cultural processes might change their dynamics, and this is the problem today typically discussed under the rubric of reproduction (and traditionally referred to in terms of the transmission of culture). In either case, the question is, how do small groups, especially families, the classical loci of socialization, deal with these new global realities as they seek to reproduce themselves and, in so doing, by accident reproduce cultural forms themselves? In traditional anthropological terms, this could be phrased as the problem of enculturation in a period of rapid culture change. So the problem is hardly novel. But it does take on some novel dimensions under the global conditions discussed so far in this chapter.

First, the sort of transgenerational stability of knowledge that was presupposed in most theories of enculturation (or, in slightly broader terms, of socialization) can no longer be assumed. As families move to new locations, or as children move before older generations, or as grown sons and daughters return from time spent in strange parts of the world, family relationships can become volatile; new commodity patterns are negotiated, debts and obligations are recalibrated, and rumors and fantasies about the new setting are maneuvered into existing repertoires of knowledge and practice. Often, global labor diasporas involve immense strains on marriages in general and on women in particular, as marriages become the meeting points of historical patterns of socialization and new ideas of proper behavior. Generations easily divide, as ideas about property, propriety, and collective obligation wither under the siege of distance and time. Most important, the work of cultural reproduction in new settings is profoundly complicated by the politics of representing a family as normal (particularly for the young) to neighbors and peers in the new locale. All this is, of course, not new to the cultural study of immigration.

What is new is that this is a world in which both points of departure and points of arrival are in cultural flux, and thus the search for steady points of reference, as critical life choices are made, can be very difficult. It is in this atmosphere that the invention of tradition (and of ethnicity, kinship, and other identity markers) can become slippery, as the search for certainties is regularly frustrated by the fluidities of transnational communication. As group pasts become increasingly parts of museums, exhibits, and collections, both in national and transnational spectacles, culture becomes less what Pierre Bourdieu would have called a habitus (a tacit realm of reproducible practices and dispositions) and more an arena for conscious choice, justification, and representation, the latter often to multiple and spatially dislocated audiences.

The task of cultural reproduction, even in its most intimate arenas, such as husband-wife and parent-child relations, becomes both politicized and exposed to the traumas of deterritorialization as family members pool and negotiate their mutual understandings and aspirations in sometimes fractured spatial arrangements. At larger levels, such as community, neighborhood, and territory, this politicization is often the emotional fuel for more explicitly violent politics of identity, just as these larger politics sometimes penetrate and ignite domestic politics. When, for example, two offspring in a household split with their father on a key matter of political identification in a transnational setting, preexisting localized norms carry little force. Thus a son who has joined the Hezbollah group in Lebanon may no longer get along with parents or siblings who are affiliated with Amal or some other branch of Shi'i ethnic political identity in Lebanon. Women in particular bear the brunt of this sort of friction, for they become pawns in the heritage politics of the household and are often subject to the abuse and violence of men who are themselves torn about the relation between heritage and opportunity in shifting spatial and political formations.

The pains of cultural reproduction in a disjunctive global world are, of course, not eased by the effects of mechanical art (or mass media), for these media afford powerful resources for counternodes of identity that youth can project against parental wishes or desires. At larger levels of organization, there can be many forms of cultural politics within displaced populations (whether of refugees or of voluntary immigrants), all of which are inflected in important ways by media (and the mediascapes and ideoscapes they offer). A central link between the fragilities of cultural reproduction and the role of the mass media in today's world is the politics of gender and violence. As fantasies of gendered violence dominate the B-grade film industries that blanket the world, they both reflect and refine gendered violence at home and in the streets, as young men (in particular) are swayed by the macho politics of self-assertion in contexts where they are frequently denied real agency, and women are forced to enter the labor force in new ways on the one hand, and continue the maintenance of familial heritage on the other. Thus the honor of women becomes not just an armature of stable (if inhuman) systems of cultural reproduction but a new arena for the formation of sexual identity and family politics, as men and women face new pressures at work and new fantasies of leisure.

Because both work and leisure have lost none of their gendered qualities in this new global order but have acquired ever subtler fetishized representations, the honor of women becomes increasingly a surrogate for the identity of embattled communities of males, while their women in reality have to negotiate increasingly harsh conditions of work at home and in the nondomestic workplace. In short, deterritorialized communities and displaced populations, however much they may enjoy the fruits of new kinds of earning and new dispositions of capital and technology, have to play out the desires and fantasies of these new ethnoscapes, while striving to reproduce the family-as-microcosm of culture. As the shapes of cultures grow less bounded and tacit, more fluid and politicized, the work of cultural reproduction becomes a daily hazard. Far more could, and should, be said about the work of reproduction in an age of mechanical art: the preceding discussion is meant to indicate the contours of the problems that a new, globally informed theory of cultural reproduction will have to face.

Shape and Process in Global Cultural Formations

The deliberations of the arguments that I have made so far constitute the bare bones of an approach to a general theory of global cultural processes. Focusing on disjunctures, I have employed a set of terms (*ethnoscape, financescape, technoscape, mediascape*, and *ideoscape*) to stress different streams or flows along which cultural material may be seen to be moving across national boundaries. I have also sought to exemplify the ways in which these various flows (or landscapes, from the stabilizing perspectives of any given imagined world) are in fundamental disjuncture with respect to one another. What further steps can we take toward a general theory of global cultural processes based on these proposals?

The first is to note that our very models of cultural shape will have to alter, as configurations of people, place, and heritage lose all semblance of isomorphism. Recent work in anthropology has done much to free us of the shackles of highly localized, boundary-oriented, holistic, primordialist images of cultural form and substance (Hannerz 1989; Marcus and Fischer 1986; Thornton 1988). But not very much has been put in their place, except somewhat larger if less mechanical versions of these images, as in Eric Wolf's work on the relationship of Europe to the rest of the world (1982). What I would like to propose is that we begin to think of the configuration of cultural forms in today's world as fundamentally fractal, that is, as possessing no Euclidean boundaries, structures, or regularities. Second, I would suggest that these cultural forms, which we should strive to represent as fully fractal, are also overlapping in ways that have been discussed only in pure mathematics (in set theory, for example) and in biology (in the language of polythetic classifications). Thus we need to combine a fractal metaphor for the shape of cultures (in the plural) with a polythetic account of their overlaps and resemblances. Without this latter step, we shall remain mired in comparative work that relies on the clear separation of the entities to be compared before serious comparison can begin. How are we to compare fractally shaped cultural forms that are also polythetically overlapping in their coverage of terrestrial space?

Finally, in order for the theory of global cultural interactions predicated on disjunctive flows to have any force greater than that of a mechanical metaphor, it will have to move into something like a human version of the theory that some scientists are calling chaos theory. That is, we will need to ask not how these complex, overlapping, fractal shapes constitute a simple, stable (even if large-scale) system, but to ask what its dynamics are: Why do ethnic riots occur when and where they do? Why do states wither at greater rates in some places and times than in others? Why do some countries flout conventions of international debt repayment with so much less apparent worry than others? How are international arms flows driving ethnic battles and genocides? Why are some states exiting the global stage while others are clamoring to get in? Why do key events occur at a certain point in a certain place rather than in others? These are, of course, the great traditional questions of causality, contingency, and prediction in the human sciences, but in a world of disjunctive global flows, it is perhaps important to start asking them in a way that relies on images of flow and uncertainty, hence *chaos*, rather than on older images of order, stability, and systematicness. Otherwise, we will have gone far toward a theory of global cultural systems but thrown out process in the bargain. And that would make these notes part of a journey toward the kind of illusion of order that we can no longer afford to impose on a world that is so transparently volatile.

Whatever the directions in which we can push these macrometaphors (fractals, polythetic classifications, and chaos), we need to ask one other old-fashioned question out of the Marxist paradigm: is there some pregiven order to the relative determining force of these global flows? Because I have postulated the dynamics of global cultural systems as driven by the relationships among flows of persons, technologies, finance, information, and ideology, can we speak of some structural-causal order linking these flows by analogy to the role of the economic order in one version of the Marxist paradigm? Can we speak of some of these flows as being, for a priori structural or historical reasons, always prior to and formative of other flows? My own hypothesis, which can only be tentative at this point, is that the relationship of these various flows to one another as they constellate into particular events and social forms will be radically context-dependent. Thus, while labor flows and their loops with financial flows between Kerala and the Middle East may account for the shape of media flows and ideoscapes in Kerala, the reverse may be true of Silicon Valley in California, where intense specialization in a single technological sector (computers) and particular flows of capital may well profoundly determine the shape that ethnoscapes, ideoscapes, and mediascapes may take.

This does not mean that the causal-historical relationship among these various flows is random or meaninglessly contingent but that our current theories of cultural chaos are insufficiently developed to be even parsimonious models at this point, much less to be predictive theories, the golden fleeces of one kind of social science. What I have sought to provide in this chapter is a reasonably economical technical vocabulary and a rudimentary model of disjunctive flows, from which something like a decent global analysis might emerge. Without some such analysis, it will be difficult to construct what John Hinkson calls a "social theory of postmodernity" that is adequately global (1990, 84).

3

Global Ethnoscapes: Notes and Queries for a

Transnational Anthropology

In chapter 2, I use the term *ethnoscape*. This neologism has certain ambiguities deliberately built into it. It refers, first, to the dilemmas of perspective and representation that all ethnographers must confront, and it admits that (as with landscapes in visual art) traditions of perception and perspective, as well as variations in the situation of the observer, may affect the process and product of representation. But I also intend this term to indicate that there are some brute facts about the world of the twentieth century that any ethnography must confront. Central among these facts is the changing social, territorial, and cultural reproduction of group identity. As groups migrate, regroup in new locations, reconstruct their histories, and reconfigure their ethnic projects, the *ethno* in ethnography takes on a slippery, nonlocalized quality, to which the descriptive practices of anthropology will have to respond. The landscapes of group identity—the ethnoscapes—around the world are no longer familiar anthropological objects, insofar as groups are no longer tightly territorialized, spatially bounded, historically unselfconscious, or culturally homogeneous. We have fewer cultures in the world and more internal cultural debates (Parkin 1978).[1] In this chapter, through a series of notes, queries, and vignettes, I seek to reposition some of our disciplinary conventions, while trying to show that the ethnoscapes of today's world are profoundly interactive.

A central challenge for current anthropology is to study the cosmopolitan (Rabinow 1986) cultural forms of the contemporary world without logically or chronologically presupposing either the authority of the Western experience or the models derived from that experience. It seems impossible to study these new cosmopolitanisms fruitfully without analyzing the transnational cultural flows within which they thrive, compete, and feed off one another in ways that defeat and confound many verities of the human sciences today. One such truth concerns the link between space, stability, and cultural reproduction. There is an urgent need to focus on the cultural dynamics of what is now called deterritorialization. This term applies not only to obvious examples such as transnational corporations and money markets but also to ethnic groups, sectarian movements, and political formations, which increasingly operate in ways that transcend specific territorial boundaries and identities. Deterritorialization (of which I offer some ethnographic profiles in chap. 2) affects the loyalties of groups (especially in the context of complex diasporas), their transnational manipulation of currencies and other forms of wealth and investment, and the strategies of states. The loosening of the holds between people, wealth, and territories fundamentally alters the basis of cultural reproduction.

At the same time, deterritorialization creates new markets for film companies, impresarios, and travel agencies, which thrive on the need of the relocated population for contact with its homeland. But the homeland is partly invented, existing only in the imagination of the deterritorialized groups, and it can sometimes become so fantastic and one-sided that it provides the fuel for new ethnic conflicts.

The idea of deterritorialization may also be applied to money and finance, as money managers seek the best markets for their investments, independent of national boundaries. In turn, these movements of moneys are the basis for new kinds of conflict, as Los Angelenos worry about the Japanese buying up their city, and people in Bombay worry about the rich Arabs from the Gulf states, who have not only transformed the price of mangoes in Bombay but have also substantially altered the profile of hotels, restaurants, and other services in the eyes of the local population—just as they have in London. Yet most residents of Bombay are ambivalent about the Arabs there, for the flip side of their presence is the absent friends and kinsfolk earning big money in the Middle East and bringing back both money and luxury commodities to Bombay and other cities in

India. Such commodities transform consumer taste in these cities. They often end up smuggled through air- and seaports and peddled in the gray markets of Bombay's streets. In these gray markets (a coinage that allows me to capture the quasi-legal characteristic of such settings), some members of Bombay's middle classes and its lumpen proletariat can buy goods, ranging from cartons of Marlboro cigarettes to Old Spice shaving cream and tapes of Madonna. Similar gray routes, often subsidized by moonlighting sailors, diplomats, and airline stewardesses, who get to move in and out of the country regularly, keep the gray markets of Bombay, Madras, and Calcutta filled with goods not only from the West, but also from the Middle East, Hong Kong, and Singapore. It is also such professional transients who are increasingly implicated in the transnational spread of disease, not the least of which is AIDS.

The vision of transnational cultural studies suggested by the discussion so far appears at first sight to involve only modest adjustments of anthropologists' traditional approaches to culture. In my view, however, a genuinely cosmopolitan ethnographic practice requires an interpretation of the terrain of cultural studies in the United States today and of the status of anthropology within such a terrain.[2]

Cultural Studies in a Global Terrain

As this volume concerns anthropologies of the present, it may be important to ask about the status of anthropology in the present and in particular about its now embattled monopoly over the study of "culture" (from now on, without quotation marks). The following discussion sets the stage for the critique of ethnography contained in subsequent sections.

As a topic, culture has many histories, some disciplinary, some that function outside the academy. Within the academy, there are certain differences between disciplines in the degree to which culture has been an explicit topic of investigation and the degree to which it has been understood tacitly. In the social sciences, anthropology (especially in the United States but less so in England) has made culture its central concept, defining it as some sort of human substance—even though ideas about this substance have shifted, over the course of a century, roughly from E. B. Tylor's ideas about custom to Clifford Geertz's ideas about meaning. Some anthropologists have worried that the meanings given to *culture* have been far too diverse for a technical term; others have made a virtue of that diversity. At the same time, the other social sciences have not been unconcerned with culture: in sociology, Max Weber's sense of *verstehen* and George Simmel's various ideas have mediated between the German neo-Kantian ideas of the late nineteenth century and sociology as a social science discipline. As in many other cases, culture is now a subfield within sociology, and the American Sociological Association has legitimized this segregation by creating a subunit in the sociology of culture, where persons concerned with the production and distribution of culture, especially in Western settings, may freely associate with one another.

At the epicenter of current debates in and about culture, many diverse streams flow into a single, rather turbulent river of many poststructuralisms (largely French) of Jacques Lacan, Jacques Derrida, Michel Foucault, Pierre Bourdieu, and their many subschools. Some of these streams are self-conscious about language as their means and their model, while others are less so. The current multiplicity of uses that surrounds the three words *meaning*, *discourse*, and *text* should be sufficient to indicate that we are not only in an era of blurred genres (as Geertz [1980] said presciently more than a decade ago), but we are in a peculiar state that I would like to call "postblurring," in which ecumenism has—happily, in my opinion—given way to sharp debates about the word, the world, and the relationship between them.

In this postblur blur, it is crucial to note that the high ground has been seized by English literature (as a discipline) in particular and by literary studies in general. This is the nexus where the word *theory*, a rather prosaic term in many fields for many centuries, suddenly took on the sexy ring of a trend. For an anthropologist in the United States today, what is most striking about the past decade in the academy is the hijack of culture by literary studies—although we no longer have a one-sided Arnoldian gaze, but a many-sided hijack (where a hundred Blooms flower) with many internal debates about texts and antitexts, reference and structure, theory and practice. Social scientists look on with bewilderment as their colleagues in English and comparative literature talk (and fight) about matters that, until as recently as fifteen years ago, would have seemed about as relevant to English departments as, say, quantum mechanics.

The subject matter of cultural studies could roughly be taken as the relationship between the word and the world. I understand these two terms in their widest sense, so that *word* can encompass all forms of textualized expression and *world* can mean anything from the means of production and the organization of life-worlds to the globalized relations of cultural reproduction discussed here.

Cultural studies conceived this way could be the basis for a cosmopolitan (global? macro? translocal?) ethnography. To translate the tension between the word and the world into a productive ethnographic strategy requires a new understanding of the deterritorialized world that many persons inhabit and the possible lives that many persons are today able to envision. The terms of the negotiation between imagined lives and deterritorialized worlds are complex, and they surely cannot be captured by the localizing strategies of traditional ethnography alone. What a new style of ethnography can do is to capture the impact of deterritorialization on the imaginative resources of lived, local experiences. Put another way, the task of ethnography now becomes the unraveling of a conundrum: what is the nature of locality as a lived experience in a globalized, deterritorialized world? As I will suggest in the next section, the beginnings of an answer to this puzzle lie in a fresh approach to the role of the imagination in social life.

The master narratives that currently guide much ethnography all have Enlightenment roots, and all have been called into serious question. Foucault's searing critique of Western humanism and its hidden epistemologies has made it difficult to retain much faith in the idea of progress in its many old and new manifestations. The master narrative of evolution, central to anthropology in the United States, suffers from a profound gap between its short-run, culturally oriented versions (as in the work of Marvin Harris) and its long-run, more appealing, but less anthropological versions as in the biogeological fables of Stephen Jay Gould. The emergence of the individual as a master narrative suffers not only from the counterexamples of our major twentieth-century totalitarian experiences but also from the many deconstructions of the idea of self, person, and agency in philosophy, sociology, and anthropology (Parfit 1986; Giddens 1979; Carrithers, Collins, and Lukes 1985). Master narratives of the iron cage and the march of bureaucratic rationality are constantly refuted by the irrationalities, contradictions, and sheer brutality that are increasingly traceable to the pathologies of the modern nation-state (Nandy 1987). Finally, most versions of the Marxist master narrative find themselves embattled as contemporary capitalism takes on a more and more disorganized and deterritorialized look (Lash and Urry 1987) and as cultural expressions refuse to bend to the requirements of even the least parochial Marxist approaches. (For example, see the debate between Frederic Jameson and Aijaz Ahmad in *Social Text* [Jameson 1986; Ahmad 1987].)

Cosmopolitan ethnography, or what might be called macroethnography, takes on a special urgency given the ailments of these many post-Enlightenment master narratives. It is difficult to be anything but exploratory about what such a macroethnography (and its ethnoscapes) might look like, but the following section seeks by illustration to point to its contours.

We live in a world of many kinds of realism, some magical, some socialist, some capitalist, and some that are yet to be named. These generic realisms have their provinces of origin: magical realism in Latin American fiction in the past two decades; socialist realism in the Soviet Union of the 1930s; and capitalist realism, a term coined by Michael Schudson (1984), in the visual and verbal rhetoric of contemporary American advertising. In much aesthetic expression today, the boundaries between these various realisms have been blurred. The controversies over Salman Rushdie's *The Satanic Verses*, over the Robert Mapplethorpe photographic exhibition in Cincinnati, and over many other works of art in other parts of the world remind us that artists are increasingly willing to place high stakes on their sense of the boundaries between their art and the politics of public opinion.

More consequential to our purposes is the fact that the imagination has now acquired a singular new power in social life. The imagination—expressed in dreams, songs, fantasies, myths, and stories—has always been part of the repertoire of every society, in some culturally organized way. But there is a peculiar new force to the imagination in social life today. More persons in more parts of the world consider a wider set of possible lives than they ever did before. One important source of this change is the mass media, which present a rich, ever-changing store of possible lives, some of which enter the lived imaginations of ordinary people more successfully than others. Important also are contacts with, news of, and rumors about others in one's social neighborhood who have become inhabitants of these faraway worlds. The importance of media is not so much as direct sources of new images and scenarios for life possibilities but as semiotic diacritics of great power, which also inflect social contact with the metropolitan world facilitated by other channels.

One of the principal shifts in the global cultural order, created by cinema, television, and video technology (and the ways in which they frame and energize other, older media), has to do with the role of the imagination in social life. Until recently, whatever the force of social change, a case could be made that social life was largely inertial, that traditions provided a relatively finite set of possible lives, and that fantasy and imagination were residual practices, confined to special persons or domains, restricted to special moments or places. In general, imagination and fantasy were antidotes to the finitude of social experience. In the past two decades, as the deterritorialization of persons, images, and ideas has taken on new force, this weight has imperceptibly shifted. More persons throughout the world see their lives through the prisms of the possible lives offered by mass media in all their forms. That is, fantasy is now a social practice; it enters, in a host of ways, into the fabrication of social lives for many people in many societies.

I should be quick to note that this is not a cheerful observation, intended to imply that the world is now a happier place with more choices (in the utilitarian sense) for more people, and with more mobility and more happy endings. Instead, what is implied is that even the meanest and most hopeless of lives, the most brutal and dehumanizing of circumstances, the harshest of lived inequalities are now open to the play of the imagination. Prisoners of conscience, child laborers, women who toil in the fields and factories of the world, and others whose lot is harsh no longer see their lives as mere outcomes of the givenness of things, but often as the ironic compromise between what they could imagine and what social life will permit. Thus, the biographies of ordinary people are constructions (or fabrications) in which the imagination plays an important role. Nor is this role a simple matter of escape (holding steady the conventions that govern the rest of social life), for in the grinding of gears between unfolding lives and their imagined counterparts a variety of imagined communities (Anderson 1983) is formed, communities that generate new kinds of politics, new kinds of collective expression, and new needs for social discipline and surveillance on the part of elites.

All this has many contexts and implications that cannot be pursued here. But what does it imply for ethnography? It implies that ethnographers can no longer simply be content with the thickness they bring to the local and the particular, nor can they assume that as they approach the local, they approach something more elementary, more contingent, and thus more real than life seen in larger-scale perspectives. For what is real about ordinary lives is now real in many ways that range from the sheer contingency of individual lives and the vagaries of competence and talent that distinguish persons in all societies to the realisms that individuals are exposed to and draw on in their daily lives.

These complex, partly imagined lives must now form the bedrock of ethnography, at least of the sort of ethnography that wishes to retain a special voice in a transnational, deterritorialized world. For the new power of the imagination in the fabrication of social lives is inescapably tied up with images, ideas, and opportunities that come from elsewhere, often moved around by the vehicles of mass media. Thus, standard cultural reproduction (like standard English) is now an endangered activity that succeeds only by conscious design and political will, where it succeeds at all.

Indeed, where insulation from the larger world seems to have been successful and where the role of the global imagination is withheld from ordinary people (in places like Albania, North Korea, and Burma), what seems to appear instead is a bizarre state-sponsored realism, which always contains within it the possibility of the genocidal and totalizing lunacies of a Pol Pot or of long-repressed desires for critique or exit, as are emerging in Albania and Myanmar (Burma).

The issue, therefore, is not how ethnographic writing can draw on a wider range of literary models, models that too often elide the distinction between the life of fiction and the fictionalization of lives, but how the role of the imagination in social life can be described in a new sort of ethnography that is not so resolutely localizing. There is, of course, much to be said for the local, the particular, and the contingent, which have always been the forte of ethnographic writing at its best. But where lives are being imagined partly in and through realisms that must be in one way or another official or large-scale in their inspiration, then the ethnographer needs to find new ways to represent the links between the imagination and social life. This problem of representation is not quite the same as the familiar problem of micro and macro, small and large scale, although it has important connections to it. The connection between the problem of ethnographically representing imagined lives and the difficulty of making the move from local realities to large-scale structures is implicit in Sherry Ortner's article "Reading America" (1991). Taken together, Ortner's argument and mine point to the importance of embedding large-scale realities in concrete life-worlds, but they also open up the possibility of divergent interpretations of what *locality* implies.

The link between the imagination and social life, I would suggest, is increasingly a global and deterritorialized one. Thus, those who represent real or ordinary lives must resist making claims to epistemic privilege in regard to the lived particularities of social life. Rather, ethnography must redefine itself as that practice of representation that illuminates the power of large-scale, imagined life possibilities over specific life trajectories. This is thickness with a difference, and the difference lies in a new alertness to the fact that ordinary lives today are more often powered not by the givenness of things but by the possibilities that the media (either directly or indirectly) suggest are available. Put another way, some of the force of Bourdieu's idea of the habitus can be retained (1977), but the stress must be put on his idea of improvisation, for improvisation no longer occurs within a relatively bounded set of thinkable postures but is always skidding and taking off, powered by the imagined vistas of mass-mediated master narratives. There has been a general change in the global conditions of life-worlds: put simply, where once improvisation was snatched out of the glacial undertow of habitus, habitus now has to be painstakingly reinforced in the face of life-worlds that are frequently in flux.

Three examples will suggest something of what I have in mind. In January 1988, my wife (who is a white American female historian of India) and I (a Tamil Brahman male, brought up in Bombay and turned into *homo academicus* in the United States), along with our son, three members of my eldest brother's family, and an entourage of his colleagues and employees, decided to visit the Meenaksi Temple in Madurai, one of the great pilgrimage centers of South India. My wife has done research there off and on for the past two decades.

Our purposes in going were various. My brother and his wife were worried about the marriage of their eldest daughter and were concerned to have the good wishes of as many powerful deities as possible in their search for a good alliance. For my brother, Madurai was a special place because he spent most of his first twenty years there with my mother's extended family. He thus had old friends and memories in all the streets around the temple. Now he had come to Madurai as a senior railway official, with business to conduct with several private businessmen who wished to persuade him of the quality of their bids. Indeed, one of these potential clients had arranged for us to be accommodated in a garishly modern hotel in Madurai, a stone's throw from the temple, and drove him around in a Mercedes, while the rest of us took in our own Madurai.

Our eleven-year-old son, fresh from Philadelphia, knew that he was in the presence of the practices of heritage and dove to the ground manfully, in the Hindu practice of prostration before elders and deities, whenever he was asked. He put up graciously with the incredible noise, crowding, and sensory rush that a major Hindu temple involves. For myself, I was there to embellish my brother's entourage, to add some vague moral force to their wishes for a happy marriage for their daughter, to reabsorb the city in which my mother grew up (I had been there several times before), to share in my wife's excitement about returning to a city and a temple that are possibly the most important parts of her imagination, and to fish for cosmopolitanism in the raw.

So we entered the fourteen-acre temple compound as an important entourage, although one among many, and were soon approached by one of the several priests who officiate there. This one recognized my wife, who asked him where Thangam Bhattar was. Thangam Bhattar was the priest with whom she had worked most closely. The answer was "Thangam Bhattar is in Houston." This punch line took us all a while to absorb, and then it all came together in a flash. The Indian community in Houston, like many communities of Asian Indians in the United States, had built a Hindu temple, this one devoted to Meenaksi, the ruling deity in Madurai. Thangam Bhattar had been persuaded to go there, leaving his family behind. He leads a lonely life in Houston, assisting in the complex cultural politics of reproduction in an overseas Indian community, presumably earning a modest income, while his wife and children stay on in their small home near the temple. The next morning my wife and niece visited Thangam Bhattar's home, where they were told of his travails in Houston, and they told the family what had gone on with us in the intervening years. There is a transnational irony here, of course: Carol Breckenridge, American historian, arrives in Madurai waiting with bated breath to see her closest informant and friend, a priest, and discovers that he is in faraway Houston, which is far away even from faraway Philadelphia.

But this transnational irony has many threads that unwind backward and forward in time to large and fluid structures of meaning and communication. Among these threads are my brother's hopes for his daughter, who subsequently married a Ph.D. candidate in physical chemistry in an upstate New York university and recently came to Syracuse herself; my wife's recontextualizing of her Madurai experiences in a world that, at least for some of its central actors, now includes Houston; and my own realization that Madurai's historical cosmopolitanism has acquired a new global dimension and that some key lives that constitute the heart of the temple's ritual practices now have Houston in their imagined biographies. Each of these threads could and should be unwound. They lead to an understanding of the globalization of Hinduism, the transformation of "natives" into cosmopolites of their own sort, and the fact that the temple now not only attracts persons from all over the world but also itself reaches out. The goddess Meenaksi has a living presence in Houston.

Meanwhile, our son now has in his repertoire of experiences a journey of the *Roots* variety. He may remember this as he fabricates his own life as an American of partly Indian descent. But he may remember more vividly his sudden need to go to the bathroom while we were going from sanctum to sanctum in a visit to another major temple in January 1989 and the bathroom at the guesthouse of a charitable foundation in which he found blissful release. But here, too, is an unfinished story, which involves the dynamics of family, memory, and tourism, for an eleven-year-old hyphenated American who has to go periodically to India, whether he likes it or not, and encounter the many webs of shifting biography that he finds there.

This account, like the ones that follow, needs not only to be thickened but to be stirred, but it must serve for now as one glimpse of an ethnography that focuses on the unyoking of imagination from place.

My second vignette comes from a collection of pieces of one kind of magical realism, a book by Julio Cortázar called A Certain Lucas (1984). Because there has been much borrowing of literary models and metaphors in recent anthropology but relatively little anthropology of literature, a word about this choice of example seems appropriate. Fiction, like myth, is part of the conceptual repertoire of contemporary societies. Readers of novels and poems can be moved to intense action (as with The Satanic Verses of Salman Rushdie), and their authors often contribute to the construction of social and moral maps for their readers. Even more relevant to my purposes, prose fiction is the exemplary province of the post-Renaissance imagination, and in this regard it is central to a more general ethnography of the imagination. Even small fragments of fantasy, such as Cortázar constructs in this brief story, show the contemporary imagination at work.

Magical realism is interesting not only as a literary genre but also as a representation of how the world appears to some people who live in it. (For an interesting commentary on one aspect of this approach to literary narrative, see Felman 1989.) Cortázar is doubtless a unique person, and not everyone imagines the world his way, but his vision is surely part of the evidence that the globe has begun to spin in new ways. Like the myths of small-scale society as rendered in the anthropological classics of the past, contemporary literary fantasies tell us something about displacement, disorientation, and agency in the contemporary world. (For an excellent recent example of this approach in the context of cultural studies, see Rosaldo 1989, chap. 7.)

Because we have now learned a great deal about the writing of ethnography (Clifford and Marcus 1986; Marcus and Fischer 1986; Geertz 1988), we are in a strong position to move to an anthropology of representation that would profit immensely from our recent discoveries about the politics and poetics of "writing culture." In this view, we can restore to the recent critiques of ethnographic practice the lessons of earlier critiques of anthropology as a field of practices operating within a larger world of institutional policies and power (Hymes 1969). The Cortázar story in question, which is both more light-handed and more heavy-hitting than some other, larger chunks of magical realism, is called "Swimming in a Pool of Gray Grits." It concerns Professor Jose Migueletes's 1964 discovery of a swimming pool containing gray grits instead of water. This discovery is quickly noticed by the world of sports, and at the Ecological Games in Baghdad the Japanese champion, Akiro Tashuma, breaks the world record by "swimming five meters in one minute and four seconds" (Cortázar 1984, 80). Cortázar's piece goes on to speak of how Tashuma solved the technical problem of breathing in this semisolid medium. The press then enters the picture, in Cortázar's own irreducibly spare words:

> Asked about the reasons why many international athletes show an ever-growing proclivity for swimming in grits, Tashuma would only answer that after several millennia it has finally been proven that there is a certain monotony in the act of jumping into the water and coming out all wet without anything having changed very much in the sport. He let it be understood that the imagination is slowly coming into power and that it's time now to apply revolutionary forms to old sports whose only incentive is to lower records by fractions of a second, when that can be done, which is quite rare. He modestly declared himself unable to suggest equivalent discoveries for soccer and tennis, but he did make an oblique reference to a new development in sports, mentioning a glass ball that may have been used in a basketball game in Naga, and whose accidental but always possible breakage brought on the act of hara-kiri by the whole team whose fault it was. Everything can be expected of Nipponese culture, especially if it sets out to imitate the Mexican. But to limit ourselves to the West and to grits, this last item has begun to demand higher prices, to the particular delight of countries that produce it, all of them in the Third World. The death by asphyxiation of seven Australian children who tried to practice fancy dives in the new pool in Canberra demonstrates, however, the limitations of this interesting product, the use of which should not be carried too far when amateurs are involved. (82–83)

Now this is a very funny parable, and it could be read at many levels, from many points of view. For my purposes, I note first that it is written by an Argentine, born in Brussels, who lived in Paris from 1952 until his death in 1984. The link between magical realism and the self-imposed exile in Paris of many of its finest voices deserves further exploration, but what else does this vignette have to offer for the study of the new ethnoscapes of the contemporary world? The story is partly about a crazy invention that captures the faraway imagination of Tashuma, a person who believes that "the imagination is slowly coming into power." It is also about the transnational journey of ideas that may begin as playful meditations and end up as bizarre technical realities that can result in death. Here, one is forced to think about the trajectory of *The Satanic Verses*, which began as a satiric meditation on good, evil, and Islam, and ended up a weapon in group violence in many parts of the world.

The vignette is also about the internationalization of sport and the spiritual exhaustion that comes from technical obsession with small differences in performance. Different actors can bring their imaginations to bear on the problem of sport in various ways. The Olympic Games of the past are full of incidents that reveal complex ways in which individuals situated within specific national and cultural trajectories imposed their imaginations on global audiences. In Seoul in 1988, for instance, the defeated Korean boxer who sat in the ring for several hours to publicly proclaim his shame as a Korean and the Korean officials who swarmed into the ring to assault a New Zealand referee for what they thought was a biased decision were bringing their imagined lives to bear on the official Olympic narratives of fair play, good sportsmanship, and clean competition. The whole question of steroids, including the case of Canadian runner Ben Johnson (see MacAloon 1990), is also not far from the technical absurdities of Cortázar's story, in which the body is manipulated to yield new results in a world of competitive and commoditized spectacle. The vision of seven Australian children's diving into a pool of grits and dying also deserves to be drawn out into the many stories of individual abnegation and physical abuse that sometimes power the spectacles of global sport.

Cortázar is also meditating on the problems of imitation and cultural transfer, suggesting that they can lead to violent and culturally peculiar innovations. The adjective *cultural* appears gratuitous here and needs some justification. That Tokyo and Canberra, Baghdad and Mexico City are all involved in the story does not mean that they have become fungible pieces of an arbitrarily shifting, delocalized world. Each of these places does have complex local realities, such that death in a swimming pool has one kind of meaning in Canberra, as do hosting large spectacles in Iraq and making bizarre technical innovations in Japan. Whatever Cortázar's idea about these differences, they remain cultural, but no longer in the inertial mode that the word previously implied. Culture does imply difference, but the differences now are no longer taxonomic; they are interactive and refractive, so that competing for a swimming championship takes on the peculiar power that it does in Canberra partly because of the way some transnational forces have come to be configured in the imagination of its residents. Culture thus shifts from being some sort of inert, local substance to being a rather more volatile form of difference. This is an important part of the reason for writing against culture, as Lila Abu-Lughod (1991) has suggested.

There are surely other macronarratives that spin out of this small piece of magical realism, but all of them remind us that lives today are as much acts of projection and imagination as they are enactments of known scripts or predictable outcomes. In this sense, all lives have something in common with international athletic spectacle, as guest workers strive to meet standards of efficiency in new national settings, and brides who marry into households at large distances from home strive to meet the criteria of hypercompetence that these new contexts often demand. The deterritorialized world in which many people now live—some moving in it actively, others living with their absences or sudden returns—is, like Cortázar's pool of grits, ever thirsty for new technical competences and often harsh with the unprepared. Cortázar's vignette is itself a compressed ethnographic parable, and in teasing out the possible histories of its protagonists and their possible futures, our own ethnographies of literature can become exercises in the interpretation of the new role of the imagination in social life. There is in such efforts a built-in reflexive vertigo as we contemplate Cortázar's inventing of Tashuma, but such reflexivity leads not only into reflections on our own representational practices as writers but also into the complex nesting of imaginative appropriations that are involved in the construction of agency in a deterritorialized world.

But not all deterritorialization is global in its scope, and not all imagined lives span vast international panoramas. The world on the move affects even small geographical and cultural spaces. In several different ways, contemporary cinema represents these small worlds of displacement. Mira Nair's films capture the texture of these small displacements, whose reverberations can nevertheless be large. One of her films, *India Cabaret*, is what I have called an ethnodrama.[3] Made in 1984, it tells about a small group of women who have left towns and villages, generally in the southern part of India, to come to Bombay and work as cabaret dancers in a seedy suburban bar and nightclub called the Meghraj. The film contains (in the style of the early Jean-Luc Godard) extended conversations between the filmmaker and a few of these women, who are presented facing the camera as if they are talking to the viewer of the film. These interview segments, which are richly narrative, are intercut with dance sequences from the cabaret and extended treatments of the sleazy paradoxes of the lives of some of the men who are regulars there. The film also follows one of the women back to her natal village, where we are shown the pain of her ostracism, as her occupation in Bombay is known to everyone. It is rumored that this scene was staged for the benefit of the filmmaker, but if anything this replaying adds to the awkwardness and pain of the sequence. The film is not about happy endings, and it leaves us with possibilities of various sorts in the lives of these women, all of whom are simultaneously proud and ashamed, dignified and defiant de facto prostitutes who have fabricated identities as artists.

For our purposes, what is most important about this film is the way in which it shows that the cabaret club is not simply a marketplace for desire but also a place where imagined lives are negotiated: the dancers act out their precarious sense of themselves as dancers; the second-rate band tries to work up its musical passions, which are fed by the aspirations of the Catholic community in Goa (western India) to play European and American instrumental music well. The men who come as customers clearly see themselves as participants in something larger than life, and they behave exactly like the customers in cabaret scenes in many Hindi commercial films. In fact, the scenario that provides the meeting ground for all these characters is provided by the cabaret sequences from Hindi commercial cinema.

In many such stock scenes, a tawdry nightclub quartet plays an oppressively sensuous melody combining Western and Indian instruments and tonalities, while the villain and his cronies consume obviously nasty alcoholic drinks and watch a painfully explicit dance routine by a vamp star. The hero is usually insinuated into the action in some way that simultaneously emphasizes his virility and his moral superiority over the tawdry environment. These scenes are usually filled with extras from the film studio, who struggle to maintain the sophisticated visage of persons habituated to the high life. These scenes are stereotypically vicarious in their approach to drink, dance, and sound and are somehow depressing. The clients, the dancers, and the band at the Meghraj seem to play out a slightly out-of-step, somnambulistic version of such classic Hindi film sequences.

Life in the Meghraj is surely driven by commercial cinematic images, but their force is inadequate to cover the anxieties, the self-abasement, and the agonized drama of leisure in which the characters are all engaged. Yet the characters in this ethnodrama have images and ideas of themselves that are not simply contingent outcomes of their ordinary lives (or simple escapes from them) but are fabrications based on a subtle complicity with the discursive and representational conventions of Hindi cinema. Thus, although this film is a documentary in conventional terms, it is also an ethnodrama, in the sense that it shows us the dramatic structure and the characters that animate a particular strand of Bombay's ways of life. These actors are also characters, not so much because they have obvious idiosyncrasies attached to them but because they are fabrications negotiated in the encounter between the efforts of cinema to represent cabaret and of real cabarets to capture the excitement of cinema. It is this negotiation, not only the negotiation of bodies, that is the real order of business at the Meghraj. The women who work in the cabaret are deterritorialized and mobile: they are guest workers in Bombay. It is hard to see in them the discourse of resistance (though they are cynical about men, as prostitutes everywhere are), although their very bodily postures, their linguistic aggressiveness, their bawdy, quasi-lesbian play with each other imply a kind of raunchy and self-conscious counterculture. What we have is a sense that they are putting lives together, fabricating their own characters, using the cinematic and social materials at their disposal.

There are individuals here, to be sure, and agency as well, but what drives these individuals and their agency are the complex realisms that animate them: a crude realism about men and their motives; a sort of capitalist realism that inspires their discourse about wealth and money; a curious socialist realism that underlies their own categorizations of themselves as dignified workers in the flesh trade (not very different from the housewives of Bombay). They constitute a striking ethnographic example for this chapter because the very displacement that is the root of their problems (although their original departures turn out usually to be responses to even worse domestic horrors) is also the engine of their dreams of wealth, respectability, and autonomy.

Thus, pasts in these constructed lives are as important as futures, and the more we unravel these pasts the closer we approach worlds that are less and less cosmopolitan, more and more local. Yet even the most localized of these worlds, at least in societies like India, has become inflected— even afflicted—by cosmopolitan scripts that drive the politics of families, the frustrations of laborers, the dreams of local headmen. Once again, we need to be careful not to suppose that as we work backward in these imagined lives we will hit some local, cultural bedrock, made up of a closed set of reproductive practices and untouched by rumors of the world at large. (For a different but complementary angle on these facts, see Hannerz 1989.) Mira Nair's *India Cabaret* is a striking model of how ethnography in a deterritorialized world might handle the problems of character and actor, for it shows how self-fabrication actually proceeds in a world of types and typification. It retains the tension between global and local that drives cultural reproduction today.

The vignettes I have used here have two purposes. One is to suggest the sorts of situations in which the workings of the imagination in a deterritorialized world can be detected. The second is to suggest that many lives are now inextricably linked with representations, and thus we need to incorporate the complexities of expressive representation (film, novels, travel accounts) into our ethnographies, not only as technical adjuncts but as primary material with which to construct and interrogate our own representations.

Conclusion: Invitations and Exhortations

Although the emergent cosmopolitanisms of the world have complex local histories, and their translocal dialogue has a complex history as well (Islamic pilgrimage is just one example), it seems advisable to treat the present as a historical moment and use our understanding of it to illuminate and guide the formulation of historical problems. This is not perverse Whiggishness; it is, rather, a response to a practical problem: in many cases it is simply not clear how or where one would locate a chronological baseline for the phenomena we wish to study. The strategy of beginning at the beginning becomes even more self-defeating when one wishes to illuminate the lived relationships between imagined lives and the webs of cosmopolitanism within which they unfold. Thus, not to put too fine a point on it, we need an ethnography that is sensitive to the historical nature of what we see today (which also involves careful comparison, as every good historian knows), but I suggest that we cut into the problem through the historical present.

While much has been written about the relationship between history and anthropology (by practitioners of both disciplines) in the past decade, few have given careful thought to what it means to construct genealogies of the present. Especially in regard to the many alternative cosmopolitanisms that characterize the world today, and the complex, transnational cultural flows that link them, there is no easy way to begin at the beginning. Today's cosmopolitanisms combine experiences of various media with various forms of experience—cinema, video, restaurants, spectator sports, and tourism, to name just a few—that have different national and transnational genealogies. Some of these forms may start out as extremely global and end up as very local—radio would be an example—while others, such as cinema, might have the obverse trajectory. In any particular ethnoscape (a term we might wish to substitute for earlier wholes such as villages, communities, and localities), the genealogies of cosmopolitanism are not likely to be the same as its histories: while the genealogies reveal the cultural spaces within which new forms can become indigenized (for example, as tourism comes to inhabit the space of pilgrimage in India), the histories of these forms may lead outward to transnational sources and structures. Thus, the most appropriate ethnoscapes for today's world, with its alternative, interactive modernities, should enable genealogy and history to confront each other, thus leaving the terrain open for interpretations of the ways in which local historical trajectories flow into complicated transnational structures. Of course, this dialogue of histories and genealogies itself has a history, but for this latter history we surely do not yet possess a master narrative. For those of us who might wish to move toward this new master narrative, whatever its form, new global ethnoscapes must be the critical building blocks. Michel-Rolph Trouillot (1991) suggests that the historical role of anthropology was to fill the "savage slot" in an internal Western dialogue about utopia. A recuperated anthropology must recognize that the genie is now out of the bottle and that speculations about utopia are everyone's prerogative. Anthropology can surely contribute its special purchase on lived experience to a wider, transdisciplinary study of global cultural processes. But to do this, anthropology must first come in from the cold and face the challenge of making a contribution to cultural studies without the benefit of its previous principal source of leverage—sightings of the savage.

4

Consumption, Duration, and History

Consumption as a topic has always come equipped with an optical illusion. This illusion, especially fostered by the neoclassical economics of the past century or so, is that consumption is the end of the road for goods and services, a terminus for their social life, a conclusion to some sort of material cycle. My main concern in this chapter is to show that this view is indeed an illusion, and that in order to get rid of it we need to resituate consumption in time—time conceived multiply—as history, periodicity, and process. From this view follows a series of methodological suggestions and a preliminary proposal about a way to conceptualize what is new about consumerism after the advent of electronic media.

Repetition and Regulation

Like breathing, consumption is a self-effacing habit that becomes noticeable only when contextually ostentatious. But it is only in ostentation that we often take notice of consumption, and this is the first of the methodological traps we need to avoid, a trap that pertains to many other topics as well. That is, we need to resist the temptation to construct a general theory of consumption around what Neil McKendrick and colleagues called the "Veblen effect" (McKendrick, Brewer, and Plumb 1982; Veblen 1912), namely, the tendency of mobility patterns to be organized around the imitation of social superiors. The fact that consumption may sometimes be conspicuous and imitative should not tempt us to regard it as always being so, not least because various forms of abstinence can be equally conspicuous and socially consequential (Appadurai 1986).

As a general feature of the cultural economy, consumption must and does fall into the mode of repetition, of habituation. In this regard, the observation by Fredric Jameson (1990), building on Jean Baudrillard, Sigmund Freud, Søren Kierkegaard, and others, that repetition characterizes the commodity culture of consumer capitalism, can be situated in a wider anthropology of the relationship between consumption and repetition. Even in the most fashion-ridden of contexts, as I shall suggest in the next section of this chapter, consumption leans toward habituation through repetition. The principal reason for this is that consumption, in all social contexts, is centered around what Marcel Mauss called the "techniques of the body" (Mauss 1973), and the body calls for disciplines that are repetitious, or at least periodic. This is not because the body is everywhere the same biological fact and thus demands the same disciplines. On the contrary, because the body is an intimate arena for the practices of reproduction, it is an ideal site for the inscription of social disciplines, disciplines that can be widely varied. Playing on one of the etymological roots of the word *consume*, it is worth noting that eating—unlike, say, tattooing—calls for habituation, even in the most upscale environments where food has become largely dominated by ideas of bodily beauty and comportment rather than by ideas of energy and sufficiency (Bourdieu 1984).

But even where hedonistic and antinomian consumption practices have taken deep hold, there remains a tendency for those practices of consumption that are closest to the body to acquire uniformity through habituation: food, dress, hairstyling. I stress the force of habituation, as it has frequently been lost sight of in favor of the forces of imitation or opposition. These latter forces can often be very important, but they always encounter the social inertia of bodily techniques. Thus, even among monks, vegetarians, food faddists, and counterconsumers of every sort, it is extremely difficult to maintain an anarchic consumption regime. The techniques of the body, however peculiar, innovative, and antisocial, need to become social disciplines (Asad 1987), parts of some habitus, free of artifice or external coercion, in order to take on their full power. The core of consumption practices being the body, the habituation that requires bodily disciplines to be successful entails consumption patterns that will always tend to repetition, at least in some regards. This is the inner paradox of hedonism especially in its anarchic dimensions: even hedonistic consumption requires its bodily disciplines, and these disciplines encourage repetition and discourage inventiveness by their nature (Campbell 1987). Even an unkempt beard must be maintained.

Naturally, not all consumption need be repetitive or habitual, but any consumption system that strives for freedom from habit is pushed toward an aesthetic of the ephemeral, as I will suggest in the course of this chapter. This accounts for some important features of the relation among consumption, fashion, and pleasure, discussed in my conclusion. All consumption practices that endure at all must pay some tribute to bodily inertia, even if this inertia affects very different areas and is anchored in dramatically different ideologies across time and space. On this inertial base can be built a variety of different periodicities and temporal rhythms, including some driven by Thorstein Veblen's type of conspicuous consumption.

In any socially regulated set of consumption practices, those that center around the body, and especially around the feeding of the body, take on the function of structuring temporal rhythm, of setting the minimum temporal measure (by analogy to musical activity) on which much more complex and chaotic patterns can be built. Pushing the analogy a step further, the small habits of consumption, typically daily food habits, can perform a percussive role in organizing large-scale consumption patterns, which may be made up of much more complex orders of repetition and improvisation. The methodological moral here may be put as follows: where imitation seems to dominate, repetition might be lurking.

The inertial logic of repetition is a resource around which societies and their ruling classes build larger regimes of periodicity, typically around some form of seasonality. Our experience of the Christmas gifting frenzy in the United States exemplifies this sort of regime very well. In many societies, important rites of passage have consumption markers, often cohering around obligatory or near-obligatory patterns of gift giving, typically between predesignated categories of socially linked persons, often kinsfolk. But this does not imply a mechanical marriage of Arnold van Gennep and Marcel Mauss (van Gennep 1965; Mauss 1976). In fact, the seasonalities that organize consumption are more complicated and less mechanical than is at first apparent.

The acts of consumption that surround routine rites of passage are often less mechanically prescriptive than they might appear. Pierre Bourdieu has shown this very well in his discussion of the gifts between affines in Kabyle marriage alliances in Algeria (1977). What Bourdieu is able to show, as an instance of what he calls the regulated improvisations of the habitus, is that what appears to be a fixed set of prescriptions that govern gift transactions between affines is governed by an extremely complex set of strategic interactions, whose sequence, because improvisatory, is unpredictable, although its general social morphology is known to the actors at the very outset. A crucial source of uncertainty, which can be treated as a strategic resource by the key actors, is the *lapse of time* between various acts of gifting. Bronislaw Malinowski had earlier noted this key role of timing in gift giving (1922), and so had Mauss, while Marshall Sahlins gave it greater typological force (Mauss 1976; Sahlins 1972). For our purposes, it suggests that the rhythms of accumulation and divestiture that generate particular states of material wealth in many societies are products not of mechanical distributions of goods or of predictable patterns of gifting but of complex calculative sequences, built, like other agonistic forms, on shared understandings of style but considerable latitude in strategy.

This calculative dimension of gift giving offers a more complex perspective on the relationship between consumption and rites of passage. Acts of gift exchange, with their attendant implications for consumption and production, are often seen in the context of rites of passage as highly conventionalized markers (in Charles Pierce's term, as icons) of these rites. But it may be more useful to see these consumption strategies as *indexically* related to rites of passage, that is, as creating the meaning of these rites by the way in which they point to their meaning. Let me elaborate. The basic package of rites described by van Gennep (1965), those having to do with birth, initiation, marriage, and death, are usually regarded as cultural regularities with a remarkable degree of universality owing, in van Gennep's argument, to the physiological and cosmological uniformities on which they are built. Using Mauss's ideas about the techniques of the body (1973) to turn van Gennep on his head, I suggest that consumption periodicities, mediated by strategies of accumulation and divestiture, often constitute the principal significance of these "natural" events rather than simply marking them in some loose, "symbolic" manner. This is very clear in initiation and marriage, where issues of time and timing are obviously salient, given the degree of play available to key actors in determining when and who these events shall affect. With birth and death, the biological clock seems primary, and yet even here we know that the ritual marking of these events, which can be lengthy, debated, and highly idiosyncratic, defines their social salience (Geertz 1973). What affects social salience is the nature, timing, scale, and social visibility of the material transactions that constitute the ritual process of these rites. The argument would be simpler still in the case of the other rites of passage that van Gennep discussed, rites involving transitions in space, territory, group membership, agriculture, and the like. In a word, the socially organized periodicities of consumption, and the calculative strategies that give them agency and amplitude, are constitutive of the social meanings of rites of passage, and not simply symbolic markers of these meanings. Thus, on the larger seasonal scales of seasons, biographies, and group histories discussed by van Gennep and others, consumption regulates the more tight periodicities of temporal rites of passage. In this sense, consumption creates time and does not simply respond to it.

To make this maxim clearer, I return to Christmas. In the United States, as the range of commodities grows, as families find themselves with larger lists of goods and services that might fulfill the desires of family members, and as fashions, particularly for youth, shift mercurially, those who play the crucial Santa role find themselves shopping earlier for Christmas. Timing is a delicate problem, as everyone wants to get his or her shopping done before the Christmas rush, and the ideal thing would be to do your Christmas shopping while you are sweltering in June or July. Absurd as this already seems, it is made doubly difficult by the fact that it is not until September or October that the fashion cycle, especially for such items as children's toys, starts issuing clear signals. So, you have to know how long to wait before deciding that this year's favorites have been established, but not so long that the stores have run out of them. At the other end of the process, all large stores run after-Christmas sales, but frequently, because of low shopper turnout in some parts of the country, there are pre-Christmas sales, further distorting the periodicity of prices and sentiments that have to be juggled by American families. The shrewd shopper has always known that the best time to shop for Christmas gifts (especially if you are not worried about goods subject to short fashion cycles) is in the immediate post-Christmas potlatches at the big stores. So Christmas is obviously not a simple seasonal fact. From one point of view, it may be seen as a yearlong celebration, with more and less frenzied periods of conscious activity. In this case, it is a lot more like Trobriand yam gardening than like birth by cesarean section. The difference lies in the larger social logics of acquisition and divestiture that are coordinated for the particular rite of passage to be successful. The methodological maxim here somewhat complicates the previous one: where repetition in consumption seems to be determined by natural or universal seasonalities of passage, always consider the reverse causal chain, in which consumption seasonalities might determine the style and significance of "natural" passages.

But the seasonalities of consumption themselves are carved out of more open-ended, more circumstantial, more contingent temporal processes, and we generally choose to call these historical. History, in all societies, irrespective of whether they are hot or cool, literate or not, is by definition the story of the *longue durée*, whether or not we know enough about all the histories we encounter. In regard to consumption the structures of the long run have not been as elaborately studied in terms of the world outside the West as they have been for Europe and the world that Europe encountered after 1500. Yet we know enough about at least some of the histories of the rest of the world over long spans of time (Curtin 1984; Hodgson 1974; Perlin 1983; Schafer 1963; Wolf 1982) to know that rather than clear units of spatiotemporal process, the world has for a very long time been constituted by overlapping congeries of cultural ecumenes. Central to the cultural economy of distance has been the driving force of merchants, trade, and commodities, especially of the luxury variety (Curtin 1984; Helms 1988; Mintz 1985; Schafer 1963). Nevertheless, not all structures of the long run are characterized by the same turns, or contingencies, that in retrospect take on the appearance of necessity. Literacy did not appear everywhere and neither did bubonic plague or the idea of democratic rights. So patterns in the *longue durée* must be considered, in the first instance, locally, that is, within fairly well-observed and documented spheres of interaction. With regard to consumption, long-term change is not everywhere equally rapid, although it seems increasingly foolish to contrast static with changing societies. The question seems to be the pace and intensity of change, as well as the alacrity with which it is invited.

What we know of Europe allows us to watch a society of sumptuary law slowly changing into a society of fashion. In general, all socially organized forms of consumption seem to revolve around some combination of the following three patterns: interdiction, sumptuary law, and fashion. The first pattern, typical of small-scale, low-tech, ritually oriented societies, organizes consumption through a fairly large list of dos and don'ts, many of them combining cosmology and etiquette in a special way. In these societies, what used to be called taboos in an older anthropology frequently regulate consumption for certain social categories, for certain temporal contexts, for certain goods (Douglas and Isherwood 1981). The social life of things in small-scale societies appears to have been driven largely by the force of interdiction. Yet as we learn more from the archaeological record, small societies in places like Melanesia seem to have long been characterized by long-distance flows, both maritime and land-based, of at least some kinds of goods. In such societies, interdiction structures of various sorts appear to have successfully accommodated new commodities into existing structures of exchange and polity, partly because the quantitative explosion associated with the commodity world had not yet appeared. Even in such low-tech societies, particular conjunctures of commodity flow and trade can create unpredicted changes in value structures (Sahlins 1981).

At this point it is tempting to pose Colin Campbell's version of the Weberian question regarding the historical conditions for the rise of capitalism, that is, to ask it in a way that highlights the consumption side of things. There seems to be widespread agreement among historians and sociologists working in Europe and the United States that a major transformation on the demand side appears to have taken place in Europe sometime after the fifteenth century (Campbell 1987; Mukerji 1983; McKendrick et al. 1982; McCracken 1988; Williams 1982). There is, however, no unanimity on the nature of the conditions that enabled the consumer revolution, except a broad sense that it was associated with the relationships between traditional aristocracies and ascendant bourgeoisies in the early modern period. But is there a more sharply articulated way to ask the question, when and under what sorts of conditions do consumer revolutions occur?

I will eventually suggest that the idea of consumer revolution is itself in some ways inadequate to the electronic present. Yet it might be of some preliminary value to define *consumer revolution* in a sufficiently narrow way so as to make comparison appealing and in a sufficiently broad way so as to avoid the tautologous question, why did the history of Europe (or England) happen only in Europe (or England)? I suggest that we define *consumer revolution* as a cluster of events whose key feature is a *generalized* shift from the reign of sumptuary law to the reign of fashion. This detaches consumer revolutions from any particular temporal sequence involving a mobile society, sophisticated marketing on the Josiah Wedgwood model, rising wages, mass merchandising, and class conflict. It also detaches consumer revolutions from specific historical sequences and conjunctures involving literacy, numeracy, expert knowledge, the book trade, and other forms of commoditized information of the sort relevant to England, France, and the United States in the past three centuries. Instead, this definition opens up the possibility that large-scale changes in consumption may be associated with various sequences and conjunctures of these factors. Thus, in India department stores are a very late development, coming after advertising had been for at least forty years a well-established commercial practice, in contrast to France, where department stores (Miller 1981; Williams 1982) seem to have preceded the modern form of the advertising industry, in conjunction with national expositions and other phenomena of leisure and spectacle. The relationship of conjuncture and sequence between the English and French consumer revolutions seems itself to be complex and contestable. In Japan after World War II, there is good evidence that mass consumption emerged substantially as a result of television viewing (often of situation comedies from the United States), and that advertising followed as a postmodernist commentatorial mode on such consumption rather than as a primary causal factor (Ivy 1989). Such differences are, of course, in part a product of the complexities of cultural flow after 1800, whereby many countries have evolved sophisticated technologies of marketing before becoming massively industrial economies. Thus, if you compare Elizabethan England with India, the right comparison would have to be with India in the late eighteenth century, when the sumptuary reach of the Mughal sovereign was both imitated and contested by all sorts of commercial and political groups in North India (Bayly 1986). Likewise, the role of class conflicts and sumptuary battles between old and new aristocracies can have very different weight, if you compare Japan and India, where the dissolution of monarchical ideas and the rise of industrial capitalism have very different internal causal and temporal relationships. Such examples could be multiplied.

The general methodological point is clear: just as we have learned, partly through the protoindustrialization debate, not to prejudge the links between European commercial forms and the rise of capitalist modes of production and exchange, likewise with consumption: what we need to avoid is the search for preestablished sequences of institutional change, axiomatically defined as constitutive of *the* consumer revolution. What this might encourage is a multiplication of scenarios concerning the appearance of consumer society, in which the rest of the world will not simply be seen as repeating, or imitating, the conjunctural precedents of England or France. Having explored such conjunctural variations in the links between class, production, marketing, and politics over long stretches of any particular history, we might be in a better position to construct models of global interaction in the realm of consumption, both before and after the great maritime expansion of Europe in the sixteenth century.

In comparing consumer revolutions in this manner, we can maintain the tension between the *longue durée* of localities and the variable duration of various world processes by making a distinction that has proved useful in another context (chap. 3), the distinction between history and genealogy. While each of these words has a host of meanings (depending on your jargon of choice), my own usage is as follows: history leads you outward, to link patterns of changes to increasingly larger universes of interaction; genealogy leads you inward, toward cultural dispositions and styles that might be stubbornly embedded both in local institutions and in the history of the local habitus. Thus, the history of Mahatma Gandhi's ascetical relationship to the world of goods might lead outward to John Ruskin, Henry David Thoreau, and others in the West who articulated a pastoral, anti-industrial vision. But the genealogy of Gandhi's hostility to goods and possessive individualism generally probably leads inward, to a longstanding Indic discomfort with attachment to sensory experience at large. Furthermore, history and genealogy may, in regard to particular practices or institutions, reinforce each other, to the point where one may disguise the other or contradict one another, as in the following example, also from India. When Indians began to enter the British world of clothing in the nineteenth century, certain desirable items of clothing acquired a history that indigenous elites found appealing but a genealogy that was more troubling. For Brahman elites, for example, the history of hat wearing linked them to a narrative of their own cosmopolitan, colonial past, but its genealogy was probably less comforting, for it juxtaposed very different ideas about hair and headgear, also crucial to the Brahman habitus. In general, in any given social and temporal location, the study of the *longue durée* with respect to consumption should involve the simultaneous exploration of the histories and genealogies of particular practices. This double historicizing is likely to reveal multiple processual flows that underwrite any given conjuncture and simultaneously make it possible to compare without sacrificing contrast, in regard to the study of consumer revolutions.

Returning then to the relationship between the small cycles, anchored in the techniques of the body, which constitute the core of all durable consumption practices, and in the more open-ended historical sequences in which they are embedded, it is important to see that the tempo of these small-scale periodicities may be set in more than one *longue durée*, with the processes implied by history and genealogy creating multiple temporalities for any given practice (Halbwachs 1980). It further follows that in studying the consumption practices of distinct societies, we must be prepared to encounter a host of different histories and genealogies present at the same moment. Thus, in France the consumption of perfume in 1880 (Corbin 1986) may be underpinned by one kind of history of bodily discipline and aesthetics, while the consumption of meat may respond to wholly other histories and genealogies. The more diverse a society and the more complex the story of its interactions with other societies, the more fragmented the history of its consumption practices is likely to be, even if broad styles, trends, and patterns are discernible. The move from small to large temporal consumption rhythms is a move from more to less patterned periodicities. Writing the history of "distinction" in the sense of Bourdieu (1984) will entail openness to such multiplicity. In the following sections, I confine myself to those societies in which fashion, at least for some classes, has become the dominant mechanism driving consumption and in which commodification is a critical feature of social life.

Fashion and Nostalgia

While much has been said about fashion (McCracken 1988; Miller 1987; Simmel 1957), it is still not fully understood as a feature of the temporal rhythms of industrial and postindustrial societies. Although it has been widely noted that fashion is the crucial link between production, merchandising, and consumption in capitalist societies, the relationship of fashion to what has recently been called "patina" by Grant McCracken has not been fully explored. The problem of patina, which McCracken proposes as a general term to deal with that property of goods by which their age becomes a key index of their high status, disguises a deeper dilemma, the dilemma of distinguishing wear from tear. That is, while in many cases wear is a sign of the right sort of duration in the social life of things, sheer disrepair or decrepitude is not. Wear, as a property of material objects, is thus itself a very complicated property that requires considerable maintenance. The polishing of old silver, the dusting of old furniture, the patching of old clothes, the varnishing of old surfaces—these are all part of the embodied practice of the upper classes in many societies, or, more exactly, of their servants. We might say, paraphrasing the well-known aphorism, "as for patina, our servants will provide it for us." But poorly maintained patina can become itself a sign either of poor breeding, outright social counterfeiting (Goffman 1951), or, worse still, complete penury. In short, patina is a slippery property of material life, ever open to faking as well as to crude handling. The patina of objects takes on its full meaning only in a proper context, of both other objects and spaces for these assemblies of objects and persons who know how to indicate, through their bodily practices, their relationships to these objects; the English country house comes to mind as a good example of this complex set of relationships. When all these conditions are felicitous, then the transposition of temporality, the

subtle shift of patina from the object to its owner or neighbor, is successful, and the person (or family or social group) himself or herself takes on
the invisible patina of reproduction well managed, of temporal continuity
undisturbed. But patina, the gloss of age, cannot by itself generate the
right temporal associations for human beings. Here, as in so many other
matters involving material life, context is everything. The distinction between an heirloom and junk is not patina as such, but also the successful
semiotic management of the social context. There is, too, a delicate temporal rhythm to be managed, particularly where membership in elites is
partly constructed through patina. Because all things have a "cultural biography" (Kopytoff 1986), even those objects that have the most unchange-
able patina have possible histories, some of which include theft, sale, or
other improper modes of acquisition. As the nouveaux riches know, the
important thing is to regulate the pace at which an ensemble of objects
with patina is assembled. If you are too slow, only your descendants will
know the pleasures of the right gloss, but if you are too quick, George Bab-
bitt's fate awaits you, surrounded as you might be with the right things.
Thus, the management of temporal rhythms is critical to the exploitation
of patina.

As a key to the material life of aristocracies (and would be aristocrats),
patina feeds a deeper stream in the social life of things, and that is the capability of certain things to evoke nostalgia, a syndrome Marcel Proust immortalized. Objects with patina are perpetual reminders of the passage of
time as a double-edged sword, which credentials the "right" people, just as
it threatens the way they lived. Whenever aristocratic lifestyles are threatened, patina acquires a double meaning, indexing both the special status of
its owner and the owner's special relationship to a way of life that is no
longer available. The latter is what makes patina a truly scarce resource,
for it always indicates the fact that a way of living is now gone forever. Yet
this very fact is a guarantee against the newly arrived, for they can acquire
objects with patina, but never the subtly embodied anguish of those who
can legitimately bemoan the loss of a way of life. Naturally, good impostors may seek to mimic this nostalgic posture as well, but here both performances and reviews are a more tightly regulated affair. It is harder to
pretend to have lost something than it is to actually do so or to claim to
have found it. Here, material wear cannot disguise social rupture.

The effort to inculcate nostalgia is a central feature of modern merchandising and is best seen in the graphics and texts of gift-order catalogs
in the United States. These catalogs use a variety of rhetorical devices, but
especially when it comes to clothing, furniture, and design, they play with

many kinds of nostalgia: nostalgia for bygone lifestyles, material assemblages, life stages (such as childhood), landscapes (of the Currier and Ives variety), scenes (of the Norman Rockwell small-town variety), and so on. Much has been written about these matters, and we now have some excellent work on the relationship of nostalgia and authenticity to collections, toys, and spectacles (Breckenridge 1989; Stewart 1984). But what has not been explored is the fact that such nostalgia, as far as mass merchandising is concerned, does not principally involve the evocation of a sentiment to which consumers who really have lost something can respond. Rather, these forms of mass advertising teach consumers to miss things they have never lost (Halbwachs 1980). That is, they create experiences of duration, passage, and loss that rewrite the lived histories of individuals, families, ethnic groups, and classes. In thus creating experiences of losses that never took place, these advertisements create what might be called "imagined nostalgia," nostalgia for things that never were. This imagined nostalgia thus inverts the temporal logic of fantasy (which tutors the subject to imagine what could or might happen) and creates much deeper wants than simple envy, imitation, or greed could by themselves invite.

The final twist in the peculiar logic of nostalgia in the politics of mass consumption involves what Fredric Jameson has called "nostalgia for the present," a term he uses to discuss certain recent films that project a future from whose perspective the present is not only historicized but also misrecognized as something the viewer has already lost (1989). Jameson's idea, illuminating in regard to certain strands in popular cinema and literature today, can be extended more widely to the world of mass merchandising. Nostalgia for the present, the stylized presentation of the present as if it has already slipped away, characterizes a very large number of television advertisements, especially those directed at the youth market. A whole new video aesthetic has emerged, most notably in the campaigns for Pepsi, Levi jeans, and Ralph Lauren outfits, in which contemporary scenes are lit, choreographed, and shot in a way that creates a sort of back-to-the-future ethos: spare, surreal, science-fictionish in certain regards, unmistakably evocative of the sixties (or fifties) in other regards. We may wish to label much of this aesthetic as based on a kind of "histoire noire." Bracketing the present in this peculiar way, and thus making it already the object of a historical sensibility, these images put the consumer in an already periodized present, thus even readier prey to the velocity of fashion. Buy now, not because you will otherwise be out of date but because your period will soon be out of date.

Thus, nostalgia and fashion creep up unknowingly on one another, not just because nostalgia is a clever instrument of the merchandiser's toolbox, but because the continuous change of small features (that is at the heart of fashion) now has acquired a recycling dimension, especially in the United States, that is remarkable. Rummaging through history has become a standard technique of advertising, especially of visual and electronic ads, as a way to draw on the genuine nostalgia of age-groups for pasts they actually know through other experiences, but also as a way to underline the inherent ephemerality of the present. Catalogs that exploit the colonial experience for merchandising purposes are an excellent example of this technique (Smith 1988). This inculcated sentiment, calculated to intensify the tempo of purchasing by toying with the merchandiser's version of the end of history, is the latest twist in the compact between nostalgia and fantasy in modern merchandising. Rather than expecting the consumer to supply memories while the merchandiser supplies the lubricant of nostalgia, now the viewer need only bring the faculty of nostalgia to an image that will supply the memory of a loss he or she has never suffered. This relationship might be called armchair nostalgia, nostalgia without lived experience or collective historical memory. One methodological issue here is interpretive: when we consider those images to which modern consumers respond, we need to distinguish different textures of temporality from one another. We need to discriminate between the force of nostalgia in its primary form and the ersatz nostalgia on which mass merchandising increasingly draws and to attend to how these two might relate in the consumption patterns of different groups. The other methodological issue is simply a matter of paying attention to the paradoxical regularity with which patina and fashion in societies of mass consumption feed and reinforce one other. Mass-merchandising techniques not only construct time, as was suggested earlier, but also influence periodization as a mass experience in contemporary societies.

Let us return briefly to the issue of repetition in relation to consumption, touched on in the previous discussion. How can we connect the problem of repetition to the issues of fantasy, nostalgia, and consumption in contemporary consumer societies? Insofar as consumption is increasingly driven by rummaging through imagined histories, repetition is not simply based on the functioning of simulacra *in* time, but also on the force of the simulacra *of* time. That is, consumption not only creates time, through its periodicities, but the workings of ersatz nostalgia create the simulacra of periods that constitute the flow of time, conceived as lost, absent, or distant. Thus, the forward-looking habituation to predictable styles, forms, and genres, which drives commodity consumption onward as a multiplicative and open-ended activity, is powered by an implosive, retrospective construction of time, in which repetition is itself an artifact of ersatz nostalgia and imagined precursory moments.

The Commodification of Time

Consumption not only creates time, but consumer revolutions are also responsible for the commodification of time in a variety of ways. The general lead in this area is, of course, owed to E. P. Thompson, who, building on Karl Marx, showed how the disciplines of the industrial workplace create needs for the regimentation of labor by the prior restructuring of time itself. Extending the transformation of labor into a commodity, labor time becomes an abstract dimension of time experienced as fundamentally productive and industrial. Thompson identifies the logic that leads to later Taylorean ideas about the body, motion, and productivity (Thompson 1967). Modern ideas of production thus have time as a salable entity at their heart, evoking Benjamin Franklin's homily that "time is money."

But we have had fewer fundamental insights into the commodification of time seen from the consumer's point of view. In early industrial societies, where industrial time sets the rhythm of the work cycle, production defines work, and consumption is rendered residual along with leisure, which comes to be recognized logically as the reward for production time well used. Consumption evolves as the phenomenological marker of time left over from work, produced by work, and justified by work. Leisure activities become the very definition of discretionary consumption (Rojek 1987), and consumption becomes the process that creates the conditions for the renewed labor or entrepreneurial energy required for production. Thus, consumption is seen as the required interval between periods of production.

But once time is commodified, it affects consumption in new ways. First, the degree of time over which one has discretionary control becomes an index for ranking and distinguishing various kinds of work, class, and occupation. "Free" time, whether for workers, professionals, or school-children, is seen as quintessentially the time of consumption, and because discretionary consumption calls both for free time (time freed of commodified constraints) and free money, at least to some degree, consumption becomes a temporal marker of leisure, of time away from work. When consumption is transformed into contemporary forms of leisure, where both space and time mark distance from work, we enter the world of the luxury cruise and the packaged vacation, commodified as "time out of time." But everyone who has taken a vacation within the highly constrained circumstances of an industrial society knows that the commodity clock of productive time never ceases to operate. This sometimes leads to the paradox increasingly characteristic of industrial leisure: the harried vacation, packed with so many activities, scenes, and choices, whose purpose is to create a hypertime of leisure, that the vacation indeed becomes a form of work, of frenetic leisure—leisure ever conscious of its forthcoming rendezvous with work time.

In fact, there is really little escape from the rhythms of industrial production, for wherever leisure is reliably available, and socially acceptable, what is required is not only free time but disposable income. To consume, whether in search of subsistence or leisure, we have to learn to contain money, that most fluid of values. As Mary Douglas has pointed out, money always threatens to slip through the cracks of the structures we build to dam, husband, and restrict its erratic flows (1967). In those industrial societies where consumer debt has become monstrously large, financial institutions have exploited the proclivity of consumers to spend before rather than after they save. From the consumers' point of view, they are not simple dupes of an exploitative system of financial lending. The credit economy is also a way of enhancing buying power in the face of huge salary differentials, an explosive growth in what is buyable, great intensification in the speed with which fashions change, and the like. Debt is income expansion by other means. Of course, from certain perspectives, paying large amounts of interest to service consumer debt is not healthy. But from whose point of view? The consumer can ratchet up his or her purchases, financial institutions make a killing, and there is periodic bloodletting, in the form of either major collapses like the recent savings and loan catastrophe in the United States or brutal increases in interest rates that asphyxiate consumer expenditure for a while.

In fact, as the immense popularity of magazines such as *Money* in the United States attests, consumption in complex industrial societies is now a very complicated skill that requires knowledge of a large variety of fiscal and economic mysteries, ranging from stock-market volatilities to housing starts and M-1. In the past decade, more American consumers have had to become literate in the mysteries of macroeconomics than ever before, at least to the degree that they are forced to enter the maze of consumer lending. Of course, there is a growing group at the bottom, notably the homeless, who have spent their chips and must now watch, or die, on the sidelines, as their friends and colleagues struggle with the roulette of consumer debt management. The relevance of these processes to the argument at hand is that in societies like the United States, there is emerging a gigantic, if silent, struggle between consumers and major lenders, where at issue are rival understandings of the future as a commodity. Where bankers and other lenders are eager to encourage borrowing (their major challenge is to minimize bad loans), the consumer has to define an open-ended temporal horizon within which the discounting of the future is an extremely tricky business. Recent debates in the United States over reductions in the Social Security tax reveal that most American consumers are prey to a variety of distorted perceptions about the taxes to which they are subject. A good part of this confusion is rooted in the deformation of the experience of time by the structures that currently organize consumer debt. Notable among these is the type of credit line, based on home equity, through which consumers can simply write checks against some specified large sum that defines the bank's sense of their ability to pay. What this involves is taking the small periodicities of the average credit card and turning them into a seductive vista of flexible purchasing power, which ultimately profits banks and retail businesses while putting increasing strain on household incomes to service these loans.

This feature of the creation of time discipline on the consumption side of advanced industrial societies is not a simple reflex, or inversion, of the logic of industrial production. The peculiar commodification of the future, which is at the heart of current consumer debt, is intimately tied to the structure of merchandising, fashion, and fantasy that were discussed in the previous section. Late industrial consumption relies on a peculiar tension between fantasy and nostalgia that gives substance (and sustenance) to consumer uncertainty about commodities, money, and the relationship between work and leisure. It is not simply the case that consumption plays the central role in societies where production once did, as Baudrillard has argued (1975); more to the point, consumption has become the civilizing work of postindustrial society (Elias 1978). To speak of contemporary industrial societies as consumer societies is to create the illusion that they are simply extensions of earlier consumer revolutions. But consumption today transforms the experience of time in a way that fundamentally distinguishes it from its eighteenth- and nineteenth-century predecessors.

Thus, large-scale innovations in lending have had a remarkable cultural effect. They have created an open-ended rather than cyclic climate for consumer borrowing; they have thereby linked borrowing to the long, linear sense of a lifetime of potential earnings and the equally open-ended sense of the growth value of assets such as houses, rather than to the short and inherently restrictive cycles of monthly or annual income. Consumption has thus become not the horizon of earning but its engine for a vast number of consumers in contemporary industrial societies. For the anthropologist, what is striking here (apart from the many implications for savings, productivity, investment, cross-generational entitlements, and the like) is that the small periodicities (typically daily ones) of consumption have now become subtly contextualized in an open, linear sense of the very rhythm of consumer life. The equivalent of Thompson's time discipline now reigns not just in the realm of production but also in the realm of consumption. But tied as it is to uneven, complex, and often long periodicities, these temporal disciplines of consumption are more powerful because they are less transparent than the disciplines of production. Anyone who has tried to figure out the exact logic of the finance charge on a monthly MasterCard bill will know about the uncertainty to which I refer.

But it is not simply the case that consumption has now become the driving force of industrial society. The fact is that consumption is now the social practice through which persons are drawn into the work of fantasy (chaps. 1 and 2). It is the daily practice through which nostalgia and fantasy are drawn together in a world of commodified objects. In the previous discussion, I argued that a sort of ersatz nostalgia—nostalgia without memory—was increasingly central to mass merchandising and that the interplay of patina and fashion was thus paradoxical. I would now suggest that the commodification of time on the consumption side implies more than the simple expansion of wants, styles, objects, and choices witnessed in earlier consumer revolutions. What we have now is something beyond a consumer revolution, something we may call a "revolution of consumption," in which consumption has become the principal work of late industrial society. By this I do not mean that there have not been important changes in production or in the sites, methods, technologies, and organizations for manufacturing commodities.

Consumption has now become a serious form of work, however, if by *work* we mean the disciplined (skilled and semiskilled) production of the means of consumer subsistence. The heart of this work is the social discipline of the imagination, the discipline of learning to link fantasy and nostalgia to the desire for new bundles of commodities. This is not to reduce work to a pale metaphor, mirroring its strong anchorage in production. It is to suggest that learning how to navigate the open-ended temporal flows of consumer credit and purchase, in a landscape where nostalgia has become divorced from memory, involves new forms of labor: the labor of reading ever-shifting fashion messages, the labor of debt servicing, the labor of learning how best to manage newly complex domestic finances, and the labor of acquiring knowledge in the complexities of money management. This labor is not principally targeted at the production of commodities but is directed at producing the conditions of consciousness in which *buying* can occur. Every housewife knows that housekeeping is work as real as any other. We are all housekeepers now, laboring daily to practice the disciplines of purchase in a landscape whose temporal structures have become radically polyrhythmic. Learning these multiple rhythms (of bodies, products, fashions, interest rates, gifts, and styles) and how to integrate them is not just work—it is the hardest sort of work, the work of the imagination. We are back then to Durkheim and Mauss and the nature of the collective consciousness, but now with a twist. The work of consumption is as fully social as it is symbolic, no less work for involving the discipline of the imagination. But increasingly freed from the techniques of the body, the work of consumption is all the more open-ended, situated in histories and genealogies whose conjuncture has to be examined, alas, case by case. The study of consumption will need to attend to the historical, social, and cultural conditions under which such work unfolds as the central preoccupation of otherwise very different contemporary societies.

Conclusion

From two very different directions, one drawing on Max Weber and the other on Norbert Elias, Colin Campbell (1987) and Chris Rojek (1987) suggest that the key to modern forms of consumerism is *pleasure*, not leisure (the crucial alternative for Rojek) or satisfaction (the crucial alternative for Campbell). This turn to pleasure as the organizing principle of modern consumption converges with my own argument in the last two sections of this chapter, but it remains now to show how the sort of pleasure I have in mind relates to my arguments about time, work, and the body.

As far as the experience of time is concerned, the pleasure that lies at the center of modern consumption is neither the pleasure of the tension between fantasy and utility (as Campbell suggests) nor the tension between individual desire and collective disciplines (Rojek's proposal), although these latter contrasts are relevant to any larger account of modern consumerism. The pleasure that has been inculcated into the subjects who act as modern consumers is to be found in the tension between nostalgia and fantasy, where the present is represented as if it were already past. This inculcation of the pleasure of *ephemerality* is at the heart of the disciplining of the modern consumer. The valorization of ephemerality expresses itself at a variety of social and cultural levels: the short shelf life of products and lifestyles; the speed of fashion change; the velocity of expenditure; the polyrhythms of credit, acquisition, and gift; the transience of television-product images; the aura of periodization that hangs over both products and lifestyles in the imagery of mass media. The much-vaunted feature of modern consumption—namely, the search for novelty—is only a symptom of a deeper discipline of consumption in which desire is organized around the aesthetic of ephemerality. Pockets of resistance are everywhere, as aristocrats batten down their sumptuary hatches, as working classes and other disenfranchised groups appropriate and resist mass aesthetics, and as states throughout the world seek immortality by freezing cultural difference. But the dominant force, spreading through the consuming classes of the world, appears to be the ethic, aesthetic, and material practice of the ephemeral.

If this valorization of ephemerality is indeed the key to modern consumption, then the techniques of the body differ in what were earlier contrasted as sumptuary and fashion regimes. In sumptuary regimes, the body is a site for the inscription of a variety of signs and values about identity and difference, as well as about duration (through the rites of passage). In regimes of fashion, the body is the site for the inscription of a generalized desire to consume in the context of the aesthetic of ephemerality. The techniques of the body appropriate to this modern consumption regime involve what Laura Mulvey has called scopophilia (the love of gazing) (1975); a variety of techniques (ranging from diets to sex-change operations) for body change that make the body of the consumer itself potentially ephemeral and manipulable; and a system of body-related fashion practices in which *impersonation* (of other genders, classes, roles, and occupations), not indexing, is the key to distinction (Sawchuk 1988).

This notion of the manipulation of the body, as well as my general argument about consumption as work, raises the question of how the aesthetic of ephemerality, the pleasure of the gaze (particularly in relation to television advertising), and the manipulability of the body add up to anything fundamentally new; after all, consumption, particularly at the level of the household, always involved drudgery, visual pleasure is not a modern prerogative, and manipulating the body is as old as gymnastics in Sparta and yogic praxis in ancient India. What is new is the *systematic* and *generalized* linkage of these three factors into a set of practices that involve a radically new relationship among wanting, remembering, being, and buying. The histories and genealogies that crisscross (in the world of the present) to constitute this new relationship are deeply variable, although they have the valorization of ephemerality at their heart. Consumption creates time, but modern consumption seeks to replace the aesthetics of duration with the aesthetics of ephemerality.

Although the full pursuit of the relation among bodies, consumption, fashion, and temporality in late capitalism is beyond the scope of this chapter, one suggestion is worth making by way of conclusion. In her recent essay on the imagery of the immune system in contemporary scientific and popular discourses in the United States, Emily Martin (1992) has drawn on the work of David Harvey (1989) and others to show that in the context of the flexibility demanded by contemporary global capitalism, there has been a great deal of compression of time and space, and the body comes to be seen as a chaotic, hyperflexible site, ridden with contradictions and warfare. The argument I have made in this chapter is to suggest that this situation can also be looked at from the point of view of the logic of consumption in a highly globalized, unruly, late capitalism. From this perspective, the aesthetic of ephemerality becomes the civilizing counterpart of flexible accumulation, and the work of the imagination is to link the ephemerality of goods with the pleasures of the senses. Consumption thus becomes the key link between nostalgia for capitalism and capitalist nostalgia.

PART II

Modern

Colonies

5

Playing with Modernity:

The Decolonization of Indian Cricket

For the former colony, decolonization is a dialogue with the colonial past, and not a simple dismantling of colonial habits and modes of life. Nowhere are the complexities and ambiguities of this dialogue more evident than in the vicissitudes of cricket in those countries that were once part of the British Empire. In the Indian case, the cultural aspects of decolonization deeply affect every domain of public life, from language and the arts to ideas about political representation and economic justice. In every major public debate in contemporary India, one underlying strand is always the question of what to do with the shreds and patches of the colonial heritage. Some of these patches are institutional; others are ideological and aesthetic.

Malcolm Muggeridge once joked that "Indians were the last living Englishmen," thus capturing the fact—true at least of the urbanized and Westernized elites of India—that while England itself became gradually denatured as it lost its Empire, aspects of its heritage took deep root in the colonies. In the areas of politics and economics, the special relationship between India and England has very little meaning anymore, as England strives to overcome economic disaster and Indians reach out increasingly to the United States, the Middle East, and the rest of the Asian world. But there is a part of Indian culture today that seems forever to be England,

and that is cricket. It therefore is worth examining the dynamics of decolonization in this sphere, where the urge to cut the ties with the colonial past seems weakest.

The process by which cricket gradually became indigenized in colonial India can best be envisioned by making a distinction between "hard" and "soft" cultural forms. Hard cultural forms are those that come with a set of links between value, meaning, and embodied practice that are difficult to break and hard to transform. Soft cultural forms, by contrast, are those that permit relatively easy separation of embodied performance from meaning and value, and relatively successful transformation at each level. In terms of this distinction, I would suggest that cricket is a hard cultural form that changes those who are socialized into it more readily than it is itself changed.

One reason that cricket is not easily susceptible to reinterpretation as it crosses social boundaries is that the values it represents are, at their heart, puritan ones, in which rigid adherence to external codes is part of the discipline of internal moral development (James 1963, chap. 2). Not unlike the design principles of the Bauhaus, form here closely follows (moral) function. To some extent, all rule-governed sport has some of this hard quality, but it is arguably more present in those competitive forms that come to encapsulate the core moral values of the society in which they are born.

Thus, cricket as a hard cultural form ought to resist indigenization. In fact, counterintuitively, it has become profoundly indigenized and decolonized, and India is often seen as suffering from a veritable cricket "fever" (Puri 1982). There are two ways to account for this puzzle. The first, recently suggested by Ashis Nandy (1989b), is that there are mythic structures beneath the surface of the sport that make it profoundly Indian in spite of its Western historical origins. The alternative approach (although it is not entirely inconsistent with many of Nandy's insights into cricket in India) is that cricket became indigenized through a set of complex and contradictory processes that parallel the emergence of an Indian "nation" from the British Empire. The argument developed in this chapter is that indigenization is often a product of collective and spectacular experiments with modernity, and not necessarily of the subsurface affinity of new cultural forms with existing patterns in the cultural repertoire.

The indigenization of a sport like cricket has many dimensions: it has something to do with the way the sport is managed, patronized, and publicized; it has something to do with the class background of Indian players and thus with their capability to mimic Victorian elite values; it has something to do with the dialectic between team spirit and national sentiment, which is inherent in the sport and is implicitly corrosive of the bonds of empire; it has something to do with the way in which a reservoir of talent is created and nurtured outside the urban elites, so that the sport can become internally self-sustaining; it has something to do with the ways in which media and language help to unyoke cricket from its Englishness; and it has something to do with the construction of a postcolonial male spectatorship that can charge cricket with the power of bodily competition and virile nationalism. Each of these processes interacted with one another to indigenize cricket in India, in a way that is distinct from the parallel process in other British colonies. (For some sense of the diaspora of cricket through the empire as a whole, see Allen 1985.)

Obviously, the story of cricket depends on the vantage point from which it is told. The remarkable implications of the history of cricket in the Caribbean have been immortalized in the corpus of C. L. R. James (1963; see also Diawara 1990 and Birbalsingh 1986). Australians have had a long struggle—dramatized in cricket—to break free of the sanctimonious and patronizing way in which they are regarded by the English. South Africa finds in cricket yet another conflicted way to reconcile its Boer and English genealogies. But it is in the colonies occupied by black and brown peoples that the story of cricket is most anguished and subtle: in the Caribbean, Pakistan, India, and Sri Lanka (on the last, see Roberts 1985). I do not pretend that what cricket implies about decolonization from the Indian perspective holds good for every other former colony, but it is surely one part of the larger story of the construction of a postcolonial and global cultural framework for team sport.

The Colonial Ecumene

It is no exaggeration to suggest that cricket came closer than any other public form to distilling, constituting, and communicating the values of the Victorian upper classes in England to English gentlemen as part of their embodied practices, and to others as a means for apprehending the class codes of the period. Its history in England goes back into the precolonial period, and there is little doubt that the sport is English in origin. In the second half of the nineteenth century, when cricket acquired much of its modern morphology, it also took shape as the most powerful condensation of Victorian elite values. These values, about which much has been written, can be summarized as follows. Cricket was a quintessentially masculine activity, and it expressed the codes that were expected to govern all masculine behavior: sportsmanship, a sense of fair play, thorough control over the expression of strong sentiments by players on the field, subordination of personal sentiments and interests to those of the group, unquestioned loyalty to the team.

Although cricket became a central instrument of socialization for the Victorian elite, it contained from the start a social paradox. It was honed as an instrument of elite formation, but like all complex and powerful forms of play, it both confirmed and created sporting sodalities that transcended class. Thus, it was always open to the most talented (and useful) among the lower and middle classes who stumbled into it. Those among the great unwashed in Victorian England who were capable of subjecting themselves to the social and moral disciplines of the playing field could enter into a limited intimacy with their superiors. The price of admission was complete dedication to the sport and, usually, great talent on the field. In Victorian England cricket was a limited road to social mobility. Of course, no amount of shared cricket would make an Englishman confuse an Oxford Blue with a Yorkshire working-class professional cricketer. But on the playing field (where cooperation was necessary) there was some respite from the brutalities of class in England. It has also been noted that it was the presence of these lower-class players that allowed the Victorian elite to incorporate the harsh techniques required to win while retaining the idea that sportsmanship involved a patrician detachment from competitiveness. Lower-class professional players thus did the dirty subaltern work of winning so that their class superiors could preserve the illusion of a gentlemanly, noncompetitive sport (Nandy 1989b, 19–20). This inherent paradox—an elite sport whose code of fair play dictated an openness to talent and vocation in those of humble origins—is a key to the early history of cricket in India.

For much of the nineteenth century in India cricket was a segregated sport, with Englishmen and Indians playing on opposite teams when they played together at all. Cricket was associated with clubs, the central social institutions of the British in India. Indian cricket clubs (and their associated teams) were largely a product of the last quarter of the nineteenth century, although there were a number of Parsi clubs based in Bombay starting in the 1840s. In this, as in other matters, the Parsis were the bridge community between Indian and English cultural tastes. Parsi teams from India toured England in the 1880s, and in 1888–89 the first English team toured India (although the majority of its matches were against teams wholly composed of Englishmen, and only a few against teams composed of Indians). Bombay was the birthplace of cricket for Indians and still retains a preeminent place in Indian cricket culture.

Although there was never a conscious policy in regard to the support of cricket by the colonial regime in India, cricket evolved into an unofficial instrument of state cultural policy. This was largely due to the cultural commitments of those members of the Victorian elite who occupied key positions in Indian administration, education, and journalism, and who regarded cricket as the ideal way to transmit Victorian ideals of character and fitness to the colony. Lord Harris, governor of Bombay from 1890 to 1893, was perhaps the most crucial figure in the quasi-official patronage of cricket in India, and he was followed by a succession of governors, both in Bombay and in the other presidencies, who saw cricket as fulfilling the following range of tasks: solidifying the bonds of empire; lubricating state dealings between various Indian "communities," which might otherwise degenerate into communal (Hindu/Muslim) riots; and implanting English ideals of manliness, stamina, and vigor into Indian groups seen as lazy, enervated, and effete. In this regard, cricket was one of many arenas in which a colonial sociology was constructed and reified. In this sociology, India was seen as a congeries of antagonistic communities, populated by men (and women) with a variety of psychological defects. Cricket was seen as an ideal way to socialize natives into new modes of intergroup conduct and new standards of public behavior. Ostensibly concerned with recreation and competition, its underlying quasi-official charter was moral and political. The underlying contradiction, between "communally" organized teams and the ideal of creating broader civic bonds, has influenced the development of cricket from its inception to the present and is dealt with more fully in the next section of this chapter.

On the whole, from about 1870 to 1930, in the high period of the Raj, there is no doubt that for Indians to play cricket was to experiment with the mysteries of English upper-class life. Whether it was by playing teams from England, which included men who had known each other at Eton and Harrow, Oxford and Cambridge, or during tours to England, a small segment of the Indian sporting population was initiated into the moral and social mysteries and rituals of Victorian cricket (Cashman 1980; Docker 1976).

The biographies and autobiographies of the finest Indian cricketers of this era, such as Vijay Hazare (1976; 1981), L. P. Jai (Raiji 1976), and Mushtaq Ali (1981), who all had active cricket careers into the 1940s, clearly show that they were exposed (in spite of their very diverse social backgrounds) to the value commitments associated with Victorian cricket—sportsmanship, self-effacement, team spirit—as well as to the hagiography and lore of cricket throughout the empire, but especially in England.

But class and race conspired in very complex ways in the "Victorian ecumene" (Breckenridge 1989, 196) and in its Edwardian successor structures. I have already suggested that Victorian cricket involved important class distinctions in England, distinctions that to this day affect the relations there between gentlemen and professional players, coaches and players, county and league cricket. Together, white males of all classes helped to create and embody a sporting code whose patrician moral dimensions were central to upper classes, and whose "workmanlike" skills were pointers to the role of the working classes in the sport. (Clarke and Clarke 1982, 82–83 offer an interesting treatment of the peculiar inflections of the idea of manliness in English sporting ideology.) The complexity of this specific brand of colonial discourse also illustrates one variant of what has been seen, in a rather different context, as the ambivalence of colonial discourse (Bhabha 1994).

As in many other areas, including art, etiquette, language, and conduct, it is now increasingly clear that during the heyday of the modern colonialisms, a complex system of hegemonizing and hierarchizing values and practices evolved conjointly in the metropolis and its colonies (Cooper and Stoler 1989). In the case of cricket in India, the key to the complex flows that linked cricket, class, and race in the colonial ecumene was the story of patronage and coaching in India. Both the biographies referred to above and an excellent synthetic account (Cashman 1980, chap. 2) make it clear that in the period between 1870 and 1930 British involvement in Indian cricket was very complex: it involved officers of the army stationed in India, businessmen from England, and senior government officials, all of whom helped to implant the idea of cricket in various Indian settings. At the same time, however, Indian princes brought English and Australian professional cricketers to India to train their own teams.

The princely phase in the patronage of Indian cricket is in some ways the most important in the analysis of the indigenization of cricket. First, cricket as an elite sport required the sort of time and money not available to the bourgeois elites of colonial India. The princes, on the other hand, were quick to see cricket as another extension of their royal traditions, and they absorbed such sports as polo, rifle shooting, golf, and cricket into their traditional aristocratic repertoires. This permitted them to offer new kinds of spectacle to their subjects (Docker 1976, 27), to link themselves to the English aristocracy in potentially new and fruitful ways, and to ingratiate themselves to the colonial authorities in India (such as Lord Harris), who favored cricket as a means for the moral disciplining of Orientals. The princes who supported cricket were often the less grand members of the Indian aristocracy, for cricket was somewhat cheaper than other forms of royal patronage and spectacle. Cricket had three appeals as an adjunct to the lifestyle and ethos of petty kingship in India: (a) its role, especially in the North, as a manly art in the aristocratic culture of leisure; (b) its Victorian credentials, which opened doors in England that might otherwise be less well-oiled (as in the case of Ranjitsinhji); and (c) its role as a useful extension of other royal public spectacles that had been an important part of the obligations and mystique of royalty in India. Accordingly, small and large princes in many parts of India throughout this century imported coaches from England, organized tournaments and prizes, subsidized teams and coaches, developed grounds and pitches, imported equipment and expertise, and hosted English teams.

Most important, the princes provided both direct and indirect support to many cricketers (or their families) from humble backgrounds, who were eventually able to make their way to bigger cities, more important teams, and sometimes to national and international visibility. For many Indian cricketers outside the big colonial cities in the period before World War II, one or another form of subsidy from princely houses was the key to their own entry into the cosmopolitan world of big-time cricket. Such players were thus able to achieve some measure of mobility through cricket and to introduce a considerable degree of class complexity into Indian cricket, a complexity that persists today.

The groundwork for the Indianization of cricket was therefore laid through the complex, hierarchical cross-hatching of British gentlemen in India, Indian princes, mobile Indian men who were often part of the civil services and the army, and, most important, those white cricketing professionals (mainly from England and Australia) who actually trained the great Indian cricketers of the first decades of this century. These professionals, the most prominent of whom were Frank Tarrant, Bill Hitch, and Clarrie Grimmett, as well as the somewhat more socially established British army men, college principals, and businessmen who coached budding Indian cricketers seem to have been the crucial links between stardom, aristocracy, and technical skill in the colonial cricketing world at large. What these professional coaches accomplished was to provide the technical skills that were crucial for the patronage fantasies of the Indian princes (which in turn were tied to their own fantasies of a monarchical and aristocratic ideal of empire) to be translated into competitive Indian teams actually composed of Indians. Although there is no decisive evidence for the following interpretation, it is highly likely that small-town boys like Mushtaq Ali, Vijay Hazare, and Lala Amarnath would have had a hard time entering the rarefied world of world cricket (still dominated by English and Victorian sporting codes), without the translation of cricket into an embodied technical practice by these lower-class white professionals. Thus, it is not the case that an Anglophone class drama was simply reproduced in India, but that in the circulations of princes, coaches, army officials, viceroys, college principals, and players of humble class origin between India, England, and Australia a complex imperial class regime was formed, in which Indian and English social hierarchies were interlinked and cross-hatched to produce, by the 1930s, a cadre of nonelite Indians who felt themselves to be genuine cricketers and genuinely "Indian" as well.

In this light, the great princely batsman Ranjitsinhji (1872–1933) is probably a sad exception, for whom cricketing and Englishness became so deeply connected that he could never take the idea of cricket as an Indian game very seriously. He was the Jamsaheb of Nawanagar, a small kingdom in Saurashtra, on the west coast of India. Ranji has a mythic place in the annals of cricket and is even today (along with a handful of others like W. G. Grace, Don Bradman, and Gary Sobers) considered to be one of the great batsmen of all time. It is worth spending a little time on Ranji, for he exemplifies what colonial cricket was all about. Ironically, it was probably just this profound identification with the empire and the crown that allowed Ranji to become the quintessential and living trope of an "Oriental" form of cricketing skill.

Ranji was not simply a great run-getter but was also seen in cricket circles as carrying a peculiar Oriental glow. The great C. B. Fry said of him that "he moved as if he had no bones; one would not be surprised to see brown curves burning in the grass where one of his cuts had traveled or blue flame shimmering round his bat, as he made one of his strokes." Neville Cardus said that "when he batted, strange light was seen for the first time on English fields." Clem Hill, the Australian test cricketer, simply said: "He is more than a batsman, he's a juggler!" Bill Hitch, the Surrey and England fast bowler, referred to him as "the master, the magician" (all cited in de Mellow 1979, chap. 9).

Ranji was seen to bring a peculiarly Indian genius to batting, hence the reference to magic and juggling, strange light and blue flames. Ranji, in fact, represented the glamorous obverse of the effeminacy, laziness, and lack of stamina that Indians were thought by many colonial theorists to embody (Hutchins 1967, chap. 3; Nandy 1983). In Ranji, wile became guile, trickery became magic, weakness became suppleness, and effeminacy was transformed into grace. This orientalist glow, of course, had a great deal to do with Ranji's impeccable social credentials, his total devotion to English institutions (all the way from college to the crown), and his unswerving loyalty to the empire. He thus not only revolutionized cricket and offered the crowds an extraordinary treat when he was at bat, but English audiences could always read in his performances a loyal and glamorous offering of the mysterious Orient to the playing fields of Eton. Ranji was the ultimate brown Englishman. There is no doubt, however, that Ranji belonged to that generation of Indian princes for whom loyalty to the crown and their pride in being Indian were coextensive with one another, although one recent analyst has suggested that Ranji's commitments may have been expressions of deep personal doubts and conflicts (Nandy 1989b). Ranji's story is only an extreme case of a more general irony: that the Indian princes, who patronized cricket as a way to enter the patrician Victorian world, and who were largely opposed to the nationalist movement, in fact, laid the grounds for the mastery of cricket among ordinary Indians that was to blossom into a full-blown pride in Indian cricketing competence by the 1930s.

Cricket, Empire, and Nation

Today, the extraordinary popularity of cricket in India is clearly tied up with nationalist sentiment. But in the early history of cricket in India, as we have noted already, cricket fostered two other kinds of loyalty. The first was (and still is) to religious (communal) identities. The second kind of loyalty, rather more abstractly instantiated in the sport, was loyalty to empire. The interesting question here is how the idea of the Indian nation emerged as a salient cricketing entity.

As far back as the first clubs organized by Parsis in Bombay in the mid-nineteenth century, membership in religious communities became the salient principle around which Indians banded together to play cricket. And this organizing principle remained in place until it was dislodged in the 1930s. Hindus, Parsis, Muslims, Europeans, and, eventually, "the Rest" (a label for the communally unmarked groups brought together into cricket teams) were organized into cricket clubs. There was much debate from the very start about the pros and cons of this communal organization of cricket. Although elsewhere in princely India the major patrons of sport were the princes, who paid no regard to communal principles in their recruitment of players, in the presidencies of British India players were divided into religious and ethnic groupings, some of which were antagonistic in public life more generally. Thus, cricket was an important arena, in which players as well as crowds learned to think of themselves as Hindu, Muslim, and Parsi, in contrast with the Europeans.

There has been much good historical work to show that these social categories were both the creation and the instrument of a colonial sociology of rule (Appadurai 1981; Cohn 1987; Dirks 1987; Freitag 1989; Pandey 1990; Prakash 1990). But the fact is that they entered deeply into Indian self-conceptions and Indian politics and cultural life. Although it is true that census classifications, the control of religious endowments, and the issue of separate electorates were the major official arenas in which issues of communal identity were reified as part of a colonial sociology of India, the role of cricket in this process must not be underestimated. At least in Western India, British officials like Governor Harris were complacent in their view of cricket as a safety valve for communal hostility, and as a means for teaching Indians how to live amicably with communal diversity. But deeply embedded as they were in their own fictions about the fragmentation of Indian society, what they did not realize was that on the playing field (as elsewhere) they were perpetuating communal conceptions of identity that in Indian cities might have become more fluid. Thus, we have the paradox that Bombay, perhaps the most cosmopolitan colonial city, had its major elite sport organized around communal lines.

This communal principle was bound to become otiose as the seriousness and quality of cricket in India increased. Unlike cricket in India, English cricket was organized around a system in which the nation was the exemplary unit and counties, not communities, were its lower-level constituencies. In other words, territory and nationhood for England, community and cultural distinctiveness for India (see chap. 6). Thus when English teams began to tour India, the question was how to construct an "Indian" team that was a fitting opponent. In the early tours, in the 1890s, these Indian teams were largely composed of Englishmen, but as more Indians began to play the game and as more patrons and entrepreneurs began to organize teams and tournaments, it was inevitable that the full pool of Indian talent be drawn on to construct a first-rate Indian team. This process, whereby Indians increasingly came to represent India in cricket, follows not surprisingly the history of the evolution of Indian nationalism as a mass movement. Cricket in the Indian colonial context thus casts an unexpected light on the relationship between nationhood and empire. Insofar as England was not simply identical with the empire, there had to be other parallel entities in the colonies against which the English nation-state could play: thus, "India" had to be invented, at least for the purposes of colonial cricket.

Yet there was surprisingly little explicit communication between those who were responsible for organizing cricket in India on an all-India basis and those, in the all-India Congress party (and elsewhere), who (beginning in the 1880s) were professionally committed to the idea of a free Indian nation. The idea of Indian talent, an Indian team, and Indian competition in international cricket emerged relatively independently, under nonofficial stimulation by its patrons and publicists. Thus, cricket nationalism emerged as a paradoxical, although logical, outgrowth of the development of cricket in England. Rather than being a spin-off of the imagined community of nationalist politicians in India, nationally organized cricket was an internal demand of the colonial enterprise and thus required cognate national or protonational enterprises in the colonies.

Nevertheless, as cricket became more popular in the first three decades of this century, and as the nationalist movement, particularly with Mahatma Gandhi and the Indian National Congress gathered momentum in the same period, cricket nationalism and explicitly nationalist politics as such came into contact in the ordinary lives of young Indians. Thus, N. K. P. Salve, a major Indian politician and cricket entrepreneur, recalls how in the early thirties he and his friends were intimidated and prevented from playing on a fine cricket pitch in Nagpur by a certain Mr. Thomas, an Anglo-Indian sergeant in charge of the pitch, who "looked like an African cape buffalo, massive and hefty in size, otherwise possessed of offensive, uncouth and vulgar characteristics" (1987, 5). After several scary and abusive episodes involving Thomas (a classic subaltern figure keeping native urchins away from the sacrosanct spaces of imperial performance), Salve's father and his friends, all influential local followers of Gandhi, intervened on behalf of the young boys with a senior British official in Nagpur and won them the right to use the pitch when it was not in official use. Throughout Salve's narration of this story, we get a strong sense of his fear of the Anglo-Indian subaltern, the sensuous attraction of playing on an official pitch, the outrage as Indians of being kept out of a public space, and the nationalist flavor of their resentment. It is probable that cricket nationalism and official nationalist politics were rarely wedded in conscious public debates or movements, but that they affected the lived experience of play, skill, space, and rights for many young Indians in the small towns and playing fields of preindependence India. But the growth of cricket consciousness and cricket excitement cannot be understood without reference to the role of language and the media.

Vernacularization and the Media

The media have played a crucial role in the indigenization of cricket, first through the English-language cricket commentaries aired by All-India Radio, starting in 1933. Largely in English during the thirties, forties, and fifties (Cashman 1980, 145–46), radio commentary starting in the sixties was increasingly in Hindi, Tamil, and Bengali, as well as in English. Multi-lingual radio commentary is probably the single major instrument in the socialization of the Indian mass audience in the subtleties of the sport. While coverage of test matches (involving India and other countries) has been confined to English, Hindi, Tamil, and Bengali, other first-class matches are accompanied by radio commentary in all the major languages of the subcontinent. No systematic study has been made of the role of vernacular cricket commentary in socializing nonurban Indians into the cosmopolitan culture of cricket, but it was evidently a major factor in the indigenization of the sport.

Through radios, which are very widely available and which attract large crowds in train stations, cafeterias, and other public places, Indians have absorbed the English terminology of cricket, especially its noun structure, into a variety of vernacular syntactic patterns. This type of sports pidgin is crucial to the indigenization of the sport, for it permits contact with an arcane form at the same time as the form is linguistically domesticated. Thus, the elementary vocabulary of cricket terms in English is widely known throughout India (increasingly even in villages).

The complex linguistic experiences that emerged in the context of vernacular broadcasts are exemplified in the following narrative from Richard Cashman. During the 1972–73 series this conversation between Lala Amarnath, the expert, and the Hindi commentator took place after Ajit Wadekar had straight driven Pocock for four off the front foot. The dialogue illustrates this hybrid language and some of the hazards of its use:

HINDI COMMENTATOR: Lalaji, aap wo back foot straight drive ke bare me kya kahena chahte hain?
AMARNATH: Wo back foot nahin front foot drive thi . . . badi sunder thi . . . wristy thi.
COMMENTATOR: Han Badi risky thi. Wadekar ko aisa nahin khelna chahiye.
AMARNATH: Commentator sahib, risky nahin wristy. Wrist se mari hui . . .

[Translation]

COMMENTATOR: Lala, what would you like to say about that straight drive off the back foot?

AMARNATH: That was a front and not a back foot drive . . . it was beautiful . . . was wristy.

COMMENTATOR: So that was risky. Wadekar shouldn't have played like that.

AMARNATH: Mr. Commentator, risky is not wristy. It was hit with the wrist. . . . (Cashman 1980, 147)

Although Cashman's translation is not entirely sensitive, it makes it quite clear that the vernacularization of cricket has its linguistic pitfalls. What he does not note, however, is that through the discussion of such errors Hindi speakers domesticate a relatively esoteric cricket term like *wristy*.

The media hegemony of cricket (often a source of complaint on the part of partisans of other sports) has grown since the arrival of television. After a very modest start with small audiences in the late 1960s, television has now completely transformed cricket culture in India. As several commentators have pointed out, cricket is perfectly suited for television, with its many pauses, its spatial concentration of action, and its extended format. For audiences as well as advertisers it is the perfect television sport.

Television is at the cutting edge of the privatization of leisure in contemporary India (as elsewhere). As public spaces grow more violent, disorderly, and uncomfortable, those who can afford television consume their spectacles in the company of their friends and family. This is true of the two great passions of the mass audience: sport and cinema. In the one case through live coverage and in the other through reruns and videocassettes, the stadium and the cinema hall are being replaced by the living room as the setting for spectacle. Test matches are still well attended, but the crowds that show up are more volatile. No longer a complex shared experience between the rich and the poor, the stadium spectacle is a more polarized and jagged experience, which many do not prefer to the cool, private, and omniscient television screen. As elsewhere in the world in regard to large-scale spectacles, the audience of live matches is itself a prop in a grander performance staged for the benefit of television viewers. The crowd is there not to enjoy the liveness of the spectacle but to provide evidence of it for the television audience. An audience of the spectacle from its own point of view, it is part of the spectacle for those at home. This, too, is part of the process of indigenization and decolonization.

Television reduces foreign teams and stars to manageable size; it visually domesticates the exotic nature of the sport, particularly for those who might previously only have heard matches on the radio. And for a country whose cinema stars are its major celebrities, television lends cinematic authority to the sports spectacle. In a civilization where seeing (*darsan*) is the sacred instrument of communion, television has intensified the star status of the great Indian cricket players. Indian test cricketers have never been the objects of greater adulation than in the past decade of intense television viewing of major games. Television has deepened the national passion for cricket nurtured by radio, but both radio commentary and television watching have been reinforced, from the view point of audience reception and participation, by a vast growth in books, newspaper coverage, and sports-magazine consumption, not just in English but in the vernaculars.

The proliferation of news, biographies of stars, commentaries, and instructional literature, especially in the major cricket-playing areas, provides the critical backdrop for the special force of television. While this vernacular material is read and heard by those who do not themselves read, radio is heard and imagined in live form, while television coverage makes the transition to spectacle. These mass-mediated forms have created a public that is extremely large, literate in many different senses in the subtleties of the sport, and can bring to cricket the passions generated by reading, hearing, and seeing.

The role of the mass vernacular literature in this process is crucial, for what these books, magazines, and pamphlets do is to create a bridge between the vernaculars and the English language, put picture and names of foreign players into Indic scripts and syntax, and reinforce the body of contact terms (English terms transliterated into Hindi, Marathi, or Tamil) that are heard on the radio. Some of these materials also are instructional and contain elaborate diagrams and verbal texts accompanying these illustrations that explain the various strokes, styles, rules, and logic of cricket to readers who may know no English. This vernacularization process, which I have examined most closely with a body of materials in Marathi,[1] provides a verbal repertoire that allows large numbers of Indians to experience cricket as a linguistically familiar form, thus liberating cricket from that very Englishness that first gave it its moral authority and intrigue.

Vernacular commentary on radio (and later on television) provides the first step to the domestication of the vocabulary of cricket because it provides not just a contact vocabulary, but also a link between this vocabulary and the excitement of the heard or seen drama of the game, its strokes, its rhythm, its physical thrill. The Englishness of cricket terminology is drawn into the worlds of Hindi, Marathi, Tamil, and Bengali, but it is simultaneously brought into intimate contact with the actual playing of the game throughout the streets, playgrounds, and building lots of urban India and the free spaces of many villages as well. Thus, the acquisition of cricket terminology in the vernacular reinforces the sense of bodily competence in the sport, which is in turn given a hefty boost by regular spots on television. The great stars of cricket are imitated, children are nicknamed after them, and the terminology of cricket, its strokes and its stars, its rules and its rhythms, become part of vernacular pragmatics and a sense of lived physical competence.

The vast corpus of printed materials in the vernaculars reinforce this link between terminological control and bodily excitement and expertise by providing large amounts of information, statistics, and lore that further support the linguistic and pictorial competence of Indians who are only partially comfortable in the Anglophone world. In the many books, magazines, and pamphlets in the vernaculars, the rules, strokes, and terminology of cricket (most often transliterated directly from the English so that they remain part of the linguistic ecumene of international cricket) are often accompanied by schematic diagrams. Discussing at length the lives and styles of cricketers both Indian and foreign and embedding these discussions in detailed debates and dialogues about matters of judgment and regulation (such as neutral umpiring), these materials hitch cricket terminology to the body as a site of language use and experience. In addition, by locating these instructional materials in news, gossip, stars, and sensational events surrounding cricket, cricket is drawn into a wider world of celebrities, controversies, and contexts outside of sport, which further embed it in linguistically familiar terrain.

The Hindi-language magazine *Kriket-Kriket* provides an excellent example of the "interocular" world of the vernacular reader (see Appadurai and Breckenridge 1991b), for this magazine contains advertisements for Hindi pulp fiction, Hindi comic books, various body products like contact lenses and indigenous lotions, and photo albums of cricket stars. There are also advertisements for various kinds of how-to and self-help pocket books, most explaining skills like electric wiring and shorthand as well as stranger subjects like methods of making lubricating grease for machinery. Finally, many lavish color photos of cricket stars and numerous news items on specific matches and tournaments place cricket in a splendid world of semicosmopolitan glitz, in which cricket provides the textual suture for a much more diverse collage of materials having to do with modern lifestyles and fantasies. Because magazines such as *Kriket-Kriket* are relatively cheaply produced and sold, their paper and graphics quality is low, and therefore it is not at all easy to distinguish various kinds of news and opinion pieces from the advertisements for other kinds of literature and services. The total effect is of a seamless web of verbal and visual impressions of cosmopolitanism in which cricket is the connective tissue. Other vernacular magazines are more chaste and less interocular than this one, but as they are taken together with other printed materials, and especially with the adjacent experiences of radio, television, and film newsreels of cricket matches, there is little doubt that the culture of cricket that is consumed by semi-Anglophone readers is decisively postcolonial and polyglot.

Perhaps even more important are the newspaper and magazine stories, as well as the books, that tell the cricketing life stories of various stars, both old and new. What these vernacular stories do is to locate the skills and excitement of the sport in linguistically manageable narratives, thus making comprehensible not just stars but proximate cricketing lives. These readable lives then become the basis for a renewed intimacy in the reception of radio and television coverage of cricket events, and the bodily hexis of even the most rustic boy, playing with poor equipment on a fallow field, is tied at the level of language and the body to the world of highpowered cricket spectacles. The fact that many of these books and pamphlets are either ghostwritten or written with professional writers does not detract from their force as tools for understanding cricket for many readers outside the Anglophone world. By connecting the life of a star to known places, events, schools, teachers, coaches, and fellow players, a narrative structure is created in which cricket becomes enlivened just as its stars are made graspable (for an excellent example of this, see Shastri and Patil 1982).

The general force of the media experience is thus powerfully synaesthetic. Cricket is read, heard, and seen, and the force of daily life experiences of cricket, occasional glimpses of live cricket matches and stars, and the more predictable events of the cricket spectacle on television all conspire not just to vernacularize cricket but to introject the master terms and master tropes of cricket into the bodily practices and body-related fantasies of many young Indian males. Print, radio, and television reinforce each other powerfully and create an environment in which cricket is simultaneously larger than life (because of its stars, spectacles, and association with the glamour of world tests and international intrigue) and close to life, because it has been rendered into lives, manuals, and news that are no longer English-mediated. As Indians from various linguistic regions in India see and hear the cricket narratives of television and radio, they do so not as neophytes struggling to grasp an English form but as culturally literate viewers for whom cricket has been deeply vernacularized. Thus, a complex set of experiential and pedagogical loops is set up through which the reception of cricket becomes a critical instrument of subjectivity and agency in the process of decolonization.

The Empire Strikes Back

At the reception end, decolonization involves the acquisition of cultural literacy in cricket by a mass audience, and this side of decolonization involves the sort of appropriation of competence that we are all inclined to applaud. But there is also a production dimension to decolonization, and here we enter into the complex world of entrepreneurship and spectacle, of state sponsorship and vast private profits.

While it is true that poorer and less urbane Indian men were able to enter the cosmopolitan world of cricket through royal or official support in the period before World War II, the relatively wide class base of even the best Indian teams would not have lasted after the war had it not been for the fascinating and quite unusual pattern of patronage of cricket by major business corporations, especially in Bombay but also throughout India. Corporate patronage of cricket is an intriguing factor in the sociology of Indian sport. Its essentials are these: many prestigious companies made the choice to hire outstanding cricket players early in their careers, to give them considerable freedom to maintain the rigorous practice schedules ("at the nets") to assure their staying in form, and, most important, to assure them secure employment as regular members of their staffs after their cricket careers ended. Such employment of cricketers was seen, originally in Bombay in the 1950s, as a beneficial form of social advertising, accruing goodwill to the company by its support of an increasingly popular sport, of some stars, and of the health of the national image in international competition. Corporate employment of cricketers has meant not just the promotion of talent in the big cities, but in the case of the State Bank of India (a huge public-sector operation), excellent cricketers were recruited and hired in branches throughout India, so that this patron was single-handedly responsible for the nurturance of cricket far from its urban homes. Thus, corporate patronage of cricket is responsible for providing not only a quasi-professional means of security for a sport whose deepest ideals are amateur, but also a steady initiative for drawing in aspiring young men from the poorer classes and from semirural parts of India.

In turn, such corporate support has meant that the state has been able to make a relatively low investment in cricket and yet reap a large profit in terms of national sentiment. While the patronage of cricket since World War II has been largely a commercial undertaking on the part of major corporations (as part of their public-relations and advertising budgets), the state in India has been generous with its extension of media support to the game. This alliance between state-controlled investments—through media and the provision of law and order, private commercial interests in providing career security to players, and a complex public (although not governmental) body called the Board of Control—provided the infrastructure for the transformation of cricket into a major national passion in the four decades since Indian independence in 1947.

The television phase in the history of Indian cricket, of course, is part of the intense, recent commercialization of cricket and the associated commodification of its stars. Like other sports figures in the capitalist world, the best-known Indian cricket stars are now metacommodities, for sale themselves while fueling the circulation of other commodities. The sport is increasingly in the hands of advertisers, promoters, and entrepreneurs, with television, radio, and print media feeding the national passion for the sport and its stars. Such commodification of public spectacles appears at first glance to be simply the Indian expression of a worldwide process and thus to represent not decolonization or indigenization but recolonization by the forces of international capital. But what it mostly represents is the aggressive mood of Indian capitalists in seizing the potential of cricket for commercial purposes.

Transformed into a national passion by the processes of spectacle, in the past two decades cricket has become a matter of mass entertainment and mobility for some and thereby has become wrapped up with winning (Nandy 1989b). Indian crowds have become steadily more greedy for Indian victories in test matches and steadily more vituperative about losses, either at home or abroad. Thus, players, coaches, and managers walk a tighter rope than they ever have before. While they reap the benefits of stardom and commercialization, they have to be increasingly solicitous of critics and the crowd, who do not tolerate even temporary setbacks. This has meant a steady growth in the pressure for technical excellence.

After a serious slump from the midfifties to the late sixties, Indian cricketers won some extraordinary victories in 1971 over the West Indies and England, both on the home grounds of their opponents. Although the 1971 team was hailed by crowds and critics alike, there were suggestions that the victories owed much to luck and the poor form of the opposing teams. Nevertheless, 1971 marked a turning point for Indian cricket under the leadership of Ajit Wadekar. There were some real setbacks after that, and yet Indian cricketers had shown that they could beat their former colonial masters on their home grounds and the formidable Caribbean players on theirs. These 1971 victories marked the psychological inauguration of a new boldness in Indian cricket.

The seventies were a period in which every test team was humbled by the West Indies, who seemed too imposing to touch, with their brilliant batsmen, their extraordinary (and scary) fast bowlers, and their speed in the field. Cricket had become the Caribbean sport, with everyone else struggling to stay in the picture. In this context, the sweetest moment for Indian cricket was the victory over a strong West Indies team in the 1983 series. With that win, India established itself as a world force in international cricket, whose real competition was the West Indies and Pakistan rather than England and Australia. South Africa, New Zealand, and Sri Lanka remained largely outside the top rank in test cricket. By 1983, England appeared to be a spent force in test cricket (in spite of occasional stars like Ian Botham) and India a major one.

But it is important not only that the black and brown former colonies now dominate world cricket. It is significant that their triumph coincides with a period in which the impact of media, commercialization, and national passion have almost completely eroded the old Victorian civilities associated with cricket. Cricket is now aggressive, spectacular, and frequently unsporting, with audiences thirsting for national victory and players and promoters out for the buck. It is hard to escape the conclusion that the decolonization of cricket would not have occurred if the sport had not been detached from its Victorian moral integument. Nor is this process restricted to the colonies: it has been noticed that Thatcherism in England has done much to erode the ideology of "fair play" that once dominated cricket in its home country (Marshall 1987).

Cricket now belongs to a different moral and aesthetic world, far from the one imagined by Thomas Arnold of Rugby. Nothing marks this change in ethos as much as the arrival of the professionalized, strictly commercial phenomenon of World Series Cricket (WSC), a global, media-centered cricket package created by an Australian by the name of Kerry Packer. Packer's WSC was the first major threat both to the colonial ecumene of amateur sportsmanship and the post-World War II ethic of cricket nationalism, centered as it was on the major innovation in the sport since the war—one-day cricket—in which a single day's play (as opposed to five or more days) settles the outcome. One-day cricket encourages risk taking, aggressiveness, and bravado while suiting perfectly the intense attention appropriate to high-powered television advertising and a higher turnover of events and settings. Packer's WSC bypassed national loyalty in the name of media entertainment and fast economic benefits for players. West Indian, English, Australian, and Pakistani cricketers were quick to see its appeals. But in India players were slower to respond, as the structure of patronage in India gave them much more security than their counterparts enjoyed elsewhere. Still, Packer's bold enterprise was the signal that cricket had moved into yet another, postnationalist phase, in which entertainment value, media coverage, and the commercialization of players would transcend the national loyalty of the early postindependence period and the Victorian amateur ethic of the colonial period.

Today, Indian cricket represents a complex configuration of each of these historical transformations. The rule structure of the game and the codes of behavior on the field are still nominally regulated by the classic Victorian values of restraint, sportsmanship, and amateurism. At the same time, national loyalty is a powerful counterpoint to these ideals, and victory at any cost is the demand of crowds and television audiences. But from the point of view of players and promoters, the Victorian code and nationalist concerns are subordinated to the transnational flow of talent, celebrity, and money.

The new ethos is best captured in the recently created Australasia Cup, hosted by the tiny Gulf emirate of Sharjah, which has a considerable population of Indian and Pakistani migrants. This cup brings out both the commercial and nationalist logic of contemporary cricket. In an extremely exciting final sequence in the decisive match in 1986, watched by a television audience of fifteen million, Pakistan needed four runs to win and achieved them in one stroke against the last ball of the match. The live audience for the game included film stars and other celebrities from India and Pakistan, as well as South Asian migrants making their living on Gulf money.

The Sharjah cup is a long way from the playing field of Eton. The patronage of oil money, the semiproletarian audience of Indian and Pakistani migrant workers in the Persian Gulf, film stars from the subcontinent sitting on a sports field created by Islamic oil wealth, an enormous television audience in the subcontinent, prize money and advertisement revenue in abundance, bloodthirsty cricket—here, finally, is the last blow to Victorian upper-class cricket codes, and here is a different global ecumene. After Sharjah, all cricket is Trobriand cricket, not because of the dramatic rule changes associated with that famous form of cricket, but because of the successful hijacking of a ritual from its original English practical hegemony and its Victorian moral integument. From the perspective of Sharjah, it is the Etonians who seem like Trobrianders today.

Part of the decolonization of cricket is the corrosion of the myth of the Commonwealth, the loose fraternity of nations united by their previous status as parts of the British Empire. The Commonwealth has largely become a community of sport (like the Ivy League in the eastern United States). Politically, it represents a faint shadow of the civilities of empire. In trade, politics, and diplomacy it has become a farce: Fijians drive Indian immigrants out of the Fijian polity; Sinhalas and Tamils kill each other in Sri Lanka (while Sinhala cricket teams tour India); Pakistan and India teeter continuously on the edge of war; the new nations of Africa fight a variety of internecine battles.

Yet the Commonwealth Games are a serious and successful international enterprise, and global cricket is still on the face of it an affair of the Commonwealth. But the Commonwealth that is constituted by cricket today is not an orderly community of former colonies, held together by common adherence to a Victorian and colonial code. It is an agonistic reality, in which a variety of postcolonial pathologies (and dreams) are played out on the landscape of a common colonial heritage. No more an instrument for socializing black and brown men into the public etiquette of empire, it is now an instrument for mobilizing national sentiment in the service of transnational spectacles and commoditization.

The peculiar tension between nationalism and decolonization is best seen in the cricket diplomacy between India and Pakistan, which involves multiple levels of competition and cooperation. Perhaps the best example of cooperation in the spirit of decolonization is the very complex process through which politicians and bureaucrats at the highest levels of the two antagonistic nations cooperated in the mid-1980s to shift the venue of the prestigious World Cup from England to the subcontinent in 1987, with the financial backing of the Reliance Group of Industries (one of the biggest, most aggressive business houses in contemporary India) and the encouragement of the leaders of the two countries (Salve 1987). Yet in Sharjah, as well as in every venue in India, Pakistan, or elsewhere since partition, cricket matches between India and Pakistan are thinly disguised national wars. Cricket is not so much a release valve for popular hostility between the two populations as it is a complex arena for reenacting the curious mixture of animosity and fraternity that characterizes the relations between these two previously united nation-states. England, in any case, is no longer part of the equation, whether in the tense politics of Kashmir or on the cricket grounds of Sharjah.

Recent journalistic coverage of the Australasia Cup matches in Sharjah (Tripathi 1990) suggests that the Gulf states have moved into increasing prominence as venues for international cricket, and that the national rivalry between India and Pakistan has been deliberately both highlighted and contained in order to create a simulacrum of their current tension over Kashmir. While the armies face each other across the borders of Kashmir, the cricket teams provide a star-studded simulacrum of warfare on the cricket field.

Conclusion: The Means of Modernity

It remains now to return to the general issues set out in the introduction to this chapter. The example of cricket suggests something of what it takes to decolonize the production of culture in regard to what I earlier characterized as hard cultural forms. In this case, particularly from the Indian vantage point, the key forces that have eroded the Victorian moral and didactic framework of cricket are the indigenization of patronage, both in the sense of finding indigenous patrons whose styles can accommodate the form and finding audiences who can be drawn into the spectacle; state support through massive media subsidies; and commercial interest, either in the standard contemporary possibilities for commoditization forms or in the slightly more unusual form of company patronage for players. It is only this strong alliance of forces that in the Indian case has permitted the gradual unyoking of cricket from its Victorian value framework and its animation by new forces associated with merchandising and spectacle.

Yet all these factors do not get to the heart of our problem: why is cricket a national passion? Why is it not just indigenized but the very symbol of a sporting practice that seems to embody India? Why is it watched with rapt attention in stadia from Sharjah to Madras and in every other media context as well? Why are the stars of cricket worshipped, perhaps even more than their counterparts in the cinema?

Part of the answer to these questions doubtless lies in the profound links between the ideas of play in human life (Huizinga 1950), of organized sport in mobilizing simultaneously powerful sentiments of both nation and humanity (MacAloon 1984; 1990), and of agonistic sport in recalibrating the relationship between leisure and pleasure in modern industrial societies (Elias and Dunning 1986; Hargreaves 1982). From these perspectives, cricket can be seen as a form of agonistic play that has captured the Indian imagination decisively.

But to account for the central place of cricket in the Indian imagination, one must understand how cricket links gender, nation, fantasy, and bodily excitement. It is true that among the Indian upper classes, especially insofar as they are able to insulate themselves from the masses (either in their homes or in special viewing sections while watching cricket), women have become both players and aficionadas of cricket. Yet, for the nation at large, cricket is a male-dominated activity in terms of players, managers, commentators, aficionados, and live audiences. Male spectators, even when they do not dominate audiences at live or televised games, are the preferred viewers of the game because the apical spectacles, test matches or major one-day matches, involve only male players. The Indian female gaze, at least thus far, is twice removed, as they are most often watching males play but also watching males watching other males play. For the male viewer, watching cricket is a deeply engaged activity, at the level of bodily hexis (Bourdieu 1977), as most Indian males under the age of forty have either seen cricket games, have played themselves in some local version of the game, or have read about and seen its practice. Thus, the pleasure of viewing cricket for the Indian male, as with virtually no other sport, is rooted in the bodily pleasure of playing, or imagining playing, cricket.

But because cricket, through the enormous convergence of state, media, and private-sector interests, has come to be identified with "India," with "Indian" skill, "Indian" guts, "Indian" team spirit, and "Indian" victories, the bodily pleasure that is at the core of the male viewing experience is simultaneously part of the erotics of nationhood. This erotics, particularly for working-class and lumpen male youth throughout India, is connected deeply to violence, not just because all agonistic sport taps the inclination to aggressiveness but because the divisive demands of class, ethnicity, language, and region in fact make the nation a profoundly contested community. The erotic pleasure of watching cricket for Indian male subjects is the *pleasure of agency* in an imagined community, which in many other arenas is violently contested. (See Mitra 1986 for a slightly different angle on this process.) This pleasure is neither wholly cathartic nor vicarious because playing cricket is close to, or part of, the experience of many Indian males. It is, however, magnified, politicized, and spectacularized without losing its links to the lived experience of bodily competence and agonistic bonding. This set of links between gender, fantasy, nation, and excitement could not occur without a complex group of historical contingencies involving empire, patronage, media, and commerce—contingencies that set the stage for the current embodied excitement about cricket in India.

We can now return to the puzzle with which we began. How did cricket, a hard cultural form tightly yoking value, meaning, and embodied practice, become so profoundly Indianized, or, from another point of view, de-Victorianized? Because in the process of its vernacularization (through books, newspapers, radio, and television) it became an emblem of Indian nationhood at the same time that it became inscribed, as practice, onto the Indian (male) body. Decolonization in this case not only involves the creation of imagined communities through the workings of print capitalism as Anderson (1983) has suggested, but it also involves the appropriation of agonistic bodily skills that can then further lend passion and purpose to the community so imagined. This may be the special contribution of spectator sport (as opposed to the many other forms of public culture) to the dynamics of decolonization.

Because gender, body, and the erotics of nationhood can come into powerful conjuncture through other sports (such as soccer and hockey, which are very popular in India even today), one can still ask, why cricket? Here, I must make a speculative leap and suggest that cricket is the ideal focus for national attention and nationalist passion because it affords the experience of experimenting with what might be called the "means of modernity" to a wide variety of groups within Indian society. To those groups who constitute the state, particularly through their control of television, it offers the sense of being able to manipulate nationalist sentiment. To the technocrats, publicists, journalists, and publishers who directly control the media, it provides the sense of skill in handling the techniques of televising sports spectacles, of manipulating private-sector advertising, of controlling public attention, and, in general, of mastering the media themselves. To the private sector, cricket affords a means for linking leisure, stardom, and nationalism, thus providing a sense of mastery over the skills of merchandising and promotion. To the viewing public, cricket affords the sense of cultural literacy in a world sport (associated with the still-not-erased sense of the technological superiority of the West) and the more diffuse pleasure of association with glamour, cosmopolitanism, and national competitiveness. To the upper-middle-class viewer, it affords the privatized pleasures of bringing stardom and nationalist sentiment within the safe and sanitized environs of the living room. To working-class and lumpen youth, it offers the sense of group belonging, potential violence, and bodily excitement that characterizes football passion in England. To rural viewers, readers, and listeners, cricket (appropriately vernacularized) gives a sense of control over the lives of stars, the fate of nations, and the electricity of cities. In all these cases, while the ends of modernity may be understood (and contested) variously as world peace, national skill, individual fame, and team virility or mobility, the means of modernity contained in cricket involve a confluence of lived interests, where the producers and consumers of cricket can share the excitement of Indianness without its many, divisive scars. Finally, although perhaps least consciously, cricket gives all these groups and actors the sense of having hijacked the game from its English habitus into the colonies, at the level of language, body, and agency as well as competition, finance, and spectacle. If cricket did not exist in India, something like it would certainly have been invented for the conduct of public experiments with the means of modernity.

6

Number in the Colonial Imagination

In the latter part of 1990, in the last months of the regime of V. P. Singh, and in the turbulent transition to the rule of the country by S. Chandrasekhar, India (especially the Hindi-speaking North) was rocked by two major social explosions. The first, associated with the Mandal Commission Report, pitted members of different castes against each other in a manner that many feared would destroy the polity. The second, associated with the holy city of Ayodhya, pitted Hindus and Muslims against each other over the control of a sacred site. These crosscutting issues, whose interrelationship has been noted and analyzed a great deal in recent months, both involved questions of entitlement (what are your rights?) and classification (what group do you belong to and where does it fit in the political landscape?). This chapter explores the colonial roots of one dimension of the volatile politics of community and classification in contemporary India. In so doing, it follows the lead of many recent authors who have traced caste and communitarian politics to the politics of group representation in the twentieth century (Kothari 1989a, 1989b; Shah 1989) as well as to the role of the colonial census (Thapar 1989). But the precise and distinctive links between enumeration and classification in colonial India have not been specified, and that is what I propose to do in this chapter.

Edward Said's famous book (1978) is centrally concerned with the forms of knowledge that constitute what he defined as orientalism, but he does not specify how exactly the orientalist knowledge project and the colonial project of domination and extraction were connected. Nevertheless, in two ways he does set the stage for the argument of this chapter. Discussing the various ways the discourse of orientalism created a vista of exoticism, strangeness, and difference, he says that "rhetorically speaking, orientalism is absolutely anatomical and *enumerative;* to use its vocabulary is to engage in the particularizing and dividing of things Oriental into manageable parts" (1978, 72; emphasis mine). A little later in the book he suggests that in exhuming dead Oriental languages, orientalists were involved in a process in which "reconstructive precision, science, even *imagination* could prepare the way for what armies, administrations, and bureaucracies would later do on the ground, in the Orient " (123; emphasis mine).

In this chapter I want to show that the exercise of bureaucratic power itself involved the colonial imagination and that in this imagination number played a crucial role. My general argument is that exoticization and enumeration were complicated strands of a single colonial project and that in their interaction lies a crucial part of the explanation of group violence and communal terror in contemporary India. In making this argument, it might be noted that I build on David Ludden's concern with "orientalist empiricism" (1993).

My central question is simple. Is there any special force to the systematic counting of bodies under colonial states in India, Africa, and Southeast Asia, or is it simply a logical extension of the preoccupation with numbers in the metropolis, that is, in Europe in the sixteenth and seventeenth centuries? In asking this question, and in seeking to answer it, I have been inspired by two essays: one by Benedict Anderson (1991) and one by Sudipta Kaviraj (1994), which together suggest an important new agenda for a critique of European colonial rule. Taking the Indian colonial experience as my case, I shall try to elaborate the idea that we have paid a good deal of attention to the classificatory logic of colonial regimes, but less attention to the ways in which they employ quantification in censuses as well as in various other instruments like maps, agrarian surveys, racial studies, and a variety of other productions of the colonial archive.

Let me briefly anticipate my argument. I believe that the British colonial state employed quantification in its rule of the Indian subcontinent in a way that was different from its domestic counterpart in the eighteenth century (Brewer 1989) and from its predecessor states in India, including the Mughals, who certainly had elaborate apparatuses for counting, classifying, and controlling the large populations under their control. To make this case, I build two arguments and raise a number of questions for further research. The first, more extensive argument will seek to identify the place of quantification and enumeration in British classification activities in colonial India. The second, only adumbrated here, will suggest why, contrary to appearance, this variety of "dynamic nominalism" (Hacking 1986) was different from earlier state-supported numerical exercises in both the metropolis and the colonies.

Enumerative Strategies

Much has been written about the virtual obsession of the British state in India with classifying its Indian population. The locus classicus of this literature is Bernard Cohn's essay "The Census, Social Structure and Objectification in South Asia" (1987), where he shows that the Indian census, rather than being a passive instrument of data gathering, creates by its practical logic and form a new sense of category identity in India, which in turn creates the conditions for new strategies of mobility, status politics, and electoral struggle in India. The classificatory dimension of Cohn's work has been carried forward by many scholars, including Nicholas Dirks (1987), David Ludden (1993), Gyan Prakash (1990), and several historians of the subaltern school, including Ranajit Guha (1983), David Arnold (1988), and Dipesh Chakrabarty (1983). This element has also recently been resituated in a major study of the orientalist imagination in India (Inden 1990). Cohn's concern with the census has also been carried forth in an important edited collection (Barrier 1981). All these historians have shown in various ways that colonial classifications had the effect of redirecting important indigenous practices in new directions, by putting different weights and values on existing conceptions of group identity, bodily distinctions, and agrarian productivity. But less attention has been paid to the issue of numbers, measurement, and quantification in this enterprise.

The vast ocean of numbers regarding land, fields, crops, forests, castes, tribes, and so forth, collected under colonial rule from very early in the nineteenth century, was not a utilitarian enterprise in a simple, referential manner. Its utilitarianism was part of a complex including informational, justificatory, and pedagogical techniques. Particular functionaries at particular levels of the system, filling bureaucratic forms that were designed to provide raw numerical data, did see their tasks as utilitarian in a common-sense, bureaucratic way. State-generated numbers were often put to important pragmatic uses, including setting agrarian tax levels, resolving land disputes, assessing various military options, and, later in the century, trying to adjudicate indigenous claims for political representation and policy change. Numbers surely were useful in all these ways. But the less obvious point is that statistics were generated in amounts that far defeated any unified bureaucratic purpose. Agrarian statistics, for example, were not only filled with classificatory and technical errors; they also encouraged new forms of agrarian practice and self-representation (Smith 1985).

Thus, although early colonial policies of quantification were utilitarian in design, I would suggest that numbers gradually became more importantly part of the illusion of bureaucratic control and a key to a colonial imaginary in which countable abstractions, of people and resources at every imaginable level and for every conceivable purpose, created the sense of a controllable indigenous reality. Numbers were part of the recent historical experience of literacy for the colonial elite (Money 1989; Thomas 1987), who had thus come to believe that quantification was socially useful. There is ample evidence that the significance of these numbers was often either nonexistent or self-fulfilling, rather than principally referential to a complex reality external to the activities of the colonial state. In the long run, these enumerative strategies helped to ignite communitarian and nationalist identities that in fact undermined colonial rule. One must therefore ask how the idea of number as an instrument of colonial control might have entered the imagination of the state.

In regard to England, the answer to this question must go back to the story of numeracy, literacy, state fiscalism, and actuarial thinking in the seventeenth and eighteenth centuries (Hacking 1975, chap. 12; 1982; 1986; Brewer 1989). This is a very complex story indeed, but by the end of the eighteenth century, number, like landscape, heritage, and the people, had become part of the language of the British political imagination (Ludden 1993), and the idea had become firmly implanted that a powerful state could not survive without making enumeration a central technique of social control. Thus, the census in Britain made rapid technical strides throughout the nineteenth century and doubtless provided the broad scaffolding for the late-nineteenth-century census in India. One overview of material on the nineteenth-century census in Britain (Lawton 1978) suggests that, operating as it did within a framework of commonsense classifications shared by officialdom with ordinary people, the British census did not have the refractive and generative effects that it did in India.

While I cannot decisively show here that the operations of the British census at home were different from those in India, there are three sound reasons to suppose that there were important differences. First, the basis of the British census was overwhelmingly territorial and occupational rather than ethnic or racial.[1] Second, insofar as its concerns were sociological in England, the census tended to be directly tied to the politics of representation, as in the issue of rotten boroughs. Finally, and most important, both British and French census projects (as well as the embryonic social sciences with which they were associated), tended to reserve their most invasive investigations for their social margins: the poor, the sexually profligate, the lunatic, and the criminal. In the colonies, by contrast, the entire population was seen as different in problematic ways, this shift lying at the very heart of orientalism (Nigam 1990, 287). Furthermore, in India this orientalist inclination was preordained to meet its indigenous counterpart in the apparent cardinality of difference in the indigenous ideology of caste, as it appeared to Western eyes. The similarities and differences between the British and French colonial projects in this regard have yet to be worked out, but it is clear that the concern with deviance and marginality at home was extended to the management of entire populations in the Orient (Armstrong 1990; Rabinow 1989). While there were clear and important connections between the enterprises of classification, science, photography, criminology, and so on, in the metropolis and in the colonies it does not appear that enumerative activities took the same cultural form in England and in India, if for no other reason because the English did not see themselves as a vast edifice of exotic communities, devoid of a polity worth the name.

In a colonial setting such as the Indian one, the encounter with a highly differentiated, religiously Other set of groups must have built on the metropolitan concern with occupation, class, and religion, all of which were a prominent part of the British census in the nineteenth century. This created a situation in which the hunt for information and archives for this information took on enormous proportions, and numerical data became crucial to this empiricist drive. By this time, statistical thinking had become allied to the project of civic control, both in England and France, in projects of sanitation, urban planning, criminal law, and demography (Canguilheim 1989; Ewald 1986; Hacking 1975, 1982, 1986). It would thus have been tempting for European bureaucrats to imagine that good numerical data would make it easier to embark on projects of social control or reform in the colonies.

This argument raises two separate but related issues. Was India a *special* case or a *limiting* case in regard to the role of enumeration, exoticization, and domination in the techniques of the modern nation-state? I would argue that it was a special case because in India the orientalist gaze encountered an indigenous system of classification that seemed virtually invented by some earlier, indigenous form of orientalism. I do not subscribe to the view that early Hindu texts constitute a simple variation on later orientalist texts, thus justifying the exoticizing tendencies of, for example, the colonial legal digests. Making this case fully would take me too far afield in this context, but let me simply note that essentialism, too, is a matter of context and that the relationship between Hindu stereotyping and British essentialism in the matter of caste cannot be considered apart from a thoroughgoing comparison of state and religious formations in very different historical contexts.

Nevertheless, it would be foolish to pretend that British orientalism did not encounter in India an indigenous social imaginary that appeared to valorize group difference in a remarkable way. Caste in India, even if it was itself a very complicated part of the Indian social imaginary and was refracted and reified in many ways through British techniques of observation and control, was nevertheless not a figment of the British political imagination. In this regard, Oriental essentializing in India carried a social force that can come only when two theories of difference share a critical assumption: that the bodies of certain groups are the bearers of social difference and moral status. This is where India is a special case. But looked at from the vantage point of the present, India may also be regarded as a limiting case of the tendency of the modern nation-state to draw on existing ideas of linguistic, religious, and territorial difference to "produce the people" (Balibar 1990).[2]

The role of numbers in complex information-gathering apparatuses such as the colonial one in India had two sides that in retrospect need to be distinguished. The one side may be described as justificatory and the other as disciplinary. A very large part of the statistical information gathered by British functionaries in India did not just facilitate learning or discovery in regard to ruling Indian territories. These statistical data also assisted in arguing and teaching in the context of bureaucratic discourse and practice, first between the East India Company and the English parliament and later between the officials of the crown in India and their bosses in London. (Smith 1985 is a classic statement of the general logic that knits together reports, manuals, and records in nineteenth-century India.) Numbers were a critical part of the discourse of the colonial state because its metropolitan interlocutors had come to depend on numerical data, however dubious their accuracy and relevance, for major social or resource-related policy initiatives. This justificatory dimension of the use of numbers in colonial policy, of course, also relates to the different levels of the British state in India, where numbers were the fuel for a series of nested struggles between

Indian officials at the lowest levels of the bureaucracy, up the system to the governor-general of India, through a series of crosscutting committees, boards, and individual officeholders, who conducted a constant internal debate about the plausibility and relevance of various classifications and the numbers attached to them (Dirks 1987, chaps. 10 and 11; Hutchins 1967, 181; Presler 1987, chap. 2).

Numbers regarding castes, villages, religious groups, yields, distances, and wells were part of a language of policy debate, in which their referential status quickly became far less important than their discursive importance in supporting or subverting various classificatory moves and the policy arguments based on them. It is important to note here that numbers permitted comparison between kinds of places and people that were otherwise different, that they were concise ways of conveying large bodies of information, and that they served as a short form for capturing and appropriating otherwise recalcitrant features of the social and human landscape of India. It is not so much that numbers did not serve a straightforward referential purpose in colonial pragmatics, serving to indicate features of the Indian social world to bureaucrats and politicians, but that this referential purpose was often not as important as the rhetorical purpose. This is in part due to the fact that the sheer vastness of the numbers involved in major policy debates in the nineteenth century often made their strictly referential or informational dimension unmanageable.

Yet the justificatory functions of these numerical strategies seem to have been no more important than their pedagogical and disciplinary ones. With regard to this latter function, Foucault's ideas about biopolitics certainly are most relevant, given that the colonial state saw itself as part of the Indian body politic while it was simultaneously engaged in reinscribing the politics of the Indian body, especially in its involvement with sati, hook swinging, possession rites, and other forms of body manipulation (Dirks 1989; Mani 1990). I will return to this point later. But the numerical issue complicates matters somewhat. For what is involved here are not simply the logistical needs of the state but also its discursive needs construed centrally as statistical needs.

Moreover, this was not just a matter of providing the numerical grist for a policy apparatus whose discursive form had been constructed through a complex European development involving probabilistic thinking and civic policy. It was also a matter of disciplining the vast officialdom of the colonial state (see also Smith 1985 and Cohn 1987), as well as the population that these officials wished to control and reform, so that numbers could become an indispensable part of its bureaucratic practices and style.

Number and Cadastral Politics

The instance of rupture between the empiricist and disciplinary moments of colonial numerology can be seen in the many technical documents produced in the middle of the nineteenth century. There are many ways in which this shift can be conceptualized, including the one that sees it as a "transformation of the census as an instrument of tax to an instrument of knowledge," in the words of Richard Smith (1985, 166), who identifies this shift as occurring in the Punjab around 1850. In the discussion that follows, I use a document from roughly the same period from western India to illustrate the formation of the new sort of numerical gaze of the colonial state in the middle of the nineteenth century.

This document, published under the title *The Joint Report of 1847*, was actually published as a book in 1975 by the Land Records Department of the state of Maharashtra in western India (Government of Maharashtra 1975). Its subtitle is *Measurement and Classification Rules of the Deccan, Gujarat, Konkan and Kanara Surveys*. It belongs to a class of documents that show the East India Company seeking to standardize its land-revenue practices across the full extent of its territories and to rationalize practices generated in the latter part of the eighteenth and in the early part of the nineteenth century in the heat of conquest. It is, par excellence, a document of bureaucratic rationalization, which seeks to create and standardize revenue rules for all the land under East India Company jurisdiction in the Deccan region. But it also contains a series of letters and reports from the early part of the 1840s that reveal a serious debate between local and central officialdom about the minutiae of mapping the agricultural terrain of western India, and its larger purposes, such as assessment and dispute settlement. It is a quintessential document of cadastral politics.

Following Ranajit Guha's characterization of "the prose of counterinsurgency" (Guha 1983), we may call the *Joint Report* a classic example of the prose of cadastral domination. This is prose composed partly of rules, partly of orders, partly of appendices, and partly of letters and petitions, which must be read together. In this prose, the internal debates of the revenue bureaucracy, the pragmatics of rule formation, and the rhetoric of utility always accompanied the final recommendations by authorities at various levels of new technical practices. These are documents whose manifest rhetoric is technical (that is, positivist, transparent, and neutral) but whose subtext is contestatory (in regard to superiors) and disciplinary (in regard to inferiors).

The bulk of the document, like most others of its ilk, is truly Borgesian, struggling to find textual methods and representations adequate to capturing both the scope and the minutiae of the Indian agriterrain. The analogy to Jorge Luis Borges's classic story of the map that had to be as large as the domain it iconicized is not fanciful, as is evidenced by the following complaint by one official about an earlier technique of mapping:

> At the time of Mr. Pringle's survey of the Deccan there were some very detailed and intricate records prepared, under the name of kaifiats, which we have also found it expedient to do away with as useless, and tending by their great length and complexity to involve in obscurity, rather than elucidate, the subjects of which they treat, and by their very bulk to render the detection of errors a matter of impossibility (1975 footnote: the kaifiats prepared for many of the villages assessed by Mr. Pringle were upwards of 300 yards in length). (*Joint Report*, 55)

Notwithstanding this complaint in 1840 about the Borgesian absurdities of earlier mapping efforts, the tension between representational economy and detail does not disappear. Throughout the 1840s, a battle continues between the survey authorities of the Deccan and the Board of Revenue, which has somewhat more synoptic and panoptic aspirations for its surveys. First, there is the relationship between measurement and classification, which is itself an explicit subject of discussion in many of the letters and reports leading up to the *Joint Report*, which fixed the basic rules of survey for this region for several subsequent decades. As regards measurement, the British officials directly responsible for the assessment perceived it as a problem of adapting existing trigonometric, topographic, and protraction methods to create maps that they saw as both accurate and functional. They were concerned to "multiply copies of these maps in the most economical and accurate manner, as well as to guard against any future fraudulent attempt at alteration," and therefore these officers suggested that "they should be lithographed" (*Joint Report*, 9–10). Their concern for accuracy in measurement already incorporated existing statistical ideas about percentages of error and "average error," which they wanted to reduce.

These officers recognized that classification was a much trickier issue than measurement; regarding measurement, however, they were naively positivist: "These results are of an absolute and invariable character, capable of being arrived at with equal certainty by many modes" (10). The classification of fields for purposes of a fair assessment posed a host of problems involving the typification of variation for purposes of classification, so that the classification could be general enough to apply to a large region, yet specific enough to accommodate important variations on the ground. The resulting solution involved a ninefold classification of soils, a complex system of notation for field assessors, and an intricate algorithm for translating such qualitative variation into quantitative values relevant to revenue assessment.

Put another way, the detailed disciplines of measurement and classification (the one relying on the iconic practices of trigonometry and surveying in general and the other on numerical and statistical ideas of average and percentage error), were the twin techniques through which an equitable policy of revenue was envisioned, based on principles of the most general applicability that would simultaneously be as sensitive as possible to local variation. This mentality—generality of application and sensitivity to minute variations—was the central tension not just of cadastral surveys but of all the informational aspirations of the colonial state. As I explain below, this mentality is also the crucial link between the cadastral logic of the first half of the century and the human censuses of the latter part of the century, in terms of enumeration and exoticization.

The exchanges surrounding the 1847 report also reveal the emergent tension between the varieties of knowledge that constituted orientalist empiricism. It should not be very surprising that officials more closely concerned with local variation and on the-ground accuracy and fairness were resentful of the obsessive panoptical needs of the higher levels of the bureaucracy. Illustrating literally the power of the textual "supplement" (in the deconstructionist usage), numerical tables, figures, and charts allowed the contingency—the sheer narrative clutter of prose descriptions of the colonial landscape—to be domesticated into the abstract, precise, complete, and cool idiom of number. Of course, numbers could be fought over, but this battle had an instrumental quality, far removed from the heat of the novel, the light of the camera, and the colonial realism of administrative ethnographies.

These properties were of particular value to those who sought to tame the very diversities of the land and the people that other aspects of the Oriental episteme such as photography, travelogs, engravings, and exhibitions did so much to create. In 1840, Lieutenant Wingate, the official most responsible for translating the assessment needs of the colonial state into locally feasible technical and bureaucratic practices in the Deccan, wrote to the revenue commissioner in Poona, his immediate superior, clearly expressing frustration with the changing interests of the central bureaucracy: "The present survey, moreover, was instituted for purely revenue purposes, and the question of rendering it subservient to those of Geography and Topography is now mooted for the first time. It can hardly therefore be in fairness objected to the plan of operations that it does not include the accomplishment of objects that were not contemplated at the time of its formation" (69).

The official at the next level up in the revenue bureaucracy, although less forthright than Wingate, nevertheless makes it clear that he is puzzled by the relation between the revenue needs and the "scientific" needs of his superiors. Mediating between two important levels of the bureaucracy, he adds, at the conclusion of an important letter, that "for every purpose for which a Revenue Officer can desire a map, those already furnished by the late survey under Major Jopp, and those now making out [sic] by the Deccan Revenue Surveys, of which a specimen is annexed, seem to me amply sufficient; and if anything more accurate or detailed be required, it must be, I conclude for some purpose of speculative science, on the necessity or otherwise of which I am not required to express an opinion" (81–82).

Documents such as the *Joint Report* were crucial in the disciplining of lower-level, especially native functionaries in the empiricist practices of colonial rule. In the collection of maps, measures, and statistics of every sort, these documents, and the rules contained and debated within them, show that junior European officials were critically concerned with making sure that the standards of colonial administrative practice were drilled into the minutest bodily techniques of these measurers. These techniques could be seen as disciplinary techniques applied both to lower-level European officialdom and to their Indian subordinates. But there was an important difference. Whereas the former might not recognize their own subjection to the regime of number in the idioms of science, patriotism, and imperial hegemony (with which they were racially identified), for Indian officialdom these practices were a direct inscription onto their bodies and minds of practices associated with the power and foreignness of their rulers. In this, as in other aspects of the control of colonial labor and resources, not all subalternities are identical.

The vast apparatus of revenue assessment was in fact part of a complex system of discipline and surveillance in and through which native functionaries were instilled with a whole series of numerical habits (tied to other habits of description, iconography, and distinction); these habits in turn involved number through a complex set of roles, including those of classification, ordering, approximation, and identification. The political arithmetic of colonialism was taught quite literally on the ground and translated into algorithms that could make future numerical activities habitual and instill bureaucratic description with a numerological infrastructure.

In each of these important ways, the prose of cadastral control set the grounds, and constituted a rehearsal, for later discourse concerning human communities and their enumeration. This rehearsal had three components: it set the stage for the widespread use of standardizing enumerative techniques to control on-the-ground material variations; it treated the physical features of the landscape, as well as its productivity and ecological variability, as separable (to some extent) from the complex social rights involved in its use and meaning for rural Indians; and it constituted a pedagogical preparation for the kind of disciplinary regime that would later be required for human census takers and tabulators at all levels.

Number (and the statistical ideology underlying number) was the ligature of these cadastral texts and provided the key links between these texts and the debates that they reported and the practices they were designed to discipline. Thus, through a careful reading of these apparently simply technical documents, one can unearth ideological tensions and fractures as well as practices of teaching and surveillance, in which it is not only the case that "land is to rule" (Neale 1969). Colonial rule had a pedagogical and disciplinary function, so that "land is to teach": the measurement and classification of land was the training ground for the culture of number in which statistics became the authorizing discourse of the appendix (giving indirect weight to the verbal portion of the text) at the same time that it gave higher-level officials a pedagogical and disciplinary sense of controlling not just the territory over which they sought to rule, but also the native functionaries through which such rule needed to be effected. As far as the native is concerned, the regime of number, as every page of such documents makes clear, is partly there to counteract the mendacity that is seen as constitutional to most natives, both farmers and measurers.

We thus have one part of an answer to the question with which we began, namely, what special role does the enumeration of bodies have under colonial rule? I have suggested that numbers were a changing part of the colonial imaginary and function in justificatory and pedagogical ways as well as in more narrowly referential ones. The history of British rule in the nineteenth century may be read in part as a shift from a more functional use of number in what has been called the fiscal militarism of the British state at home (Brewer 1989) to a more pedagogical and disciplinary role. Indian bodies were gradually not only categorized but given quantitative values (Bayly 1988, 88–89), increasingly associated with what Ian Hacking has called "dynamic nominalism" (1986), that is, the creation of new kinds of self by officially enforced labeling activities.

Number played a critical role in such dynamic nominalism in the colonial setting, partly because it provided a shared language for information transfer, disputation, and linguistic commensuration between center and periphery, and for debates among a huge army of mediating bureaucrats in India. Number was thus part of the enterprise of *translating* the colonial experience into terms graspable in the metropolis, terms that could encompass the ethnological peculiarities that various orientalist discourses provided. Numerical glosses constituted a kind of metalanguage for colonial bureaucratic discourse within which more exotic understandings could be packaged, at a time when enumerating populations and controlling and reforming society had come together in Europe. These numerical glosses that appear as accompanying data for discursive descriptions and recommendations are best regarded as a normalizing frame for the stranger discursive realities that the verbal portions of many colonial texts needed to construct. This normalizing frame functions at three of the levels discussed by Foucault, those of knowledge and power, text and practice, reading and ruling. Following Richard Smith's distinction (1985) between rule-by-record and rule-by-report, it can be seen that numbers in *records* provided the empirical ballast for the descriptivist thrust of the colonial gaze, whereas numbers in *reports* provided more of a normalizing frame, balancing the contestatory and polyphonic aspects of the narrative portions of these reports, which shared some of the tensions of the "prose of counterinsurgency" (Guha 1983).

Colonial Body Counts

These enumerative practices, in the setting of a largely agricultural society that was already to a large degree practically prepared for cadastral control by the Mughal state, had another major consequence. They were not merely a rehearsal for the counting practices of the Indian national census after 1870. They also accomplished a major and hitherto largely unnoticed task. The huge apparatus of revenue settlements, land surveys, and legal and bureaucratic changes in the first half of the nineteenth century did something beyond commoditizing land (Cohn 1969); transforming "lords into landlords" and peasants into tenants (Prakash 1990); and changing reciprocal structures of gift and honor into salable titles, which were semiotically fractured and were rendered marketable, while retaining some of the metonymic force that tied them to named persons. They also unyoked social groups from the complex and localized group structures and agrarian practices in which they had previously been embedded, whether in the context of the "silent settlement" of *inams* in South India (Frykenberg 1977; Dirks 1987), of *inams* in Maharashtra (Preston 1989), of bonded laborers in Bihar (Prakash 1990), or of Julahas in Uttar Pradesh (Pandey 1990). The huge diversity of castes, sects, tribes, and other practical groupings of the Indian landscape were thus rendered into a vast categorical landscape un-tethered to the specificities of the agrarian terrain.

This unyoking occurs in two major steps, one associated with the pe-riod before 1870, during which issues of land settlement and taxation are dominant colonial projects, and the other with the period from 1870 to 1931, the era of the great All-India Census, of which the enumeration of human populations is the dominant project. The years from about 1840 to 1870 mark the transition from one major orientation to the other. The first period sets the stage for the second in that it is dominated by a concern for the physical and ecological basis of land productivity and revenue; as I have already suggested, the first era to some extent unyokes this variability from the social and human world associated with it, in the context of ef-forts to wage a battle of standardization against on-the-ground variation. In the second period, so usefully explored by Rashmi Pant (1987) in the context of the North-West Provinces and Oudh, the reverse move occurs, and human groups (castes) are treated to a considerable extent as ab-stractable from the regional and territorial contexts in which they func-tion. It is of course important to note that these colonial projects were con-currently plagued by internal contradictions (the urge to specificity and generalizability in the names of castes for the All-India Census, for exam-ple), by inconsistencies among different colonial projects, and, most im-portant, by the fact that colonial bureaucratic operations did not necessar-ily transform practices or mentalities on the ground. I shall return to this issue toward the end of this chapter in a discussion of the colonial subject.

Pant's seminal essay discusses the way in which caste became a crucial site for the activities of the national censuses after 1870 against other sites. Along with the essay by Smith (1985), Pant's argument allows us to see that colonial bureaucratic practice, as a contingent and historically shaped locus of agency in its own right, helped to create a special and powerful re-lationship among essentialization, discipline, surveillance, objectification, and group consciousness by the last decades of the nineteenth century.

Numbers played a crucial role in this conjuncture, and the earlier statis-tical panopticon was a critical factor in the gravitation of the census to-ward caste as a key site of social classification, as caste appeared to be the key to Indian social variability as well as to the Indian mentality. Pant, who builds on the earlier work of Smith, points out that the use of caste for "dif-ferentiating a stream of data" was first applied in the realm of sex statistics from this region (1987, 148). Specifically, it was argued in the 1872 report of the All-India Census for the North-West Provinces and Oudh that certain hypotheses about sex ratios in relation to female infanticide could only be explained by reference to caste. This concern with explaining and controlling exotic behaviors is a crucial piece of evidence that empiricism and exoticization were not disconnected aspects of the colonial imaginary in India. This linkage of empirical statistics and the management of the exotic was the basis for a more general policy orientation—that much of what needed to be known about the Indian population would become intelligible only by the detailed enumeration of the population in terms of caste.

Although the subsequent history of the All-India Census shows that in practice there were enormous difficulties and anomalies involved with the effort to construct an all-India grid of named and enumerated castes, the principle was not abandoned until the 1930s. As Pant shows, "by the turn of the century, the epistemological status of caste as a locale for recognizing qualified and socially effective units of the Indian population was well established—as our Census Reports of 1911–1931 confirm" (149). But it is also worth noting that because the hunt for data about caste created a huge and unmanageable flow of information, even as early as the 1860s, only "numerical majorities" were given prominence in the census reports. Thus, the concern with numerical majorities emerged as a principle for organizing census information. This apparently innocuous bureaucratic principle, of course, is a logical basis for the ideas of majority and minority groups that subsequently affected Hindu-Muslim politics in colonial India and caste politics in India during the twentieth century up to the present.

While it is true that caste as *the* master trope with which to taxonomize the Indian landscape is a relatively late product of colonial rule (Pant 1987), the more general essentialization of Indian groups goes back at least to the beginnings of the nineteenth century, if not earlier, as Gyan Pandey has shown with the weaving castes of Uttar Pradesh (Pandey 1990). Until the last decades of the nineteenth century, however, the essentialization of groups in orientalist and administrative discourse was largely separate from the enumerative practices of the state, except insofar as they were directly linked to localized revenue purposes. An analysis of an 1823 colonial census in South India (Ludden 1988) shows that the late-nineteenth-century preoccupation with social classification and enumeration is anticipated very early. But this early census seems, on the whole, pragmatic, localistic, and relational in its treatment of groups, rather than abstract, uniformitarian, or encyclopedic in its aspirations. This was still a census oriented to *taxation* rather than to *knowledge*, to use Smith's terms.

After 1870, however, not only had numbers become an integral part of the colonial imaginary and the practical ideologies of its low-level functionaries, but Indian social groups had become both functionally and discursively unyoked from local agrarian landscapes and set adrift in a vast pan-Indian social encyclopedia. This release was a function of the growing sense that the social morphology of caste could provide an overall grid through the census for organizing knowledge about the Indian population. These are the conditions for the special force of the Indian census after 1870, which was intended to quantify previously set classifications but in fact had just the reverse effect—to stimulate the self-mobilization of these groups into a variety of larger translocal political forms.

Here also is the place to note the key difference between the British and their Mughal predecessors: while the Mughals did a great deal to map and measure the land under their control for revenue purposes (Habib 1963), thus generating a large part of the revenue vocabulary alive in India and Pakistan even today, they conducted no known census of persons, a fact noted by Irfan Habib as the central reason why it is difficult to estimate the population of Mughal India (Habib 1982, 163). Enumeration of various things was certainly part of the Mughal state imaginary as was the acknowledgment of group identities, but not the enumeration of group identities. As for the other major precolonial political formations of the subcontinent, such as the Vijayanagara kingdom, they do not appear to have shared the linear, centralizing, record-keeping modes of the Mughals and were oriented to number as a far more subtle cosmopolitics of names, territories, honors, shares, and relations (Breckenridge 1983). In this regard, non-Mughal states in the Indian subcontinent before colonial rule, including those like the Marathas who ran elaborately monetized political domains (Perlin 1987), do not seem to have been concerned with number as a direct instrument of social control. In these precolonial regimes, enumerative activities were tied to taxation, accounting, and land revenue, but the linkage of enumeration to group identity seems very weak indeed. Where it did exist, it seems to have been connected to very specific social formations, such as *akharas* (wrestling and gymnastic sodalities), and not to the enumeration of the population at large (Freitag 1990).

For this last, totalizing thrust to enter the imaginary of the state, the crucial intervening step was the essentializing and taxonomizing gaze of early orientalism (of the European variety), followed by the enumerative habit applied to the land in the first half of the nineteenth century, and finally the idea of political representation as tied, not to essentially similar citizens and individuals but to communities conceived as inherently special. The essentializing and exoticizing gaze of orientalism in India in the eighteenth and nineteenth centuries provides the crucial link between census classifications and caste and community politics. Here, we are finally at the heart of the argument, both regarding the differences between the colonial regime in India (and its metropolitan counterparts as well as its indigenous predecessors) and the link between colonial classificatory politics and contemporary democratic politics. The enumeration of the social body, conceived as aggregations of individuals whose bodies were inherently both collective and exotic, sets the stage for group difference to be the central principle of politics. Linking the idea of representation to the idea of communities characterized by bioracial commonalities (internally) and bioracial differences (externally) seems to be the critical marker of the colonial twist in the politics of the modern nation-state.

What occurred in the colony was a conjuncture that never occurred at home: the idea that techniques of measurement were a crucial way to normalize the variation in soil and land, conjoined with the idea that numerical representation was a key to normalizing the pathology of difference through which the Indian social body was represented. Thus, the idea of the "average man" (*l'homme moyen* of Quetelet), smuggled in through statistics (as its epistemological underbelly), was brought into the domain of group difference. This sets up an orientalist extension of the metropolitan idea of the numerical representation of groups (conceived as composed of average individuals) and the idea of separate electorates, which is a natural outgrowth of the sense that India was a land of groups (both for civil and political purposes) and that Indian social groupings were inherently special. Thus, under colonial rule, at least in British India, the numerical dimension of classification carries the seeds of a special contradiction, as it was brought to bear on a world conceived as one of incommensurable group differences.

Nationalism, Representation, and Number

The communitarian approach, which later (in the first part of the twentieth century) has its most dramatic manifestation in separate electorates for Hindus and Muslims (Hasan 1979; Pandey 1990; Robinson 1974), was by no means restricted to them. It was built on earlier ideas about caste as the critical principle of a general morphology of the Indian population (as known through the census) and still earlier ideas about the powers of enumeration in grasping the variability and the tractability of India's land and resources. This communitarian approach was also crucial in defining the dynamics of ideas of *majority* and *minority* as culturally coded terms for dominant and disenfranchised groups in South India (Frykenberg 1987; Saraswathi 1974; Washbrook 1976, chap. 6) and elsewhere. It is thus very plausible to argue, as Rajni Kothari (1989a, 1989b) and others have done, that the very fabric of Indian democracy remains adversely affected by the idea of numerically dominated bloc voting, as opposed to more classically liberal ideas of the bourgeois individual's casting his vote as a democratic citizen.

Although it is beyond the scope of this chapter to show in a detailed way how the cognitive importance of caste in the census of India in the 1870s anticipates the communitarian politics of this century, it should be noted that even after 1931, when caste ceased to be a central concern of the Indian census, the idea of politics as the contest of essentialized and enumerated communities (the latter being a concept I owe to Kaviraj 1994) had already taken firm hold of local and regional politics and thus no longer required the stimulation of the census to maintain its hold on Indian politics. As Shah (1989) has noted, there has been a steady (and successful) effort in the past few decades to reverse the post-1931 policy of eliminating caste counts from the census.

Hannah Pitkin (1967) and others have written eloquently about the complex relationships among representation in its moral, aesthetic, and political senses. I need not repeat this Western genealogy here, except to note that fairly early in the history of the Enlightenment the idea of democracy became tied to an idea of the representative sovereignty of subjects. Thus, as Robert Frykenberg (1987) has pointed out for the Indian context, electoral politics became both a politics of *representation* (of the people to the people—a game of mirrors in which the state is made virtually invisible) and a politics of *representativeness*, that is, a politics of statistics, in which some bodies could be held to stand for other bodies because of the numerical principle of metonymy rather than the varied cosmopolitical principles of representation that had characterized ideas of divine rule in many premodern polities.

During the nineteenth and early twentieth century, the colonial state found itself in an interesting contradiction in India as it sought to use ideas of representation and representativeness at lower levels of India's political order, with paternalist, monarchic, and qualitative principles at the top. The story of Indian self-government (which was confined to a variety of village- and district-level bodies during the bulk of the second half of the nineteenth century) became transformed steadily into the logic of Indian nationalism, which co-opted the colonial logic of representativeness and used it to annex the democratic idea of representation as self-representation.

Thus, the counting of bodies that had served the purposes of colonial rule at lower levels in the last half of the nineteenth century turned gradually into the idea of the representation of Indian selves (self-rule) as nationalism became a mass movement. Of course, in hindsight, as Partha Chatterjee has helped us see, nationalism suffered from sharing the basic thematic of colonialist thought and thus could not generate a thoroughgoing critique of it (Chatterjee 1986). So, the politics of numbers, especially in regard to caste and community, is not only the bane of democratic politics in India, but these older identities have become politicized in ways that are radically different from other local conceptions of the relationship between the order of *jatis* and the logic of the state. The process by which separate Hindu and Muslim identities were constructed at a macro level and transformed not just into imagined communities but also into enumerated communities is only the most visible pathology of the transfer of the politics of numerical representation to a society in which representation and group identity had no special numerical relationship to the polity.

But it could still be said that colonial rule, either of the British in India or of other European regimes elsewhere in the world, was not alone in generating enumerated communities. Many large non-European states, including the Ottomans, Mughals, and various Chinese dynasties, had numerical concerns. Where lies the *colonial* difference? For the mature colonial state, numbers were part of a complex imaginary in which the utilitarian needs of fiscal militarism in the world system, the classificatory logics of orientalist ethnology, the shadow presence of Western democratic ideas of numerical representation, and the general shift from a classificatory to a numerical biopolitics created an evolving logic that reached a critical conjunctural point in the last three decades of the nineteenth century and the first two decades of the twentieth.

The net result was something critically different from all other complex state apparatuses in regard to the politics of the body and the construction of communities as bodies. Put very simply, other regimes may have had numerical concerns and they may also have had classificatory concerns. But these remained largely separate, and it was only in the complex conjuncture of variables that constituted the project of the mature colonial state that these two forms of dynamic nominalism came together to create a polity centered around self-consciously enumerated communities. When these communities were also embedded in a wider official discourse of space, time, resources, and relations that was also numerical in critical ways, a specifically colonial political arithmetic was generated, in which essentializing and enumerating human communities became not only concurrent activities but unimaginable without one another.

This arithmetic is a critical part of colonial biopolitics (at least in terms of the British in India) not only because it involved abstractions of number whereas other state regimes had more concrete numerical purposes (such as taxes, corvée labor, and the like). The modern colonial state brings together the exoticizing vision of orientalism with the familiarizing discourse of statistics. In the process, the body of the colonial subject is made simultaneously strange and docile. Its strangeness lies in the fact that it comes to be seen as the site of cruel and unusual practices and bizarre subjectivities. But colonial body counts create not only types and classes (the first move toward domesticating differences) but also homogeneous bodies (within categories) because number, by its nature, flattens idiosyncrasies and creates boundaries around these homogeneous bodies as it performatively limits their extent. In this latter regard, statistics are to bodies and social types what maps are to territories: they flatten and enclose. The link between colonialism and orientalism, therefore, is most strongly reinforced not at the loci of classification and typification (as has often been suggested) but at the loci of enumeration, where bodies are counted, homogenized, and bounded in their extent. Thus, the unruly body of the colonial subject (fasting, feasting, hook swinging, abluting, burning, and bleeding) is recuperated through the language of numbers that allows these very bodies to be brought back, now counted and accounted, for the humdrum projects of taxation, sanitation, education, warfare, and loyalty.

My argument thus far might be read as implying that the colonial project of essentializing, enumerating, and appropriating the social landscape was wholly successful. In fact, that is not the case, and there is ample evidence from a variety of sources that the projects of the colonial state were by no means completely effective, especially in regard to the colonizing of the Indian consciousness. In various kinds of peasant and urban revolt, in various kinds of autobiographic and fictional writing, in many different sorts of domestic formation and expression, and in various kinds of bodily and religious practices Indians of many classes continued practices and reproduced understandings that far predated colonial rule. Moreover, Indian men and women deliberately recast their conceptions of body, society, country, and destiny in movements of protest, internal critique, and outright revolt against colonial authorities. It is indeed from these various sources that the energies of local resistance were drawn—energies and spaces (ranging from prayer groups and athletic associations to ascetic orders and mercantile orders) that provided the social basis of the nationalist movement. These energies permitted someone like Gandhi, and many other lesser-known figures, to recapture social and moral ground from the British (and from the discourse of orientalism itself). These reflections bring us back to a problem raised earlier, that of the colonial subject in relation to the enumerative and classificatory projects of the state.

There is of course no easy generalization to be made about the degree to which the effort to organize the colonial project around the idea of essentialized and enumerated communities made inroads into the practical consciousness of colonial subjects in India. It is easy enough, however, to say that the results must have varied according to various dimensions of the position of the colonial subject: her gender, her closeness to or distance from the colonial gaze, her involvement with or detachment from colonial politics, her participation in or distance from the bureaucratic apparatus itself. It is also true that various Indian persons and groups did remain (in memory if not in empirical reality) tied to locality, whatever the panopticon saw or said. Also, while certain components of the colonial state were active propagators of the discourses of group identity, others, such as those involved with education, law, and moral reform, were implicated in the creation of what might be called a colonial bourgeois subject, conceived as an individual. This problem is not resolvable here, but it needs to be remarked as an important issue that any interpretation of enumerated communities will eventually have to engage.

But even if various spaces remained free of the colonial panopticon (whether through the agency of resisting colonial subjects or the incapacities and contradictions of the colonial juggernaut), the fact is that the colonial gaze, and its associated techniques, have left an indelible mark on Indian political consciousness. Part of this indelible heritage is to be seen in the matter of numbers. It is enumeration, in association with new forms of categorization, that creates the link between the orientalizing thrust of the British state, which saw India as a museum or zoo of difference and of differences, and the project of reform, which involved cleaning up the sleazy, flabby, frail, feminine, obsequious bodies of natives into clean, virile, muscular, moral, and loyal bodies that could be moved into the subjectivities proper to colonialism (Arnold 1988). With Gandhi, we have a revolt of the Indian body, a reawakening of Indian selves, and a reconstitution of the loyal body into the unruly and sign-ridden body of mass nationalist protest (Amin 1984; Bondurant 1958). But the fact that Gandhi had to die after watching bodies defined as "Hindu" and "Muslim" burn and defile one another reminds us that his success against the colonial project of enumeration, and its idea of the body politic, was not and is not complete.

The burning body of Roop Kanwar (associated with the renascent Rajput consciousness of urban males in small-town Rajasthan), the self-immolations of young, middle-class men and women after the Mandal Commission Report was revitalized, and the bodies of the *kar sewaks* in Ayodhya and of Muslims in Lucknow and elsewhere suggest that indigenous ideas of difference have become transformed into a deadly politics of community, a process that has many historical sources. But this cultural and historical tinder would not burn with the intensity we now see, but for contact with the techniques of the modern nation-state, especially those having to do with number. The kinds of subjectivity that Indians owe to the contradictions of colonialism remain both obscure and dangerous.

PART III

Postnational

Locations

7

Life after Primordialism

The contemporary world is filled with examples of ethnic consciousness that are closely linked to nationalism and violence.[1] It will no longer serve to look at ethnicity as just another principle of group identity, as just another cultural device for the pursuit of group interests, or as some dialectical combination of the two. We need an account of ethnicity that explores its modernity.[2] Perhaps the most clear index of modern ethnicity is that it draws together groups that by their sheer spatial spread and numerical strength are vastly larger than the ethnic groups of traditional anthropology. Tamils, Serbs, Sikhs, Malaysians, Basques, and others are all very large groups, are all claimants to nationhood, and are all involved in violent confrontations with existing state structures and other large-scale ethnic groupings. This matrix of large size, nationalist aspiration, and violence characterizes these new ethnicities. It is to this matrix that this chapter is addressed, although I recognize that the term *ethnicity* may also be relevant to smaller, less volatile, more instrumentally organized groupings.

The Black Box of Primordialism

The primordialist thesis in virtually all of its many forms (Apter 1965; Isaacs 1975; Shils 1957) is of little use in accounting for the ethnicities of the twentieth century. This thesis distracts us from certain important facts, especially about the new ethnicities of Asia and Europe in the past decade. In fleshing out this claim, I shall propose the skeleton of a new approach to ethnic movements, especially in their violent and destructive moments. Both in arguing that the primordialist thesis is deeply flawed and in seeing in ethnicity a historically constituted form of social classification that is regularly misrecognized and naturalized as a prime mover in social life, I build on important earlier work in anthropology (Comaroff and Comaroff 1992b; Barth 1969; Geertz 1963).[3]

The first step toward my case is to outline the primordialist argument. In essence, it says the following: all group sentiments that involve a strong sense of group identity, of we-ness, draw on those attachments that bind small, intimate collectivities, usually those based on kinship or its extensions. Ideas of collective identity based on shared claims to blood, soil, or language draw their affective force from the sentiments that bind small groups. This deceptively simple thesis has certain special qualities that deserve to be noted. It is usually cited to account for certain aspects of politics, notably those that show groups engaging in various forms of behavior that in terms of the model are considered irrational.

Here, two very different poles of irrationality are collapsed. One pole, which holds the greatest appeals to our common sense, is the pole of group violence, ethnocide, and terror. The other pole is constituted by any form of behavior that appears antimodern, whether it involves sluggish participation in elections, corruption in bureaucracy, resistance to modern educational techniques, or refusal to comply with modern state policies, ranging from birth control to monolingualism. Modernization theory, especially as it was applied to the new, postcolonial nations by American political scientists, was largely responsible for defining this antimodern symptom of primordialism. In recent efforts to explain ethnic violence, the two explanatory targets of primordialist theory have become subtly fused, so that the primordialism of resistance to modernization and the primordialism of ethnic violence have become loosely identified. The linkage of certain religious fundamentalisms to acts of political violence has lent renewed credibility to these two very different symptoms of primordialism. The bombings at the World Trade Center in New York brought out various popular forms of this primordialist theorizing in full force.

The primordialist perspective on matters of group mobilization brings together ontogenetic and phylogenetic ideas about human development. That is, just as the individual in Western psychology is seen to carry deep within him or her an affective core that can rarely be transformed and can always be ignited, so social collectivities are seen to possess a collective conscience whose historical roots are in some distant past and are not easily changeable but are potentially available to ignition by new historical and political contingencies. It is not surprising that this linkage of the infancy of individuals and the immaturity of groups is made with the greatest comfort about the nations of the non-Western world, although the explosion of ethnic conflicts in Eastern (and even in Western) Europe is blurring the line between the West and the non-West in regard to the primordialist thesis. The fact that the old language of modernization has been replaced by new talk of the obstacles to civil society and sustainable democracy should not obscure the persistence of the primordialist thesis. A quick word search for *tribe* and *tribalism* in the American press should clinch the case.

What is wrong with the primordialist thesis? One problem is a logical one and lies buried in the universalist assumptions of the primordialist argument, especially in its more radical Enlightenment-derived forms. If all societies and nations are composed of smaller units based on primordial ties, and if there are ethnic animosities buried in every national closet, why do only some explode into explicit primordialist fury? This is a comparative question, and a large part of the literature of comparative politics in the past three decades has tried to answer this question, sometimes with reference to structural factors and sometimes to cultural factors. These answers have generally proven bankrupt because there is growing evidence that the problem and the solution are uncomfortably complicit. Let me be more concrete: there is increasing evidence that Western models of political participation, education, mobilization, and economic growth, which were calculated to distance the new nations from their most retrograde primordialisms, have had just the opposite effect. These medicines appear increasingly to create iatrogenic disorders. This latter argument, which has much merit, has taken some moderate forms (Brass 1994; Tambiah 1986), but also some radical forms (Kothari 1989c; Nandy 1989a). But however much one may wish to blame the political context for the failures of what used to be called political development (that is, maturation away from the dangers of primordialism), there is too much evidence that the cure and the disease are difficult to disaggregate. Perhaps the single best example of this is the way in which armed forces throughout the Third World have turned out to be brutal, corrupt, anticivil, and self-expanding.

One way to handle this embarrassment for theorists who hold (even implicitly) to the primordialist thesis is the period-of-hardship theory (such as was held by various American economists in the first flush of liberalization in the former Soviet Union). It was also evidenced in Václav Havel's speech given at the end of the first year of his leadership of the then-united Czechoslovakia, which suggested that the societies of Eastern Europe must go through a painful period of detoxification that can in turn cause primordialist fevers to recur. This argument bears some curious affinities to Marxist views of the tribulations of the dictatorship of the proletariat, the period before the state withers away and socialist humanity becomes self-governing. The comparative argument also runs into difficulties because ethnic explosions today characterize such a variety of polities, for example, in India, Czechoslovakia, Indonesia, France, the United States, Egypt, South Africa. What comparative theory can show us what is common in such different cases of ethnic turbulence?

One variation on the comparativist answer is historical, and it fits with the developmentalist thrust of the primordialist case. This version of the argument would suggest that those countries that have had time to work out the Enlightenment project of political participation—based on the idea of an educated, postethnic, calculating individual, subsisting on the workings of the free market and participating in a genuine civil society—are indeed able to stave off the disorders of primordialism. Par excellence, here, are those societies that hewed closest and longest to different versions of the civil-society model, namely, the societies of Western Europe (the pre-1989 NATO societies) and the United States. Potential members of this club are the aggressively procapitalist societies of Asia and Latin America, such as Japan, Singapore, Taiwan, Korea, Chile, Argentina, Brazil, and a few others. Of course, a quick glance at this group over the past two decades suggests that the experiment is hardly uncontaminated by the active involvement of the United States in various forms of economic, political, and ideological subsidy to these societies, so that their experiences with overcoming primordialism can hardly be seen as a success for the endogenous vitality of the Enlightenment program. In any case, in many of these societies a strong dose of state authoritarianism seems to be required (following Jeanne Kirkpatrick's famous and subtle distinction between authoritarian and totalitarian states). Thus, if you cannot educate societies out of primordialism, you can certainly beat it out of them. At this point, the road to democracy is paved with the bodies of democrats. Hard states can hardly be used to showcase the road from primordialism to modernity.

Even those societies that have had the longest undisturbed periods of ethnic harmony, or, to put it another way, of successful cultural pluralism, seem one way or another to be coming apart at the seams: consider India, the former Soviet Union, Sri Lanka, the United Kingdom, and Egypt.

These are societies that differ in many regards. Each of them had certain lines of ethnic cleavage built into them, but all of them are now split not just along these predictable lines but along others as well. The efforts in England to promote multiculturalism and to improve what are termed *race relations* are clearly failing, partly in the context of what now looks like the caricature of a Third World economy. In India, the Hindu-Muslim divide is now one among several ethnic and separatist movements, crosscut by the largest caste wars ever seen in the history of the subcontinent, unleashed by the revival of the Mandal Commission Report in the early years of the 1990s. In Sri Lanka, the Tamil-Sinhala wars have yielded an increasing harvest of other lines of cleavage among Sinhala speakers and Tamil speakers, divisions that appear to generate new primordialisms (Moorish, Burgher, Buddhist, and other). As I finish this book, Buddhist monks from all over Sri Lanka have paraded through the streets of Colombo, protesting the bold new plans for decentralization of the new president of Sri Lanka, Chandrika Kumaratunga.

All that this leaves is a few European capitalist democracies (such as Germany and France), the United States, and Japan as states that appear not to be threatened by ethnic strife. Yet the prospects even in these cases are not clear. witness the problem of Koreans in Japan, of African-Americans and Hispanic-Americans in the United States, of Iranians, Jews, Turks, and other guest-worker populations in France and Germany. These suggest that even the most staunchly capitalist democracies are not eternally safe from what is seen as the primordialist bug. Right-wing racist, fascist, and fundamentalist movements in Europe and the United States certainly appear to be more primordial in their behavior than the racial minorities they openly abhor. The United States, Germany, Japan, and France are in any case enormously diverse in their histories as modern nation-states and in their commitments to political plurality as a central principle of political participation. These facts make it crucial to identify the limits of the primordialist approach to ethnic strife, as the thesis rests crucially on the view of certain populations and polities as infantile and relies implicitly on some sort of germ theory of ethnic strife in Western democracies. That is, these democracies are seen as fundamentally mature but now as at risk because they have become host to populations (typically from the Third World) that carry the primordial bug—the bug, that is, that makes them attached in infantile ways to blood, language, religion, and memory and makes them violence-prone and ill-equipped for participation in mature civic societies.

Let us summarize the central embarrassment of the primordialist perspective. Given the widespread commitment to the idea of democracy in a very large number of societies since World War II, including those in the socialist bloc, which placed heavy emphasis on the project of modernity (technology, modern science, mass participation in politics, massive investments in higher education, and immense propaganda for new ideas about citizenship, both in capitalist and socialist regimes), why are ethnic primordialisms more alive than ever? Apart from arguing that the operation was successful although the patient died, it appears that the primordialist thesis cannot account for the intensification and spread of ethnic sentiment in a world devoted to various versions of the Enlightenment project. This leaves us with two options: blaming the recipients of the theory (who received it under the guise of a variety of national and international discourses of development and modernization, usually aggressively sponsored by the apparatus of the modern nation-state), or rethinking the primordialist perspective itself. I hope that what I have said so far justifies the latter proposal.

The Politics of Affect

Underneath most primordialist models are not only the assumptions I have discussed above, but also a theory of affect in relation to politics, which we now have several excellent reasons to question. The first set of reasons, which I have adumbrated already and which I will not develop at length here, has been identified by many Marxist and nationalist critics of capitalist development. It consists of the view that the project of development, as it has been imposed on the non-Western world, has typically involved the creation of new elites and new gaps between castes and classes, which may not have arisen except for various neocolonialist projects in the new states. Modernization is held responsible for various frictions of rising expectations and for key contradictions between economic and political participation. These fuel mass frustration that can easily be translated by demagogues of all varieties into ethnicized discourse and action. I subscribe to this argument in a general way, although I do not believe it is fine-grained enough to account for the specific conjunctures that trigger ethnic violence in particular societies. Nor are these theories entirely free of the idea that there is always a real substrate of primordialist affect that is perpetual tinder waiting to be exploited by specific political interests at a given moment in the history of any given nation-state.

The second set of reasons for doubting the primordialist perspective on the role of affect in politics comes out of a broad body of literature that derives from continental political theory and some of its American variants in the past two decades. This is the literature that emphasizes not the mechanical workings of the primordial homunculus that drives group politics, especially in the Third World, but that strand of social and political theory that stresses the role of the imagination in politics. This strand, which is widely associated with the work of Benedict Anderson (1983), also has its roots in the venerable tradition of works that highlight the autonomy of ideology in political life (going back to another of the strands in the protean thought of Max Weber, as opposed to his evolutionist, primordialist ideas). It is also associated with the work of Cornelius Castoriadis on the imaginary (1987), of Claude Lefort on ideology (1986), of Ernesto Laclau and Chantal Mouffe on hegemony (1985). These works in turn draw on and complicate the work of Antonio Gramsci, Raymond Williams, and others who were concerned with the transformation of ideologies into common sense. I have emphasized the value of this perspective and my own reliance on it in chapter 1. Stressing negotiation and contestation in the life of all complex polities, these thinkers (as well as their associates in the Birmingham School in England and the subaltern school of historians in India) began to show us a new way to see subaltern consciousness. In this view, enriched by recent work on the strategies of everyday life (de Certeau 1984), popular consciousness was shown to be less a knee-jerk symptom of buried and semiconscious ideologies of identity and more a consciously worked-out strategy of irony and satire, which could critique the ruling order while experimenting with styles of identity politics (Hebdige 1979).

At the same time, the rather different work of James Scott (1985) on the "weapons of the weak," drawing on the earlier moral economy work of E. P. Thompson and others, began to show that those social orders and groupings that were apparently passive victims of larger forces of control and domination were nevertheless capable of subtle forms of resistance and "exit" (in Albert Hirschman's terms [1970]) that seemed not to be primordialist in any way. Common to a good deal of this work, which is diverse in other regards, is the idea that conceptions of the future play a far larger role than ideas of the past in group politics today, although primordialist projections onto the past are not irrelevant to the contemporary politics of the imagination.

With the recognition that imagination and agency are far more vital to group mobilization than we had hitherto imagined, we can more easily interpose the invention of tradition critique of Eric Hobsbawm and Terence Ranger (1983), which drove another nail into the coffin of the primordialist perspective. Although there have been serious criticisms of this influential thesis (not least its tendency to see some traditions as "authentic" but others as "invented"), it has alerted us to the idea that between the landscape of discourses about tradition and the sensibilities and motives of individual actors is a historical discourse that issues not from the depths of the individual psyche or from the hoary mists of tradition but from the specific, historically situated play of public and group opinions about the past. One major contribution of this work is to point to the fact that much of national and group politics in the contemporary world has to do not with the mechanics of primordial sentiment, but with what I am calling "the work of the imagination." I shall return to the theme of the imagination below.

The great irony in much of this work is that it shows beyond a doubt that very often the creation of primordial sentiments, far from being an obstacle to the modernizing state, is close to the center of the project of the modern nation-state. Thus, many racial, religious, and cultural fundamentalisms are deliberately fostered by various nation-states, or parties within them, in their efforts to suppress internal dissent, to construct homogeneous subjects of the state, and to maximize the surveillance and control of the diverse populations under their control. In these contexts, modern nation-states often draw on classificatory and disciplinary apparatuses that they inherited from colonial rulers and that in the postcolonial context have substantial inflammatory effects. An excellent example of this is the politics of number in colonial India and the politics of caste in the recent controversy over the Mandal Commission Report in India (see chap. 6). Likewise, recent work on political culture in Japan (Kelly 1990; Ivy 1995) shows that the state and major commercial interests have done a great deal to construct and energize the discourse of Japaneseness and of tradition (*furusato*) in an effort to exploit the idea of Japan as the repository of a unique, homogeneous form of cultural difference. In England, the heritage industry has worked to create a landscape of heritage, conservation, monuments, and English historical space, just as the role of Britain as a world power has faded considerably. This discourse of Englishness is only the most recent phase in the "internal colonialism" (Hechter 1975) through which a hegemonic idea of Englishness was created. This idea, regnant today, makes the discourse of multiculturalism in England strangely hollow and supports the implicit and explicit racisms that could be played on by Margaret Thatcher in the Falklands, by John Major in the Gulf War, as well as by fascist and racist hate groups in England.

It is this sort of mobilization that I characterized in chapter 1 as culturalist, which is to say, as involving ethnicities mobilized by or in relation to the practices of the modern nation-state. *Culturalism* suggests something more than either *ethnicity* or *culture*, both of which terms partake of the sense of the natural, the unconscious, and the tacit in group identity. When identities are produced in a field of classification, mass mediation, mobilization, and entitlement dominated by politics at the level of the nation-state, however, they take cultural differences as their *conscious* object. These movements can take a variety of forms: they can be directed primarily toward self-expression, autonomy, and efforts at cultural survival, or they can be principally negative in form, characterized largely by hate, racism, and the desire to dominate or eliminate other groups. This is a key distinction because culturalist movements for autonomy and dignity involving long-dominated groups (such as African-Americans in the United States and Dalits in India) are often tendentiously tarred with the same brush as those they oppose, as being somehow racist or antidemocratic.

Although modern ethnicity is in this sense culturalist and intimately linked to the practices of the nation-state, it is also worth noting that an important group of culturalist movements is today *transnational,* given that many mobilized national ethnicities, because of international migration, operate beyond the confines of a single nation-state. These transnational culturalist movements are intimately connected with what I refer to as diasporic public spheres.

The final and perhaps least obvious recent development that makes it difficult to sustain the primordialist thesis as it applies to ethnic politics is the notion, largely developed in the past decade by cultural anthropologists, that the emotions are not raw, precultural materials that constitute a universal, transsocial substrate. While it is not possible within the scope of this chapter to lay out the full contours of this argument, its main insight is that affect is in many important ways learned: what to feel sad or happy about, how to express it in different contexts, and whether or not the expression of affects is a simple playing out of inner sentiments (often assumed to be universal) are all issues that have been richly problematized (Lutz and Abu-Lughod 1990). This body of work has gone far to show that emotion is culturally constructed and socially situated and that universal aspects of affect do not tell us anything very revealing.

This work fits very well with another strand of work in recent cultural anthropology (Asad 1983; van der Veer 1989), which shows that various forms of sensory experience and bodily technique emerge as parts of historically constituted regimes of knowledge and power. This strand, which is also influenced by Michel Foucault's views of the historically constituted relations between knowledge and power, builds on the classic work of Marcel Mauss

(1973) on the techniques of the body and the suggestions of Pierre Bourdieu (1977) and others on embodied experience and its emergence within specific cultural frameworks of habit and experience. The thrust of this work is that, far from representing the projection of bodily states and experiences onto larger canvases of action and representation, bodily techniques and affective dispositions often represent just the opposite: namely, the inscription upon bodily habit of disciplines of self-control and practices of group discipline, often tied up with the state and its interests. The discussion of Indian cricket in chapter 5 fits directly in this tradition.

In turn, this work is supported not only by the insights of Foucault and others on the historical process by which the body is transformed, appropriated, and mobilized, but also by the work of Norbert Elias and his followers that shows that particular, and powerful, senses of bodily comportment and civility are the direct product of courtly and bourgeois ideas of dignity and distinction. This general orientation is not wholly problem-free: the question of how cultural and political schemata imprint themselves upon bodily experience and thus motivate agents in powerful ways is still being worked on. What does seem clear is that there is little payoff in separating the world of emotion and affect from the world of language and self-representation and that these in turn are remarkably responsive to macroconceptions of civility and dignity, as constructed by interests and ideologues that exercise power over whole social orders.

The causal chain is, if not reversed, at least problematized. Instead of moving from inner sentiments to outer displays that aggregate upward into larger forms of action and representation, this body of work works from the top down, or from the macro to the micro, suggesting that power is largely a matter of the imprinting of large-scale disciplines of civility, dignity, and bodily control onto the intimate level of embodied agents. This anthropological literature, while not yet conclusive and by no means problem-free, suggests that the feelings and sentiments of actors are largely comprehensible only within specific cultural frames of meaning and style and larger historical frames of power and discipline. It thus calls into serious question the idea of a layer of primordial sentiment that may be seen to lurk beneath the surface of cultural forms, social orders, and historical moments.

Yet crowds and the individuals who constitute them certainly seem to display the paradox of unplanned anger and coordinated targeting of victims. This mixture of combustibility and coordination is at the heart of the mystery of the crowd and the riot and has exercised observers from Gustave Le Bon onward. It is obviously a critical part of ethnic violence. In the

scripts that seem to underlie much ethnic violence (for rarely is such violence entirely chaotic) there is clearly a sort of order, which it would be
too easy to attribute to the contingencies of secret plans, outside agents,
and hidden calculations beneath the surface of group frenzy (Tambiah
1990). The challenge is to capture the frenzy of ethnic violence without
reducing it to the banal and universal core of inner, primordial sentiments.
We need to maintain the sense of psychic, and embodied, rage as well as
the intuition that the sentiments of ethnic violence (like any other sort
of sentiment) make sense only within large-scale formations of ideology,
imagination, and discipline. This seems an impossible task, but I shall suggest in the following section that the trope of implosion is a tentative way
out of the primordialist trap.

Ethnic Implosions

If the primordialist perspective is so frequently misleading, it seems important to find an equally general perspective with which to move beyond it.
The alternative is a model of ethnic implosion, a trope deliberately put forward against the connotations of explosion so often associated with the
primordialist view. As far as I know, the idea of implosion has been used in
the context of social movements only recently and rather cryptically in the
context of state violence and refugee formations in weak states (Zolberg et
al. 1989, 256–57). Linking ideas from James Scott and Albert Hirschman,
Aristide Zolberg and colleagues claim that peasants who try to dodge the
predatory actions of the state may find themselves cornered by the state
and thus forced into violence: "In this manner, withdrawal from the state
may trigger a violent implosion, a division of both rulers and ruled into
primary solidarity groups vying with each other in a desperate search for
security" (257). This cryptic use of the image of implosion is suggestive
and is related to the more deliberate use I shall make of it.

Before I go on to specify exactly how the model of implosion can provide a more useful approach to ethnic confrontations than the primordialist model, I need to set the stage for this approach in a broader way. I am
generally committed to the view that the world we live in today is global
and transnational in a way not anticipated by earlier models in the study of
international politics, as I have made clear in the first part of this book.
Not only am I convinced of the virtues of the neorealism of Robert Keohane and others, and its strong critique of the earlier, state-centered realist
view (Keohane 1986), but I am also convinced that even the neorealist
view does not go far enough to accommodate the many processes, events,

and structures that appear to work largely outside the strategic interactions of nation-states. Thus, I am sympathetic to the broad approach of James Rosenau (1990), which appeals for an entirely new view of global politics and stresses the image of turbulence, especially as it has been developed by physicists and mathematicians. Building on the idea of bifurcation and related ideas of complexity, chaos, and turbulence in complex systems, Rosenau argues that the dynamics of contemporary world politics cannot be accounted for except by seeing that there are two systems in bifurcated play in contemporary world politics: the multicentric system and the statecentric system.

Rosenau's main message is that structure and process in today's polities are artifacts of the turbulent interplay of these two bifurcated systems, each of which affects the others in multiple ways, at multiple levels, and in ways that make events enormously hard to predict. To account for event structures in the multicentric world he describes, Rosenau suggests that we replace the idea of events with the image of "cascades," action sequences in the multicentric world that "gather momentum, stall, reverse course, and resume anew as their repercussions spread among whole systems and subsystems" (299). The sorts of cascade that Rosenau identifies are a crucial component of what might be called the structure of externalities that partly account for the shape and timing of particular ethnic conflagrations. Because not all microevents associated with daily life in ethnically sensitive localities lead to ethnic violence, the cascade concept may help us understand why one particular act of religious desecration, or one particular terrorist killing, or one particular inflammatory speech ignites large-scale ethnic violence. The idea of global turbulence as a model of world politics seems also to fit a variety of other models, such as Lash and Urry's idea of "disorganized capitalism" (Lash and Urry 1987), Robertson's and Arnason's recent essays on globalization (Robertson 1990; Arnason 1990), and my own efforts to resituate the politics of cultural difference against a picture of disjunctures in the global cultural economy (see chap. 2).

But it seems a long journey from ideas of global turbulence and images of cascade and flow to the actualities of ethnic violence and concrete human brutality. To close this gap, I draw on two terms recently proposed by Tambiah (1990) in an effort to identify the dynamics of crowd behavior in the context of ethnic violence—*focalization* and *transvaluation*. He develops these terms in the context of a close reading of the riots in Karachi in 1985 between Pathans and Mohajirs (Biharis), the latter being Pakistanis who originally migrated from Eastern India:

By focalization I mean the process of progressive denudation of local incidents and disputes of their particulars of context and aggregating them, thereby narrowing their concrete richness. Transvaluation refers to the parallel process of assimilating particulars to a larger, collective, more enduring, and therefore less context-bound, cause or interest. The processes of focalization and transvaluation thereby contribute to a progressive polarization and dichotomization of issues and partisans, such that the climactic acts of violence by groups and mobs become in a short time self-fulfilling manifestations, incarnations and re-incarnations, of allegedly irresolvable communal splits between Pathans and Biharis, Sikhs and Hindus, Sinhalese and Tamils, or Malays and Chinese. (Tambiah 1990, 750)

The processes of focalization and transvaluation that Tambiah identifies are even more revealing when placed within what can be seen as the event cascades (in Rosenau's sense) that linked Karachi and its neighborhoods to developments in regional and national politics in Pakistan and in world politics as perceived by Pakistanis. Such cascades included the victory of Benazir Bhutto in the elections for the prime ministership, the reading of this victory in Karachi and elsewhere as a victory for Sind over Punjab in regional politics, the projection by various pro-Zia parties of the weakness of Bhutto as a woman and as a corrupt descendant of her father, and the parallel emergence of the MQM (Mohajir Qaumi Movement) as a major party for the formation of Mohajir identity. These readings in turn could inflame Pathan social and economic strength in Karachi and feed into the generalized anger with Bhutto's party in Karachi, especially among those, like the Pathans, who did not have a strong political voice in regional politics in Sind. Thus, the delicate and deadly interpretation (and interpenetration) of events on the streets of Karachi, which unfolded into a drama rapidly read in macro terms, could not have taken the various turns it did were it not for the implosive effects of wider action sequences on the street politics of Karachi. Of course, these very events reverberated outward and upward, through other cascades of events that created the sense that Bhutto could not maintain civil order. This perception, mobilized along with other political images and manipulations, was part of her eventual downfall in 1990, a downfall associated with major shifts in the politics of the subcontinent and in the perception of India and the United States in the aftermath of the Gulf War.

This is obviously a simplified picture into which one would want to introduce a great many other externalities, such as the strident anti-Indian and anti-Hindu note that Bhutto introduced into her speeches about Azad

Kashmir, in an effort to defuse her image as a weak woman and a person who had been soft on the Mohajirs in the context of the 1985 Karachi riots. The situation in Karachi has grown both more inviolate and more implosive in the period since 1985, and in 1995 Karachi is a scene of civil war and ethnic violence on a par with Mogadishu, Beirut of the 1980s, and one step short of Kabul in the past decade. Bhutto returned to power after being defeated in an earlier election and once again faces a volatile Karachi and a highly insecure national mandate. Much has happened in Karachi since 1985, and a series of violent battles between the forces of the state and the armed youth of the MQM has brought the death toll in Karachi to more than eight hundred persons between January and June 1995.

Much could be said about the history of violence in Karachi in the past decade that is salient to the general arguments of this book and the specific concerns of this chapter. As a city, Karachi is a depressingly forceful example of the sort of urban warfare I discuss in chapter 9, which produces locality under conditions of everyday terror and armed battle. Since the mid-1980s, the MQM, which began as a fruit of the sense of shared grievance among migrants to Pakistan from Eastern India, has itself become deeply divided, and its leadership now functions in exile in England. It is thus an excellent example of a movement that is diasporic, transnational, and anti-state without demanding national autonomy. Bhutto herself has deployed the language of terrorism and jihad against the MQM, thus blurring the lines between subcontinental politics (the MQM often being seen as tied to India, the land of origin of the Mohajirs) and Pakistani national politics.

All sides in the conflict—the state, the different factions of the MQM, and the ruling party, the Pakistan People's Party—have moved from reliance on petty arms to the use of rocket launchers, armored cars, and bunkers. There is no sharper indication of the implosion of global and national politics into the urban world of Karachi than the following quotation from one Karachi warlord, who leads a dissident MQM faction in the Landhi neighborhood: "Let them make a separate province or country or whatever they want. This area will remain my state" (Hanif 1995, 40).

The urban warfare of Karachi is linked to regional, state, national, and global politics through the drug traffic, the criminalization of politics, the efforts to enumerate the major ethnic populations by the state (see chap. 6), and the half-million migrants who come every year to this already overstretched city of twelve million.

But this is not the place for a detailed study of ethnic violence in Karachi. The key point is that both focalization and transvaluation take their energy from macroevents and processes (cascades) that link global politics to the micropolitics of streets and neighborhoods. Synchronically, these cascades provide the material for linking processes of focalization and transvaluation. That is, they provide material for the imagination of actors at various levels for reading general meanings into local and contingent events, just as they provide the alibi for inscribing long-standing scripts about ethnic manipulations and conspiracies onto apparently trivial street events.

But there is a diachronic dimension to this linkage as well. After all, the primordialist perspective was strongest (even if wrongest) in accounting for the politics of affect and thus for the violent intensity of ethnic confrontations. A new perspective of the sort proposed here must provide an alternative etiology of what Raymond Williams would have called the "structure of feeling" in ethnic violence. Macroevents, or cascades, work their way into highly localized structures of feeling by being drawn into the discourse and narratives of the locality, in casual conversations and low-key editorializing of the sort that often accompanies the collective reading of newspapers in many neighborhoods and on many front stoops of the world. Concurrently, the local narratives and plots in terms of which ordinary life and its conflicts are read and interpreted become shot through with a subtext of interpretive possibilities that is the direct product of the workings of the *local* imagining of broader regional, national, and global events.

The trouble with such local readings is that they are often silent and literally unobservable, except in the smallest of passing comments on world or national events that occur in the evanescent small talk of tea stalls, cinema houses, and urban gathering places. They are part of the incessant murmur of urban political discourse and its constant, undramatic cadences. But persons and groups at this most local level generate those structures of feeling that over time provide the discursive field within which the explosive rumors, dramas, and speeches of the riot can take hold.

This perspective does not require a primordialist assumption in order to account for the local structures of feeling that give ethnic riots and collective action their brutal and inexplicable force. These local feelings are the product of long-term interactions of local and global cascades of events that build up structures of feeling, which are both social and historical and are part of the environment within which, gradually, it becomes possible to envisage a neighbor as a fiend, a shopkeeper as a foreign traitor, and a local trader as a ruthless capitalist exploiter. Once this anthology of images is activated, the processes of which Tambiah speaks take over, and we are assured that there will be fresh episodes of recollection, interpretation, and suffering, which after the riot subsides will work their way once again into new local structures of feeling.

But there is no denying that such concepts as cascade, transvaluation, focalization, and implosion seem too abstract, too mechanistic, too general to capture the brute contingency, the raw violence, the electric blood lust, the instinct to degradation that seem to accompany the ethnic terror of such places as Rwanda and Bosnia, Karachi and Colombo. When rape, torture, cannibalism, and the brutal use of blood, feces, and body parts enter the scenario of ethnic cleansing, we are faced with the limits not just of social science but of language itself. Can one say anything useful about this sort of violence in the globalized world that this book describes?

I venture one hypothesis in the face of my own interpretive paralysis when faced with the gory group violence of today's ethnic wars.[4] The worst kinds of violence in these wars appear to have something to do with the distorted relationship between daily, face-to-face relations and the large-scale identities produced by modern nation-states and complicated by large-scale diasporas. More exactly, the most horrible fact about the rape, degradation, torture, and murder of the new ethnic wars is that they happen in many cases between actors who know, or thought they knew, one another. Our horror is sparked by the sheer intimacy that frequently frames the new ethnic violence. It is horror at the neighbor turned killer/torturer/rapist. What does this intimacy have to do with media, state-politics, and global macroevents?

The rage of those who kill, maim, and rape seems to be tied up with a profound sense of betrayal that is focused on the victims, and the betrayal is tied up with the relationship between appearance and reality. When the neighborhood merchant is revealed to be, in his heart, a Croat, when the schoolteacher turns out to be sympathetic to the Hutu, when your best friend turns out to be a Muslim rather than a Serb, when your uncle's neighbor turns out to be a hated landlord—what seems to follow is a sense of deep categorical treachery, that is, treachery about group identity as defined by states, censuses, the media, and other large-scale forces.

At heart, this sense of betrayal is about mistaken identity in a world where the stakes associated with these identities have become enormously high. The rage that such betrayal seems to inspire can of course be extended to masses of persons who may not have been intimates, and thus it can and does become increasingly mechanical and impersonal, but I would propose that it remains animated by a perceived violation of the sense of knowing who the Other was and of rage about who they really turn out to be. This sense of treachery, of betrayal, and thus of violated trust, rage, and hatred has everything to do with a world in which large-scale identities forcibly enter the local imagination and become dominant voice-overs in the traffic of ordinary life. The primary literature closest to the most brutal episodes of contemporary ethnic violence is shot through with the language of the impostor, the secret agent, and the counterfeit person. This discourse brings together uncertainty about categories and intimacy among persons—the key feature of the new violence.

There are many examples of contemporary political violence that sustain this point of view. It has a pedigree in such well-known instances as the marking of German Jews as impostors by the Nazis (Anderson 1983, 149). If we examine evidence close to the actual moments of greatest brutality in recent episodes of group violence (Das 1995; Malkki 1995; Sutton 1995), it shows that the revelation of hated and hateful official identities behind the bodily masks of real (and known) persons seems crucial to the perpetration of the worst forms of mutilation and damage. Conversely, the exposure of the individual names, histories, and memories of specific persons behind the corpses of the victims of adverse categorization is used to provoke the strongest of sentiments. These reciprocal processes—exposing impostors and restoring real persons through personalized memorials—seem to lie at the core of the embodied violence of today's ethnic battles. Remembering and forgetting are vital to nationalism (Anderson 1983), but they are even more vital to its brutal embodied politics. This view of the peculiar and stunning brutality of ethnic and racial warfare does not exclude other factors that usually figure in theories of ethnic violence—economic frustrations, manipulation by politicians, fears of religious change, aspirations for ethnic self-governance, scapegoating in times of crisis, and the like. All these factors surely account for the overall dynamics of ethnic strife in many social and historical settings. But they seem unable to account for the sheer brutality of modern ethnocide and ethnic war, and their sense of runaway contingency. This hypothesis about violence in relation to treachery, intimacy, and identity is meant to account for the transformation of ordinary people into killers, torturers, and rapists and the re-presentation of friends, neighbors, and coworkers as objects of the deepest hatred and rage.

If the hypothesis of treachery is plausible, it has much to do with the large-scale identities created, transformed, and reified by modern state apparatuses (often in a transnational and diasporic field) and circulated through the media. When these identities are convincingly portrayed as primary (indeed as primordial) loyalties by politicians, religious leaders, and the media, then ordinary people self-fulfillingly seem to act as if only this kind of identity mattered and as if they were surrounded by a world of pretenders. Such representations of identity (and identification) seem even

Life after Primordialism

more plausible in a world of migrants and mass media, which can subvert the everyday certainties that come from face-to-face knowledge of the ethnic Other.[5]

Not all culturalist movements lead to violence between ethnic groups, but culturalism—insofar as it involves identities mobilized at the level of the nation-state—has high potential for violence, especially in an era when the cultural space of the nation-state is subject to the externalities of migration and mass media. Such externalities would not necessarily increase the potential for violence except for one more contradiction that affects all nation-states in principle and most nation-states in practice. This is the contradiction between the idea that each nation-state can truly represent only one ethnos and the reality that all nation-states historically involve the amalgamation of many identities. Even where long-standing identities have been forgotten or buried, the combination of migration and mass mediation assures their reconstruction on a new scale and at larger levels. Incidentally, this is why the politics of remembering and forgetting (and thus of history and historiography) is so central to the ethnicist battles tied up with nationalism (van der Veer 1994). Culturalist movements among minorities and historically dominated groups tend to enter into a conscious dialogue with the culturalisms of numerical majorities. As these culturalisms compete for a piece of the nation (and of the resources of the state), they inevitably enter into the space of potential violence.

This proposal differs fundamentally from the primordialist perspective. It does not regard a substratum of ethnic sentiment as the bedrock of the explanation of ethnic explosions. Rather, it suggests that ethnic structures of feeling are themselves complex products of the local imagination (mediating a bewildering variety of global cascades as they move through the locality). Episodes of ethnic violence may thus be regarded as implosive in two senses: in the structural sense, they represent the folding into local politics of pressures and ripples from increasingly wider political arenas; and in the historical sense, the local political imagination is increasingly subject to the flow of large events (cascades) over time, events that influence the interpretation of mundane occurrences and gradually create a repertoire of adversarial ethnic sentiments. These can seem primordial at first sight but are surely the product of longer-term processes of action, communication, interpretation, and comment. Once these events occur, however, it is far easier to see their explosive dimensions, as they spread outward, inflaming other sectors and drawing other issues into the vortex of ethnic fury. But this explosive dimension, powered by (and empowering) the processes of focalization and transvaluation, should not blind us to its initial conditions. These conditions are better accounted for in terms of the idea of implosion proposed in this chapter than by the many versions of the primordialist perspective that satisfy our thirst for final, and ahistorical, explanations, especially of apparently irrational behavior.

Modern Ethnicity

Let me underline, even if cryptically, what is modern (in my usage, culturalist) about contemporary ethnic movements. Today's large-scale and frequently violent ethnic movements call for a new understanding of the relationship between history and agency, affect and politics, large-scale and local factors. I have suggested throughout this chapter that one way to engage these requirements is to resist the inner-outer dialectic imposed on us by the primordialist way of thinking and think instead in terms of the dialectics of implosion and explosion over time as the key to the peculiar dynamics of modern ethnicity.

Looked at in this way, modern ethnic movements (culturalisms) can be tied to the crisis of the nation-state through a series of interesting links. First, all modern nation-states have subscribed to and contributed to the idea that legitimate polities must be the outgrowth of natural affinities of some sort. Thus, even as many nation-states enter a crisis of legitimation and face the demands of migrant groups, they work within a legacy in which national self-rule must rest on some sort of tradition of natural affinity. Second, the specific projects (however successful) of the modern nation-state, ranging from sanitation to the census, from family planning to disease control, and from immigration control to language policy, have tied concrete bodily practices (speech, cleanliness, movement, health) to *large-scale* group identities, thus increasing the potential scope of embodied experiences of group affinity. Finally, whether in democratic or nondemocratic state setups, the language of rights and entitlement more generally has become inextricably linked to these large-scale identities. Today's ethnic projects are increasingly defined by these three features of the culture of the modern nation-state. Ethnic groups may imagine their futures, but even here (as with Marx's observations about men making their history) they may not do just as they please. As states lose their monopoly over the idea of nation, it is understandable that all sorts of groups will tend to use the logic of the nation to capture some or all of the state, or some or all of their entitlements from the state. This logic finds its maximum power to mobilize where the body meets the state, that is, in those projects that we call ethnic and often misrecognize as atavistic.

8

Patriotism and Its Futures

We need to think ourselves beyond the nation.[1] This is not to suggest that thought alone will carry us beyond the nation or that the nation is largely a thought or an imagined thing. Rather, it is to suggest that the role of intellectual practices is to identify the current crisis of the nation and in identifying it to provide part of the apparatus of recognition for postnational social forms. Although the idea that we are entering a postnational world seems to have received its first airings in literary studies, it is now a recurrent (if unselfconscious) theme in studies of postcolonialism, global politics, and international welfare policy. But most writers who have asserted or implied that we need to think postnationally have not asked exactly what emergent social forms compel us to do so, or in what way. This latter task is the principal focus of this chapter.

Postdiscursive Colonies

For those of us who grew up male in the elite sectors of the postcolonial world, nationalism was our common sense and the principal justification for our ambitions, our strategies, and our sense of moral well-being. Now, almost half a century after independence was achieved for many of the new nations, the nation form is under attack, and that, too, from many points of view. As the ideological alibi of the territorial state, it is the last refuge of ethnic totalitarianism. In important critiques of the postcolony (Mbembe 1992), its discourses have been shown to be deeply implicated in the discourses of colonialism itself. It has frequently been a vehicle for the staged self-doubts of the heroes of the new nations—Sukarno, Jomo Kenyatta, Jawaharlal Nehru, Gamal Abdel Nasser—who fiddled with nationalism while the public spheres of their societies were beginning to burn. So, for postcolonial intellectuals such as myself, the question is, does patriotism have a future? And to what races and genders shall that future belong?

To answer this question requires not just an engagement with the problematics of the nation form, the imagined community (Anderson 1991), the production of people (Balibar 1991), the narrativity of nations (Bhabha 1990), and the colonial logics of nationalist discourse (Chatterjee 1986). It also requires a close examination of the discourses of the state and the discourses that are contained within the hyphen that links nation to state (chap. 2; Mbembe et al. 1992). What follows is an exploration of one dimension of this hyphen.

There is a disturbing tendency in the Western academy today to divorce the study of discursive forms from the study of other institutional forms, and the study of literary discourses from the mundane discourses of bureaucracies, armies, private corporations, and nonstate social organizations. This chapter is in part a plea for a widening of the field of discourse studies: if the postcolony is in part a discursive formation, it is also true that discursivity has become too exclusively the sign and space of the colony and the postcolony in contemporary cultural studies. To widen the sense of what counts as discourse demands a corresponding widening of the sphere of the postcolony, to extend it beyond the geographical spaces of the former colonial world. In raising the issue of the *postnational*, I will suggest that the journey from the space of the former colony (a colorful space, a space of color) to the space of the postcolony is a journey that takes us into the heart of whiteness. It moves us, that is, to America, a postnational space marked by its whiteness but marked too by its uneasy engagement with diasporic peoples, mobile technologies, and queer nationalities.

The Trope of the Tribe

In spite of all the evidence to the contrary, these are hard times for patriotism. Maimed bodies and barbed wire in Eastern Europe, xenophobic violence in France, flag waving in the political rituals of the election year here in the United States—all seem to suggest that the willingness to die for one's country is still a global fashion. But patriotism is an unstable sentiment, which thrives only at the level of the nation-state. Below that level it is easily supplanted by more intimate loyalties; above that level it gives way to empty slogans rarely backed by the will to sacrifice or kill. So, when thinking about the future of patriotism, it is necessary first to inquire into the health of the nation-state.

My doubts about patriotism (patria-tism?) are tied up with my father's biography, in which patriotism and nationalism were already diverging terms. As a war correspondent for Reuters in Bangkok in 1940, he met an expatriate Indian nationalist, Subhas Chandra Bose, who split with Gandhi and Nehru on the issue of violence. Bose had escaped from British surveillance in India, with the active support of the Japanese, and established a government-in-exile in Southeast Asia. The army that Bose formed from Indian officers and enlisted men whom the Japanese had taken prisoner called itself the Indian National Army. This Indian Army was roundly defeated by the British Indian Army in Assam (on Indian soil, as my father never tired of noting) in 1944, and the provisional government of Azad Hind (Free India) in which my father was minister of publicity and propaganda soon crumbled with the defeat of the Axis powers.

When my father returned to India in 1945, he and his comrades were unwelcome heroes, poor cousins in the story of the nationalist struggle for Indian independence. They were patriots, but Bose's anti-British sentiment and his links with the Axis powers made him an embarrassment both to Gandhi's nonviolence and Nehru's Fabian Anglophilia. To the end of their lives, my father and his comrades remained pariah patriots, rogue nationalists. My sister, brothers, and I grew up in Bombay wedged between former patriotism, Bose-style, and bourgeois nationalism, Nehru-style. Our India, with its Japanese connections and anti-Western ways, carried the nameless aroma of treason, in respect to the cozy alliance of the Nehrus and Mountbattens, and the bourgeois compact between Gandhian nonviolence and Nehruvian socialism. My father's distrust of the Nehru dynasty predisposed us to imagine a strange, deterritorialized India, invented in Taiwan and Singapore, Bangkok and Kuala Lumpur, quite independent of New Delhi and the Nehrus, the Congress Party and mainstream nationalisms. So, there is a special appeal for me in the possibility that the marriage between nations and states was always a marriage of convenience and that patriotism needs to find new objects of desire.

One major fact that accounts for strains in the union of nation and state is that the nationalist genie, never perfectly contained in the bottle of the territorial state, is now itself diasporic. Carried in the repertoires of increasingly mobile populations of refugees, tourists, guest workers, transnational intellectuals, scientists, and illegal aliens, it is increasingly unrestrained by ideas of spatial boundary and territorial sovereignty. This revolution in the foundations of nationalism has crept up on us virtually unnoticed. Where soil and place were once the key to the linkage of territorial affiliation with state monopoly of the means of violence, key identities and identifications now only partially revolve around the realities and images of place. In the Sikh demand for Khalistan, in French-Canadian feelings about Quebec, in Palestinian demands for self-determination, images of a homeland are only part of the rhetoric of popular sovereignty and do not necessarily reflect a territorial bottom line. The violence and terror surrounding the breakdown of many existing nation-states are not signs of reversion to anything biological or innate, dark or primordial (Comaroff and Comaroff 1992b). What then are we to make of this renewed blood lust in the name of the nation?

Modern nationalisms involve communities of citizens in the territorially defined nation-state who share the collective experience, not of face-to-face contact or common subordination to a royal person, but of reading books, pamphlets, newspapers, maps, and other modern texts together (Habermas 1989; Calhoun 1992). In and through these collective experiences of what Benedict Anderson (1991) calls "print capitalism" and what others increasingly see as "electronic capitalism," such as television and cinema (Warner 1992; Lee 1993), citizens *imagine* themselves to belong to a national society. The modern nation-state in this view grows less out of natural facts—such as language, blood, soil, and race—and more out of a quintessential cultural product, a product of the collective imagination. This view distances itself, but not quite enough, from the dominant theories of nationalism, from those of J. G. Herder and Guiseppe Mazzini and since then from all sorts of right-wing nationalists, who see nations as products of the natural destinies of peoples, whether rooted in language, race, soil, or religion. In many of these theories of the nation as imagined, there is always a suggestion that blood, kinship, race, and soil are somehow less imagined and more natural than the imagination of collective interest or solidarity. The trope of the tribe reactivates this hidden biologism largely because forceful alternatives to it have yet to be articulated. The historical conjunctures concerning reading and publicity, texts and their linguistic mediations, nations and their narratives are only now being juxtaposed to formulate the special and specific diacritics of the national imaginary and its public spheres (Lee 1993).

The leaders of the new nations that were formed in Asia and Africa after World War II—Nasser, Nehru, Sukarno—would have been distressed to see the frequency with which the ideas of tribalism and nationalism are conflated in recent public discourse in the West. These leaders spent a great deal of their rhetorical energies in urging their subjects to give up what they saw as primordial loyalties—to family, tribe, caste, and region—in the interests of the fragile abstractions they called "Egypt," "India," and "Indonesia." They understood that the new nations needed to subvert and annex the primary loyalties attached to more intimate collectivities. They rested their ideas of their new nations on the very edges of the paradox that modern nations were intended to be somehow open, universal, and emancipatory by virtue of their special commitment to citizenly virtue but that *their* nations were nonetheless, in some essential way, different from and even better than other nations. In many ways these leaders knew what we have tended to forget, namely, that nations, especially in multiethnic settings, are tenuous collective projects, not eternal natural facts. Yet they too helped to create a false divide between the artificiality of the nation and those facts they falsely projected as primordia—tribe, family, region.

In its preoccupation with the control, classification, and surveillance of its subjects, the nation-state has often created, revitalized, or fractured ethnic identities that were previously fluid, negotiable, or nascent. Of course, the terms used to mobilize ethnic violence today may have long histories. But the realities to which they refer—Serbo-Croatian language, Basque customs, Lithuanian cuisine—were most often crystallized in the nineteenth and early twentieth centuries. Nationalism and ethnicity thus feed each other, as nationalists construct ethnic categories that in turn drive others to construct counterethnicities, and then in times of political crisis these others demand counterstates based on newfound counternationalisms. For every nationalism that appears to be naturally destined, there is another that is a reactive byproduct.

While violence in the name of Serbs and Moluccans, Khmer and Latvians, Germans and Jews tempts us to think that all such identities run dark and deep, we need only turn to the recent riots in India occasioned by the report of a government commission that recommended reserving a large percentage of government jobs for certain castes defined by the census and the constitution as "backward." Rioting and carnage, and not a few killings and suicides, took place in North India over such labels as "other backward caste," which come out of the terminological distinctions of the Indian census and its specialized protocols and schedules. How astonishing it seems that anyone would die or kill for entitlements associated with being the member of an other backward caste. Yet this case is not an exception: in its macabre bureaucratic banality it shows how the technical needs of censuses and welfare legislation, combined with the cynical tactics of electoral politics, can draw groups into quasi-racial identifications and fears. The matter is not so different as it may appear for such apparently natural labels as Jew, Arab, German, and Hindu, each of which involves people who choose these labels, others who are forced into them, and yet others who through their philological scholarship shore up the histories of these names or find them handy ways of tidying up messy problems of language and history, race and belief. Of course, not all nation-state policies are hegemonic, nor are all subaltern forms of agency impotent to resist these pressures and seductions. But it does seem fair to say that there are few forms of popular consciousness and subaltern agency that are, in regard to ethnic mobilization, free of the thought forms and political fields produced by the actions and discourses of nation-states.

Thus, minorities in many parts of the world are as artificial as the majorities they are seen to threaten. Whites in the United States, Hindus in India, Englishmen in Great Britain—all are examples of how the political and administrative designation of some groups as minorities (blacks and Hispanics in the United States, Celts and Pakistanis in the United Kingdom, Muslims and Christians in India) helps to pull majorities (silent or vocal) together under labels with short lives but long histories. The new ethnicities are often no older than the nation-states that they have come to resist. The Muslims of Bosnia are being reluctantly ghettoized although there is fear among both Serbians and Croats of the possibility of an Islamic state in Europe. Minorities are as often made as they are born.

Recent ethnic movements often involve thousands, sometimes millions of people who are spread across vast territories and often separated by vast distances. Whether we consider the linkage of Serbs divided by large chunks of Bosnia-Herzegovina, or Kurds dispersed across Iran, Iraq, and Turkey, or Sikhs spread through London, Vancouver, and California, as well as the Indian Punjab, the new ethnonationalisms are complex, large-scale, highly coordinated acts of mobilization, reliant on news, logistical flows, and propaganda across state borders. They can hardly be considered tribal, if by this we mean that they are spontaneous uprisings of closely bonded, spatially segregated, naturally allied groupings. In the case we find most frightening today, what could be called Serbian tribalism is hardly a simple thing given that there are at least 2.8 million Yugoslav families who have produced about 1.4 million mixed marriages between Serbs and Croats (Hobsbawm 1992). To which tribe could these families be said to belong? In our horrified preoccupation with the shock troops of ethnonationalism, we have lost sight of the confused sentiments of civilians, the torn loyalties of families that have members of warring groups within the same household, and the urgings of those who hold to the view that Serbs, Muslims, and Croats in Bosnia-Herzegovina have no fundamental enmity. It is harder to explain how principles of ethnic affiliation, however dubious their provenance and fragile their pedigree, can very rapidly mobilize large groups into violent action.

What does seem clear is that the tribal model, insofar as it suggests prepackaged passions waiting to explode, flies in the face of the contingencies that spark ethnic passion. The Sikhs, until recently the bulwark of the Indian army and historically the fighting arm of Hindu India against Muslim rule, today regard themselves as threatened by Hinduism and seem willing to accept aid and succor from Pakistan. The Muslims of Bosnia-Herzegovina have been forced reluctantly to revitalize their Islamic affiliations. Far from activating long-standing tribal sentiments, Bosnian Muslims are torn between their own conception of themselves as *European Muslims* (a term recently used by Ejub Ganic, vice president of Bosnia) and the view that they are part of a transnational Islam, which is already actively involved in Bosnian warfare. Wealthy Bosnians who live abroad in countries such as Turkey are already buying weapons for the defense of Muslims in Bosnia. To free us from the trope of the tribe, as the primordial source of those nationalisms that we find less civic than our own in the United States, we need to construct a theory of large-scale ethnic mobilization that explicitly recognizes and interprets its postnational properties.

Postnational Formations

Many recent and violent ethnonationalisms are not so much explosive as implosive. That is, rather than being rooted in some primordial substrate of affect deep within each of us that is brought up and out into wider sorts of social engagement and group action, the reverse is often the case. The effects of large-scale interactions between and within nation-states, often stimulated by news of events in even more distant locations, serve to cascade (Rosenau 1990) through the complexities of regional, local, and neighborhood politics until they energize local issues and implode into various forms of violence, including the most brutal ones. What were previously *cool* ethnic identities (Sikh and Hindu, Armenian and Azerbaijani, Serb and Croat) thus turn *hot*, as localities implode under the pressure of events and processes distant in space and time from the site of the implosion. Among Bosnia's Muslims it is possible to watch the temperature of these identities change before our very eyes as they find themselves pushed away from a secular, Europeanist idea of themselves into a more fundamentalist posture. They are being pushed not only by the threats to their survival from Serbs but also by pressure from their fellow Muslims in Saudi Arabia, Egypt, and Sudan, who suggest that Bosnian Muslims are now paying the price for playing down their Islamic identity under Communist rule. Bosnian Muslim leaders have begun to explicitly state that if they do not receive help quickly from the Western powers, they might have to turn to Palestinian models of terror and extremism.

One important way to account for those cases in which cool identities turn hot and implosions from one place generate explosions in others is to remind ourselves that the nation-state is by no means the only game in town as far as translocal loyalties are concerned. The violence that surrounds identity politics around the world today reflects the anxieties attendant on the search for nonterritorial principles of solidarity. The movements we now see in Serbia and Sri Lanka, Mountain Karabakh and Namibia, Punjab and Quebec are what might be called "trojan nationalisms." Such nationalisms actually contain transnational, subnational links and, more generally, nonnational identities and aspirations. Because they are so often the product of forced as well as voluntary diasporas, of mobile intellectuals as well as manual workers, of dialogues with hostile as well as hospitable states, very few of the new nationalisms can be separated from the anguish of displacement, the nostalgia of exile, the repatriation of funds, or the brutalities of asylum seeking. Haitians in Miami, Tamils in Boston, Moroccans in France, Moluccans in Holland are the carriers of these new transnational and postnational loyalties.

Territorial nationalism is the alibi of these movements and not necessarily their basic motive or final goal. In contrast, these basic motives and goals can be far darker than anything having to do with national sovereignty, as when they seem driven by the motives of ethnic purification and genocide; thus, Serbian nationalism seems to operate on the fear and hatred of its ethnic Others far more than on the sense of a sacred territorial patrimony. Or they can be simply idioms and symbols around which many groups come to articulate their desire to escape the specific state regime that is seen as threatening their own survival. Palestinians are more worried about getting Israel off their backs than about the special geographical magic of the West Bank.

While there are many separatist movements in the world today—the

Basques, the Tamils, the Québecois, the Serbs—that seem determined to lock nationhood and statehood together under a single ethnic rubric, more impressive still are the many oppressed minorities who have suffered displacement and forced diaspora without articulating a strong wish for a nation-state of their own: Armenians in Turkey, Hutu refugees from Burundi who live in urban Tanzania, and Kashmiri Hindus in exile in Delhi are a few examples of how displacement does not always generate the fantasy of state building. Although many antistate movements revolve around images of homeland, soil, place, and return from exile, these images reflect the poverty of their (and our) political languages rather than the hegemony of territorial nationalism. Put another way, no idiom has yet emerged to capture the collective interests of many groups in translocal solidarities, cross-border mobilizations, and postnational identities. Such interests are many and vocal, but they are still entrapped in the linguistic imaginary of the territorial state. This incapacity of many deterritorialized groups to think their way out of the imaginary of the nation-state is itself the cause of much global violence because many movements of emancipation and identity are forced, in their struggles against existing nation-states, to embrace the very imaginary they seek to escape. Postnational or nonnational movements are forced by the very logic of actually existing nation-states to become antinational or antistate and thus to inspire the very state power that forces them to respond in the language of counternationalism. This vicious circle can only be escaped when a language is found to capture complex, nonterritorial, postnational forms of allegiance.

Much has been said in recent years about the speed with which information travels around the world, the intensity with which the news of one city flashes on the television screens of another, of how money manipulations in one stock exchange affect finance ministries a continent away. Much has been said, too, about the need to attack global problems, such as AIDS, pollution, and terrorism, with concerted forms of international action. The democracy wave and the AIDS pandemic are to some extent caused by the same kinds of intersocietal contact and transnational human traffic.

From the perspective of the Cold War, the world may have become unipolar. But it has also become *multicentric*, to use James Rosenau's term (1990). Adapting metaphors from chaos theory, Rosenau has shown how the legitimacy of nation-states has steadily weakened, how international and transnational organizations of every type have proliferated, and how local politics and global process affect each other in chaotic but not unpredictable ways, often outside the interactions of nation-states.

To appreciate these complexities, we need to do more than what social scientists like to call comparison, putting one country or culture next to another as if they were as independent in life as in thought.[2] We need to take a fresh look at a variety of organizations, movements, ideologies, and networks of which the traditional multinational corporation is only one example. Consider such transnational philanthropic movements as Habitat for Humanity (whose volunteers seek to build new environments with fellow volunteers in far-flung locations). Take the various international terrorist organizations, which mobilize men (and sometimes women), money, equipment, training camps, and passion in a bewildering cross-hatching of ideological and ethnic combinations. Consider international fashion, which is not just a matter of global markets and cross-national-style cannibalism but is increasingly a matter of systematic transnational assemblages of production, taste transfer, pricing, and exhibition. Take the variety of Green movements that have begun to organize themselves transnationally around specific sorts of biopolitics. Consider the world of refugees. For long we have taken refugee issues and organizations to be part of the flotsam and jetsam of political life, floating between the certainties and stabilities of nation-states. What we cannot see therefore is that refugee camps, refugee bureaucracies, refugee-relief movements, refugee-oriented departments of nation-states, and refugee-oriented transnational philanthropies all constitute one part of the *permanent* framework of the emergent, postnational order. Another excellent example, closer to home perhaps, is the large number of organizations, movements, and networks of Christian philanthropy, such as World Vision, that have long blurred the boundaries between evangelical, developmental, and peace-keeping functions in many parts of the world. Perhaps the best studied of these examples is the Olympic movement, certainly the largest modern instance of a movement born in the context of European concerns with world peace in the latter part of the nineteenth century. This movement, with its special form of dialectical play between national and transnational allegiances (MacAloon 1981; Kang, MacAloon, and DaMatta 1988) represents only the most spectacular among a series of sites and formations on which the uncertain future of the nation-state will turn.

In all these cases, what we are looking at are not just international slogans, or interest groups, or image transfers. We are looking at the birth of a variety of complex, postnational social formations. These formations are now organized around principles of finance, recruitment, coordination, communication, and reproduction that are fundamentally postnational and not just multinational or international. The classic modern multinational corporation is a slightly misleading example of what is most important about these new forms precisely because it relies crucially on the legal, fiscal, environmental, and human organization of the nation-state, while maximizing the possibilities of operating both within and across national structures, always exploiting their legitimacy. The new organizational forms are more diverse, more fluid, more ad hoc, more provisional, less coherent, less organized, and simply less implicated in the comparative advantages of the nation-state. Many of them are explicitly constituted to monitor the activities of the nation-state: Amnesty International is an excellent example. Others, largely associated with the United Nations, work to contain the excesses of nation-states, for example, by assisting refugees, monitoring peace-keeping arrangements, organizing relief in famines, and doing the unglamorous work associated with oceans and tariffs, international health and labor.

Yet others, like Oxfam, are examples of global organizations that work outside the quasi-official United Nations network and rely on the growth of nongovernmental organizations (NGOs) in many parts of the developing world. These NGOs, which operate in a host of areas ranging from technology and the environment to health and the arts, grew from less than two hundred in 1909 to more than two thousand in the early 1970s. They often constitute major grassroots organizations for self-help that grow out of and contribute to a sense of the limited capability of national governments to deliver the basics of life in such societies as India.

Still other organizations, which we often call fundamentalist, such as the Muslim Brotherhood in the Middle East, the Unification Church, and any number of Christian, Hindu, and Muslim organizations, constitute full-service global movements that seek to alleviate suffering across national boundaries while mobilizing first-order loyalties across state boundaries. Some of these evangelical movements (such as the radical Hindu group known as the Ananda Marg, which has been held responsible for the assassination of Indian diplomats abroad) are aggressively opposed to specific nation-states and are frequently treated as seditious. Others, such as the Unification Church, simply work their way around the nation-state without directly questioning its jurisdiction. Such examples, which we still tend to see as exceptional or pariah organizational forms, are both instances and incubators of a postnational global order.

The Heart of Whiteness

The term *postnational*, so far used without comment, has several implications that can now be more closely examined. The first is temporal and historical and suggests that we are in the process of moving to a global order in which the nation-state has become obsolete and other formations for allegiance and identity have taken its place. The second is the idea that what are emerging are strong alternative forms for the organization of global traffic in resources, images, and ideas—forms that either contest the nation-state actively or constitute peaceful alternatives for large-scale political loyalties. The third implication is the possibility that, while nations might continue to exist, the steady erosion of the capabilities of the nation-state to monopolize loyalty will encourage the spread of national forms that are largely divorced from territorial states. These are relevant senses of the term *postnational,* but none of them implies that the nation-state in its classical territorial form is as yet out of business. It is certainly in crisis, and part of the crisis is an increasingly violent relationship between the nation-state and its postnational Others.

The United States is a particularly salient place in which to consider these propositions because, on the face of it, it has managed to retain most successfully the image of a national order that is simultaneously civil, plural, and prosperous. It appears to nurture a vibrant and complex set of public spheres, including some that have been called "alternative," "partial," or "counter" publics (Berlant and Freeman 1992; Fraser 1992; Hansen 1993; Robbins 1993; Black Public Sphere Collective 1995). It remains enormously wealthy by global standards, and although its forms of public violence are many and worrisome, its state apparatus is not generally dependent on forms of torture, imprisonment, and violent repression. When this is added to the fact that multiculturalism in the United States seems to take predominantly nonviolent forms, we appear to be faced with a great, uncontested power that dominates the new world order, that draws in immigrants in the thousands, and that seems to be a triumphant example of the classic, territorial nation-state. Any argument about the emergence of a postnational global order will have to engage its greatest apparent falsification, the contemporary United States. This last section lays the groundwork for such an engagement.

Until a few years ago, I was content to live in that special space allotted to "foreigners," especially Anglophone, educated ones like myself, with faint traces of a British accent. As a black woman at a bus stop in Chicago once said to me with approval, I was an East Indian. That was in 1972. But since that happy conversation more than two decades ago, it has become steadily less easy to see myself, armed with my Indian passport and my Anglophone ways, as somehow immune from the politics of racial identity in the United States. Not only is it that after nearly three decades of being a resident alien in the United States, married to an Anglo-Saxon American woman, the father of a bicultural teenager, my Indian passport seems like a rather slight badge of identity. The net of racial politics is now cast wider than ever before on the streets of the urban United States.

My own complexion and its role in minority politics, as well as in street encounters with racial hatred, prompt me to reopen the links between America and the United States, between biculturalism and patriotism, between diasporic identities and the (in)stabilities provided by passports and green cards. Postnational loyalties are not irrelevant to the problem of diversity in the United States. If, indeed, a postnational order is in the making, and Americanness changes its meanings, the whole problem of diversity in American life will have to be rethought. It is not just the force of certain deductions that moves me to this recommendation. As I oscillate between the detachment of a postcolonial, diasporic, academic identity (taking advantage of the mood of exile and the space of displacement) and the ugly realities of being racialized, minoritized, and tribalized in my everyday encounters, theory encounters practice.

A book recently published by Random House is *Tribes: How Race, Religion, and Identity Determine Success in the New Global Economy* (Kotkin 1993). Written by Joel Kotkin, "an internationally recognized authority on global, economic, political and social trends," as the dust jacket boasts, it traces the connections between ethnicity and business success. Kotkin's five tribes—the Jews, the Chinese, the Japanese, the British, and the Indians— are an odd group, but they represent primordialism with a high-tech face. They are Max Weber's pariah capitalists in late-twentieth-century transnational drag. Books like this are reminders that East Indians are still a tribe, as are the Jews and others, working the primordial lode to make their way to global dominance. So, the trope of the tribe can turn on its own premises, and we can have vast global tribes, an image that seeks to have it both ways, with primordial intimacy *and* high-tech strategies. However diasporic we get, like the Jews, South Asians are doomed to remain a tribe, forever fixers and dealers in a world of open markets, fair deals, and opportunity for all.

For those of us who have moved into the "national fantasy" (Berlant 1991) of America from the former colonies, there is thus the seductiveness of a plural belonging, of becoming American while staying somehow diasporic, of an expansive attachment to an unbounded fantasy space. But while we can make our identities, we cannot do so exactly as we please. As many of us find ourselves racialized, biologized, minoritized, somehow reduced rather than enabled by our bodies and our histories, our special diacritics become our prisons, and the trope of the tribe sets us off from another, unspecified America, far from the clamor of the tribe, decorous, civil, and white, a land in which we are not yet welcome.

This brings us back to the pervasive idiom and image of tribalism. Applied to New York, Miami, and Los Angeles (as opposed to Sarajevo, Soweto, or Colombo), the trope of tribalism both conceals and indulges a diffuse racism about those Others (for example, Hispanics, Iranians, and African-Americans) who have insinuated themselves into the American body politic. It allows us to maintain the idea of an Americanness that precedes (and subsists in spite of) the hyphens that contribute to it and to maintain a distinction between tribal Americans (the black, the brown, and the yellow) and other Americans. This trope facilitates the fantasy that civil society in the United States has a special destiny in regard to peaceful multiculturalism—intelligent multiculturalism for us, bloody ethnicity or mindless tribalism for them.

There has developed a special set of links between democracy, diversity, and prosperity in American social thought. Built on a complex dialogue between political science (the only genuine made-in-America social science without obvious European counterparts or antecedents) and vernacular constitutionalism, a comfortable equilibrium was established between the ideas of cultural diversity and one or another version of the melting pot. Swinging between *National Geographic* and *Reader's Digest*, this anodyne polarity has proved remarkably durable and comforting. It accommodates, sometimes on the same page or in the same breath, a sense that plurality is the American genius *and* that there is an Americanness that somehow contains and transcends plurality. This second, post-Civil War accommodation with difference is now on its last legs, and the political correctness-multiculturalism debate is its peculiar, parochial Waterloo. Parochial because it insistently refuses to recognize that the challenge of diasporic pluralism is now global and that American solutions cannot be seen in isolation. Peculiar because there has been no systematic recognition that the politics of multiculturalism is now part and parcel of the extraterritorial nationalism of populations who love America but are not necessarily attached to the United States. More bluntly, neither popular nor academic thought in this country has come to terms with the difference between being a land of immigrants and being one node in a postnational network of diasporas.

In the postnational world that we see emerging, diaspora runs with, and not against, the grain of identity, movement, and reproduction. Everyone has relatives working abroad. Many people find themselves exiles without really having moved very far—Croats in Bosnia, Hindus in Kashmir, Muslims in India. Yet others find themselves in patterns of repeat migration. Indians who went to East Africa in the nineteenth and early twentieth centuries found themselves pushed out of Uganda, Kenya, and Tanzania in the 1980s to find fresh travails and opportunities in England and the United States, and they are now considering returning to East Africa. Similarly, Chinese from Hong Kong who are buying real estate in Vancouver, Gujarati traders from Uganda opening motels in New Jersey and newspaper kiosks in New York City, and Sikh cabdrivers in Chicago and Philadelphia are all examples of a new sort of world in which diaspora is the order of things and settled ways of life are increasingly hard to find. The United States, always in its self-perception a land of immigrants, finds itself awash in these global diasporas, no longer a closed space for the melting pot to work its magic, but yet another diasporic switching point. People come here to seek their fortunes, but they are no longer content to leave their homelands behind. Global democracy fever and the breakdown of the Soviet empire have meant that most groups that wish to renegotiate their links to their diasporic identities from their American vantage points are now free to do so: thus, American Jews of Polish origin undertake Holocaust tours in Eastern Europe, Indian doctors from Michigan set up eye clinics in New Delhi, Palestinians in Detroit participate in the politics of the West Bank.

The Form of the Transnation

The formula of hyphenation (as in Italian-Americans, Asian-Americans, and African-Americans) is reaching the point of saturation, and the right-hand side of the hyphen can barely contain the unruliness of the left-hand side. Even as the legitimacy of nation-states in their own territorial contexts is increasingly under threat, the idea of the nation flourishes transnationally. Safe from the depredations of their home states, diasporic communities become doubly loyal to their nations of origin and thus ambivalent about their loyalties to America. The politics of ethnic identity in the United States is inseparably linked to the global spread of originally local national identities. For every nation-state that has exported significant numbers of its populations to the United States as refugees, tourists, or students, there is now a delocalized *transnation*, which retains a special ideological link to a putative place of origin but is otherwise a thoroughly diasporic collectivity.[3] No existing conception of Americanness can contain this large variety of transnations.

In this scenario, the hyphenated American might have to be twice hyphenated (Asian-American-Japanese or Native-American-Seneca or African-American-Jamaican or Hispanic-American-Bolivian) as diasporic identities stay mobile and grow more protean. Or perhaps the sides of the hyphen will have to be reversed, and we can become a federation of diasporas: American-Italians, American-Haitians, American-Irish, American-Africans. Dual citizenships might increase if the societies from which we came remain or become more open. We might recognize that diasporic diversity actually puts loyalty to a nonterritorial transnation first, while recognizing that there is a special American way to connect to these global diasporas. America, as a cultural space, will not need to compete with a host of global identities and diasporic loyalties. It might come to be seen as a model of how to arrange one territorial locus (among others) for a cross-hatching of diasporic communities. In this regard, the American problem resembles those of other wealthy industrial democracies (such as Sweden, Germany, Holland, and France), all of which face the challenge of squaring Enlightenment universalisms and diasporic pluralism.

The question is, can a postnational politics be built around this cultural fact? Many societies now face influxes of immigrants and refugees, wanted and unwanted. Others are pushing out groups in acts of ethnic cleansing intended to produce the very people whose preexistence the nation was supposed to ratify. But America may be alone in having organized itself around a modern political ideology in which pluralism is central to the conduct of democratic life. Out of a different strand of its experience, this society has also generated a powerful fable of itself as a land of immigrants. In today's postnational, diasporic world, America is being invited to weld these two doctrines together, to confront the needs of pluralism *and* of immigration, to construct a society *around* diasporic diversity.

But such images as the mosaic, the rainbow, the quilt, and other tropes of complexity-in-diversity cannot supply the imaginative resources for this task, especially as fears of tribalism multiply. Tribes do not make quilts, although they sometimes make confederacies. Whether in debates over immigration, bilingual education, the academic canon, or the underclass, these liberal images have sought to contain the tension between the centripetal pull of Americanness and the centrifugal pull of diasporic diversity in American life. The battles over affirmative action, quotas, welfare, and abortion in America today suggest that the metaphor of the mosaic cannot contain the contradiction between group identities, which Americans will tolerate (up to a point) in cultural life, and individual identities, which are still the nonnegotiable principle behind American ideas of achievement, mobility, and justice.

What is to be done? There could be a special place for America in the new, postnational order, and one that does not rely on either isolationism or global domination as its alternative basis. The United States is eminently suited to be a sort of cultural laboratory and a free-trade zone for the generation, circulation, importation, and testing of the materials for a world organized around diasporic diversity. In a sense, this experiment is already under way. The United States is already a huge, fascinating garage sale for the rest of the world. It provides golf vacations and real estate for the Japanese; business-management ideologies and techniques for Europe and India; soap-opera ideas for Brazil and the Middle East; prime ministers for Yugoslavia; supply-side economics for Poland, Russia, and whoever else will try; Christian fundamentalism for Korea; and postmodern architecture for Hong Kong. By also providing a set of images—Rambo in Afghanistan, "We Are the World," George Bernard Shaw in Baghdad, Coke goes to Barcelona, Perot goes to Washington—that link human rights, consumer style, antistatism, and media glitz, it might be said that the United States is partly accountable for the idiosyncrasies that attend struggles for self-determination in otherwise very different parts of the world. This is why a University of Iowa sweatshirt is not just a silly symbol in the jungles of Mozambique or on the barricades of Beirut. It captures the free-floating yearning for American style, even in the most intense contexts of opposition to the United States. The cultural politics of queer nationality is an example of this contradictory yearning in the United States (Berlant and Freeman 1992). The rest of this yearning is provoked by authoritarian state policies, massive arms industries, the insistently hungry eye of the electronic media, and the despair of bankrupt economies.

Of course, these products and ideas are not the immaculate conceptions of some mysterious American know-how but are precisely the result of a complex environment in which ideas and intellectuals meet in a variety of special settings (such as labs, libraries, classrooms, music studios, business seminars, and political campaigns) to generate, reformulate, and recirculate cultural forms that are fundamentally postnational and diasporic. The role of American musicians, studios, and record companies in the creation of world beat is an excellent example of this sort of downhome but offshore entrepreneurial mentality. Americans are loathe to admit the piecemeal, pragmatic, haphazard, flexible, and opportunistic ways in which these American products and reproducts circulate around the world. Americans like to think that the Chinese have simply bought the virtues of free enterprise; the Poles, the supply side; the Haitians and Filipinos, democracy; and everyone, human rights. We rarely pay attention to the complicated terms, traditions, and cultural styles into which these ideas are folded and thus transformed beyond our recognition. Thus, during the historic events of Tiananmen Square in 1989, when it seemed as if the Chinese people had become democratic overnight, there was considerable evidence that the ways in which different groups in China understood their problems were both internally varied and tied to various specificities of China's history and cultural style.

When Americans see transformations and cultural complications of their democratic vocabulary and style, if they notice them at all, they are annoyed and dismayed. In this misreading of how others handle what we still see as *our* national recipe for success, Americans perform a further act of narcissistic distortion: we imagine that these peculiarly American inventions (democracy, capitalism, free enterprise, human rights) are automatically and inherently interconnected and that our national saga holds the key to the combination. In the migration of our words, we see the victory of our myths. We are believers in terminal conversion.

The American "victory" in the Cold War need not necessarily turn pyrrhic. The fact is that the United States, from a cultural point of view, is already a vast free-trade zone, full of ideas, technologies, styles, and idioms (from McDonald's and the Harvard Business School to the Dream Team and reverse mortgages) that the rest of the world finds fascinating. This free-trade zone rests on a volatile economy; the major cities of the American borderland (Los Angeles, Miami, New York, Detroit) are now heavily militarized. But these facts are of little relevance to those who come, either briefly or for more extended stays, to this free-trade zone. Some, fleeing vastly greater urban violence, state persecution, and economic hardship, come as permanent migrants, legal or illegal. Others are short-term shoppers for clothes, entertainment, loans, armaments, or quick lessons in free-market economics or civil-society politics. The very unruliness, the rank unpredictability, the quirky inventiveness, the sheer cultural vitality of this free-trade zone are what attract all sorts of diasporas to the United States.

For the United States, to play a major role in the cultural politics of a postnational world has very complex domestic entailments. It may mean making room for the legitimacy of cultural rights, rights to the pursuit of cultural difference under public protections and guarantees. It may mean a painful break from a fundamentally Fordist, manufacture-centered conception of the American economy, as we learn to be global information brokers, service providers, style doctors. It may mean embracing as part of our livelihood what we have so far confined to the world of Broadway, Hollywood, and Disneyland: the import of experiments, the production of fantasies, the fabrication of identities, the export of styles, the hammering out of pluralities. It may mean distinguishing our attachment to America from our willingness to die for the United States. This suggestion converges with the following proposal by Lauren Berlant:

> The subject who wants to avoid the melancholy insanity of the self-abstraction that is citizenship, and to resist the lure of self-overcoming the material political context in which she lives, must develop tactics for refusing the interarticulation, now four hundred years old, between the United States and America, the nation and utopia. (1991, 217)

That is, it may be time to rethink monopatriotism, patriotism directed exclusively to the hyphen between nation and state, and to allow the material problems we face—the deficit, the environment, abortion, race, drugs, and jobs—to define those social groups and ideas for which we would be willing to live, and die. The queer nation may only be the first of a series of new patriotisms, in which others could be the retired, the unemployed, and the disabled, as well as scientists, women, and Hispanics. Some of us may still want to live—and die—for the United States. But many of these new sovereignties are inherently postnational. Surely, they represent more humane motives for affiliation than statehood or party affiliation and more interesting bases for debate and crosscutting alliances. Ross Perot's volunteers in 1992 give us a brief, intense glimpse of the powers of patriotism totally divorced from party, government, or state. America may yet construct another narrative of enduring significance, a narrative about the uses of loyalty after the end of the nation-state. In this narrative, bounded territories could give way to diasporic networks, nations to transnations, and patriotism itself could become plural, serial, contextual, and mobile. Here lies one direction for the future of patriotism in a postcolonial world. Patriotism—like history—is unlikely to end, but its objects may be susceptible to transformation, in theory and in practice.

It remains now to ask what transnations and transnationalism have to do with postnationality and its prospects. This relationship requires detailed engagement in its own right, but a few observations are in order. As populations become deterritorialized and incompletely nationalized, as nations splinter and recombine, as states face intractable difficulties in the task of producing "the people," transnations are the most important social sites in which the crises of patriotism are played out.

The results are surely contradictory. Displacement and exile, migration and terror create powerful attachments to ideas of homeland that seem more deeply territorial than ever. But it is also possible to detect in many of these transnations (some ethnic, some religious, some philanthropic, some militaristic) the elements of a postnational imaginary. These elements for those who wish to hasten the demise of the nation-state, for all their contradictions, require both nurture and critique. In this way, transnational social forms may generate not only postnational yearnings but also actually existing postnational movements, organizations, and spaces. In these postnational spaces, the incapacity of the nation-state to tolerate diversity (as it seeks the homogeneity of its citizens, the simultaneity of its presence, the consensuality of its narrative, and the stability of its citizens) may, perhaps, be overcome.

9

The Production of Locality

This chapter addresses related questions that have arisen in an ongoing series of writings about global cultural flows. I begin with three such questions. What is the place of locality in schemes about global cultural flow?
Does anthropology retain any special rhetorical privilege in a world where
locality seems to have lost its ontological moorings? Can the mutually
constitutive relationship between anthropology and locality survive in a
dramatically delocalized world? My argument does not stem directly from
concern with either the production of space (Lefebvre 1991) or the disciplinary anxieties of anthropology as such, although they broadly inform
my response to these questions. Rather, it engages a continuing debate
about the future of the nation-state (chap. 8). My concern is with what locality might mean in a situation where the nation-state faces particular
sorts of transnational destabilization.

I view locality as primarily relational and contextual rather than as
scalar or spatial. I see it as a complex phenomenological quality, constituted by a series of links between the sense of social immediacy, the technologies of interactivity, and the relativity of contexts. This phenomenological quality, which expresses itself in certain kinds of agency, sociality,
and reproducibility, is the main predicate of locality as a category (or subject) that I seek to explore. In contrast, I use the term *neighborhood* to refer

to the actually existing social forms in which locality, as a dimension or value, is variably realized. Neighborhoods, in this usage, are situated communities characterized by their actuality, whether spatial or virtual, and their potential for social reproduction.[1]

As part of this exploration, I address two further questions. How does *locality*, as an aspect of social life, relate to *neighborhoods* as substantive social forms? Is the relationship of locality to neighborhoods substantially altered by recent history, especially by the global crisis of the nation-state? A simpler way to characterize these multiple goals is through this question: What can locality mean in a world where spatial localization, quotidian interaction, and social scale are not always isomorphic?

Locating the Subject

It is one of the grand clichés of social theory (going back to Toennies, Weber, and Durkheim) that locality as a property or diacritic of social life comes under siege in modern societies. But locality is an inherently fragile social achievement. Even in the most intimate, spatially confined, geographically isolated situations, locality must be maintained carefully against various kinds of odds. These odds have at various times and places been conceptualized differently. In many societies, boundaries are zones of danger requiring special ritual maintenance; in other sorts of societies, social relations are inherently fissive, creating a persistent tendency for some neighborhoods to dissolve. In yet other situations, ecology and technology dictate that houses and inhabited spaces are forever shifting, thus contributing an endemic sense of anxiety and instability to social life.

Much of what we call the ethnographic record can be rewritten and reread from this point of view. In the first instance, a great deal of what have been termed *rites of passage* is concerned with the production of what we might call *local subjects*, actors who properly belong to a situated community of kin, neighbors, friends, and enemies. Ceremonies of naming and tonsure, scarification and segregation, circumcision and deprivation are complex social techniques for the inscription of locality onto bodies. Looked at slightly differently, they are ways to embody locality as well as to locate bodies in socially and spatially defined communities. The spatial symbolism of rites of passage has probably been paid less attention than its bodily and social symbolism. Such rites are not simply mechanical techniques for social aggregation but social techniques for the production of "natives," a category I have discussed elsewhere (Appadurai 1988).

What is true of the production of local subjects in the ethnographic record is as true of the processes by which locality is materially produced. The building of houses, the organization of paths and passages, the making and remaking of fields and gardens, the mapping and negotiation of transhuman spaces and hunter-gatherer terrains is the incessant, often humdrum preoccupation of many small communities studied by anthropologists. These techniques for the *spatial* production of locality have been copiously documented. But they have not usually been viewed as instances of the production of locality, both as a general property of social life and as a particular valuation of that property. Broken down descriptively into technologies for house building, garden cultivation, and the like, these material outcomes have been taken as ends in themselves rather than as moments in a general technology (and teleology) of localization.

The production of locality in the societies historically studied by anthropologists (on islands and in forests, agricultural villages and hunting camps) is not simply a matter of producing local subjects as well as the very neighborhoods that contextualize these subjectivities. As some of the best work in the social logic of ritual in the past few decades so amply shows (Lewis 1986; Munn 1986; Schieffelin 1985), space and time are themselves socialized and localized through complex and deliberate practices of performance, representation, and action. We have tended to call these practices *cosmological* or *ritual*—terms that by distracting us from their active, intentional, and productive character create the dubious impression of mechanical reproduction.

One of the most remarkable general features of the ritual process is its highly specific way of localizing duration and extension, of giving these categories names and properties, values and meanings, symptoms and legibility. A vast amount of what we know of ritual in small-scale societies can be revisited from this point of view. The large body of literature on techniques for naming places, for protecting fields, animals, and other reproductive spaces and resources, for marking seasonal change and agricultural rhythms, for properly situating new houses and wells, for appropriately demarcating boundaries (both domestic and communal) is substantially literature documenting the socialization of space and time. More precisely, it is a record of the spatiotemporal production of locality. Looked at this way, Arnold van Gennep's extraordinary and vital study of rites of passage (1965), much of James G. Frazer's bizarre encyclopedia (1900), and Bronislaw Malinowski's monumental study of Trobriand garden magic (1961) are substantially records of the myriad ways in which small-scale societies do not and cannot take locality as a given. Rather, they seem to assume that locality is ephemeral unless hard and regular work is undertaken to produce and maintain its materiality. Yet this very materiality is sometimes mistaken for the terminus of such work, thus obscuring the more abstract effects of this work on the production of locality as a structure of feeling.

Much that has been considered local knowledge is actually knowledge of how to produce and reproduce locality under conditions of anxiety and entropy, social wear and flux, ecological uncertainty and cosmic volatility, and the always present quirkiness of kinsmen, enemies, spirits, and quarks of all sorts. The locality of local knowledge is not only, or even mainly, its embeddedness in a nonnegotiable here and now or its stubborn disinterest in things at large, although these are certainly crucial properties as Clifford Geertz has reminded us in much of his work (Geertz 1975, 1983). Local knowledge is substantially about producing reliably local subjects as well as about producing reliably local neighborhoods within which such subjects can be recognized and organized. In this sense, local knowledge is what it is not principally by contrast with other knowledges—which (from some nonlocal point of view) the observer might regard as less localized—but by virtue of its local teleology and ethos. We might say, adapting Marx, that local knowledge is not only local in itself but, even more important, for itself.

Even in the smallest of societies, with the humblest of technologies and in the most desolate of ecological contexts, the relationship between the production of local subjects and the neighborhoods in which such subjects can be produced, named, and empowered to act socially is a historical and dialectical relationship. Without reliably local subjects, the construction of a local terrain of habitation, production, and moral security would have no interests attached to it. But by the same token, without such a known, named, and negotiable terrain already available, the ritual techniques for creating local subjects would be abstract, thus sterile. The long-term reproduction of a neighborhood that is simultaneously practical, valued, and taken-for-granted depends on the seamless interaction of localized spaces and times with local subjects possessed of the knowledge to reproduce locality. Problems that are properly historical arise whenever this seamlessness is threatened. Such problems do not arrive only with modernity, colonialism, or ethnography. I stress this point now because I will discuss below the special properties of the production of locality under the conditions of contemporary urban life, which involve national regimes, mass mediation, and intense and irregular commoditization.

If a large part of the ethnographic record can be reread and rewritten as a record of the multifarious modes for the production of locality, it follows that ethnography has been unwittingly complicit in this activity. This is a point about knowledge and representation rather than about guilt or violence. The ethnographic project is in a peculiar way isomorphic with the very knowledges it seeks to discover and document, as both the ethnographic project and the social projects it seeks to describe have the production of locality as their governing telos.[2] The misrecognition of this fact in both projects, as involving only more humdrum and discrete actions and settings (house building, child naming, boundary rituals, greeting rituals, spatial purifications), is the constitutive misrecognition that guarantees both the special appropriateness of ethnography to certain kinds of description and its peculiar lack of reflexivity as a project of knowledge and reproduction. Drawn into the very localization they seek to document, most ethnographic descriptions have taken locality as ground not figure, recognizing neither its fragility nor its ethos *as a property of social life*. This produces an unproblematized collaboration with the sense of inertia on which locality, as a structure of feeling, centrally relies.

The value of reconceiving ethnography (and rereading earlier ethnography) from this perspective is threefold: (1) it shifts the history of ethnography from a history of neighborhoods to a history of the techniques for the production of locality; (2) it opens up a new way to think about the complex coproduction of indigenous categories by organic intellectuals, administrators, linguists, missionaries, and ethnologists, which undergirds large portions of the monographic history of anthropology; (3) it enables the ethnography of the modern, and of the production of locality under modern conditions, to be part of a more general contribution to the ethnographic record *tout court*. Together, these effects would help guard against the too-easy use of various oppositional tropes (then and now, before and after, small and large, bounded and unbounded, stable and fluid, hot and cold) that implicitly oppose ethnographies of and in the present to ethnographies of and in the past.

The Contexts of Locality

I have so far focused on locality as a phenomenological property of social life, a structure of feeling that is produced by particular forms of intentional activity and that yields particular sorts of material effects. Yet this dimensional aspect of locality cannot be separated from the actual settings in and through which social life is reproduced. To make the link between locality as a property of social life and neighborhoods as social forms requires a more careful exposition of the problem of context. The production of neighborhoods is always historically grounded and thus contextual. That is, neighborhoods are inherently what they are because they are opposed to something else and derive from other, already produced neighborhoods. In the practical consciousness of many human communities, this something else is often conceptualized ecologically as forest or wasteland, ocean or desert, swamp or river. Such ecological signs often mark boundaries that simultaneously signal the beginnings of nonhuman forces and categories or recognizably human but barbarian or demonic forces. Frequently, these contexts, against which neighborhoods are produced and figured, are at once seen as ecological, social, and cosmological terrains.

It may be useful here to note that the social part of the context of neighborhoods—the fact, that is, of other neighborhoods—recalls the idea of *ethnoscape* (chap. 3), a term I used to get away from the idea that group identities necessarily imply that cultures need to be seen as spatially bounded, historically unselfconscious, or ethnically homogeneous forms. In this earlier usage, I implied that the idea of ethnoscape might be salient especially to the late twentieth century, when human motion, the volatility of images, and the conscious identity-producing activities of nation-states lend a fundamentally unstable and perspectival quality to social life.

Yet neighborhoods are always to some extent ethnoscapes, insofar as they involve the ethnic projects of Others as well as consciousness of such projects. That is, particular neighborhoods sometimes recognize that their own logic is a general logic by which Others also construct recognizable, social, human, situated life-worlds. Such knowledge can be encoded in the pragmatics of rituals associated with clearing forests, making gardens, building houses, which always carry an implicit sense of the teleology of locality building. In more complex societies, typically associated with literacy, priestly classes, and macro-orders for the control and dissemination of powerful ideas, such knowledges are codified, as in the case of the rituals associated with the colonization of new villages by Brahmans in precolonial India.

All locality building has a moment of colonization, a moment both historical and chronotypic, when there is a formal recognition that the production of a neighborhood requires deliberate, risky, even violent action in respect to the soil, forests, animals, and other human beings. A good deal of the violence associated with foundational ritual (Bloch 1986) is a recognition of the force that is required to wrest a locality from previously uncontrolled peoples and places. Put in other terms (de Certeau 1984), the transformation of spaces into places requires a conscious moment, which may subsequently be remembered as relatively routine. The production of a neighborhood is inherently colonizing, in the sense that it involves the assertion of socially (often ritually) organized power over places and settings that are viewed as potentially chaotic or rebellious. The anxiety that attends many rituals of habitation, occupation, or settlement is a recognition of the implicit violence of all such acts of colonization. Some of this anxiety remains in the ritual repetition of these moments, long after the foundational event of colonization. In this sense, the production of a neighborhood is inherently an exercise of power over some sort of hostile or recalcitrant environment, which may take the form of another neighborhood.

Much of the narrative material unearthed by ethnographers working in small communities, as well as much of their description of rituals of agriculture, house building and social passage, stresses the sheer material fragility associated with producing and maintaining locality. Nevertheless, however deeply such description is embedded in the particularities of place, soil, and ritual technique, it invariably contains or implies a theory of context—a theory, in other words, of what a neighborhood is produced from, against, in spite of, and in relation to. The problem of the relationship between neighborhood and context requires much fuller attention than can be afforded here. Let me sketch the general dimensions of this problem. The central dilemma is that neighborhoods both are contexts and at the same time require and produce contexts. Neighborhoods are contexts in the sense that they provide the frame or setting within which various kinds of human action (productive, reproductive, interpretive, performative) can be initiated and conducted meaningfully. Because meaningful life-worlds require legible and reproducible patterns of action, they are text-like and thus require one or many contexts. From another point of view, a neighborhood is a context, or a set of contexts, within which meaningful social action can be both generated and interpreted. In this sense, neighborhoods are contexts, and contexts are neighborhoods. A neighborhood is a multiplex interpretive site.

Insofar as neighborhoods are imagined, produced, and maintained against some sort of ground (social, material, environmental), they also require and produce contexts against which their own intelligibility takes shape. This context-generative dimension of neighborhoods is an important matter because it provides the beginnings of a theoretical angle on the relationship between local and global realities. How so? The way in which neighborhoods are produced and reproduced requires the continuous construction, both practical and discursive, of an ethnoscape (necessarily nonlocal) against which local practices and projects are imagined to take place.

In one dimension, at one moment, and from one perspective, neighborhoods as existing contexts are prerequisites for the production of local subjects. That is, existing places and spaces, within a historically produced spatiotemporal neighborhood and with a series of localized rituals, social categories, expert practitioners, and informed audiences, are required in order for new members (babies, strangers, slaves, prisoners, guests, affines) to be made temporary or permanent local subjects. Here, we see locality in its taken-for-granted, commonsensical, habitus dimension. In this dimension, a neighborhood appears to be simply a set of contexts, historically received, materially embedded, socially appropriate, naturally unproblematic: fathers yield sons, gardens yield yams, sorcery yields sickness, hunters yield meat, women yield babies, blood yields semen, shamans yield visions, and so forth. These contexts in concert appear to provide the unproblematized setting for the technical production of local subjects in a regular and regulated manner.

But as these local subjects engage in the social activities of production, representation, and reproduction (as in the work of culture), they contribute, generally unwittingly, to the creation of contexts that might exceed the existing material and conceptual boundaries of the neighborhood. Affinal aspirations extend marriage networks to new villages; fishing expeditions yield refinements of what are understood to be navigable and fish-rich waters; hunting expeditions extend the sense of the forest as a responsive ecological frame; social conflicts force new strategies of exit and recolonization; trading activities yield new commodity-worlds and thus new partnerships with as-yet-unencountered regional groupings; warfare yields new diplomatic alliances with previously hostile neighbors. And all of these possibilities contribute to subtle shifts in language, worldview, ritual practice, and collective self-understanding. Put summarily, as local subjects carry on the continuing task of reproducing their neighborhood, the contingencies of history, environment, and imagination contain the potential for new contexts (material, social, and imaginative) to be produced. In this way, through the vagaries of social action by local subjects, neighborhood as context produces the context of neighborhoods. Over time, this dialectic changes the conditions of the production of locality as such. Put another way, this is how the subjects of history become historical subjects, so that no human community, however apparently stable, static, bounded, or isolated, can usefully be regarded as cool or outside history. This observation converges with Marshall Sahlins's view of the dynamics of conjunctural change (1985).

Consider the general relationship among various Yanomami groups in the rain forests of Brazil and Venezuela. The relationship among settlements, population shifts, predatory warfare, and sexual competition can be viewed as a process in which specific Yanomami villages (neighborhoods), in and through their actions, preoccupations, and strategies, actually produce a wider set of contexts for themselves and each other. This creates a general territory of Yanomami movement, interaction, and colonization in which any given village responds to a material context wider than itself while simultaneously contributing to the creation of that wider context. In a larger-scale perspective, the overall network of space and time, in which the Yanomami produce and generate reciprocal contexts for specific acts of localization (village building), also produces some of the contexts in which the Yanomami as a whole encounter the Brazilian and Venezuelan nation-states. In this sense, Yanomami locality-producing activities are not only context-driven but are also context-generative. This is true of all locality-producing activities.

Thus, neighborhoods seem paradoxical because they both constitute and require contexts. As ethnoscapes, neighborhoods inevitably imply a relational consciousness of other neighborhoods, but they act at the same time as autonomous neighborhoods of interpretation, value, and material practice. Thus, locality as a relational achievement is not the same as a locality as a practical value in the quotidian production of subjects and colonization of space. Locality production is inevitably context-generative to some extent. What defines this extent is very substantially a question of the relationships between the contexts that neighborhoods create and those they encounter. This is a matter of social power and of the different scales of organization and control within which particular spaces (and places) are embedded.

Although the practices and projects of the Yanomami are context-producing for the Brazilian state, it is even truer that the practices of the Brazilian nation-state involve harsh, even overwhelming forces of military intervention, large-scale environmental exploitation, and state-sponsored migration and colonization that the Yanomami confront on hugely unequal terms. In this sense, which I will pursue in the next section on the conditions of locality production in the era of the nation-state, the Yanomami are being steadily *localized*, in the sense of enclaved, exploited, perhaps even cleansed in the context of the Brazilian polity. Thus, while they are still in a position to generate contexts as they produce and reproduce their own neighborhoods, they are increasingly prisoners in the context-producing activities of the nation-state, which makes their own efforts to produce locality seem feeble, even doomed.

This example has wide general applicability. The capability of neighborhoods to produce contexts (within which their very localizing activities acquire meaning and historical potential) and to produce local subjects is profoundly affected by the locality-producing capabilities of larger-scale social formations (nation-states, kingdoms, missionary empires, and trading cartels) to determine the general shape of all the neighborhoods within the reach of their powers. Thus, power is always a key feature of the contextual relations of neighborhoods, and even "first contact" always involves different narratives of firstness from the two sides involved in it.

The political economy that links neighborhoods to contexts is thus both methodologically and historically complex. Our ideas of context derive largely from linguistics. Until recently, context has been opportunistically defined to make sense of specific sentences, rituals, performances, and other sorts of text. While the production of texts has been carefully considered from several different points of view (Bauman and Briggs 1990; Hanks 1989), the structure and morphology of contexts has only lately become the focus of any systematic attention (Duranti and Goodwin 1992). Beyond anthropological linguistics, context remains a poorly defined idea, an inert concept indexing an inert environment. When social anthropologists appeal to context, it is generally to a loosely understood sense of the social frame within which specific actions or representations can best be understood. Sociolinguistics, especially as derived from the ethnography of speaking (Hymes 1974), has been the main source for this general approach.

The structure of contexts cannot and should not be derived entirely from the logic and morphology of texts. Text production and context production have different logics and metapragmatic features. Contexts are produced in the complex imbrication of discursive and nondiscursive practices, and so the sense in which contexts imply other contexts, so that each context implies a global network of contexts, is different from the sense in which texts imply other texts, and eventually all texts. Intertextual relations, about which we now know a fair amount, are not likely to work in the same way as *intercontextual* relations. Last, and most daunting, is the prospect that we shall have to find ways to connect theories of intertextuality to theories of intercontextuality. A strong theory of globalization from a sociocultural point of view is likely to require something we certainly do not now have: a theory of intercontextual relations that incorporates our existing sense of intertexts. But that is truly another project.

The relationship between neighborhood as context and the context of neighborhoods, mediated by the actions of local historical subjects, acquires new complexities in the sort of world in which we now live. In this new sort of world, the production of neighborhoods increasingly occurs under conditions where the system of nation-states is the normative hinge for the production of both local and translocal activities. This situation, in which the power relations that affect the production of locality are fundamentally translocal, is the central concern of the next section.

The Global Production of Locality

What has been discussed thus far as a set of structural problems (locality and neighborhoods, text and context, ethnoscapes and life-worlds) needs now to be explicitly historicized. I have indicated already that the relationship of locality (and neighborhoods) to contexts is historical and dialectical, and that the context-generative dimension of places (in their capacity as ethnoscapes) is distinct from their context-providing features (in their capacity as neighborhoods). How do these claims help to understand what happens to the production of locality in the contemporary world?

Contemporary understandings of globalization (Balibar and Wallerstein 1991; Featherstone 1990; King 1991; Robertson 1992; Rosenau 1990) seem to indicate a shift from an emphasis on the global journeys of capitalist modes of thought and organization to a somewhat different emphasis on the spread of the nation form, especially as dictated by the concurrent spread of colonialism and print capitalism. If one problem now appears to be the dominant concern of the human sciences, it is that of nationalism and the nation-state (Anderson 1991; Bhabha 1990; Chatterjee 1986, 1993; Gellner 1983; Hobsbawm 1990).

While only time will tell whether our current preoccupations with the nation-state are justified, the beginnings of an anthropological engagement with this issue are evident in the increasing contribution of anthropologists to the problematics of the nation-state (Borneman 1992; Moore 1993; Handler 1988; Herzfeld 1982; Kapferer 1988; Tambiah 1986; Urban and Sherzer 1991; van der Veer 1994). Some of this work explicitly considers the global context of national cultural formations (Hannerz 1992; Basch et al. 1994; Foster 1991; Friedman 1990; Gupta and Ferguson 1992; Rouse 1991; Sahlins 1992). Yet a framework for relating the global, the national, and the local has yet to emerge.

In this section, I hope to extend my thoughts about local subjects and localized contexts to sketch the outlines of an argument about the special problems that beset the production of locality in a world that has become deterritorialized (Deleuze and Guattari 1987), diasporic, and transnational.

This is a world where electronic media are transforming the relationships between information and mediation, and where nation-states are struggling to retain control over their populations in the face of a host of subnational and transnational movements and organizations. A full consideration of the challenges to the production of locality in such a world would require extended treatment beyond the scope of this chapter. But some elements of an approach to this problem can be outlined.

Put simply, the task of producing locality (as a structure of feeling, a property of social life, and an ideology of situated community) is increasingly a struggle. There are many dimensions to this struggle, and I shall focus here on three: (1) the steady increase in the efforts of the modern nation-state to define all neighborhoods under the sign of its forms of allegiance and affiliation; (2) the growing disjuncture between territory, subjectivity, and collective social movement; and (3) the steady erosion, principally due to the force and form of electronic mediation, of the relationship between spatial and virtual neighborhoods. To make things yet more complex, these three dimensions are themselves interactive.

The nation-state relies for its legitimacy on the intensity of its meaningful presence in a continuous body of bounded territory. It works by policing its borders, producing its people (Balibar 1991), constructing its citizens, defining its capitals, monuments, cities, waters, and soils, and by constructing its locales of memory and commemoration, such as graveyards and cenotaphs, mausoleums and museums. The nation-state conducts throughout its territories the bizarrely contradictory project of creating a flat, contiguous, and homogeneous space of nationness and simultaneously a set of places and spaces (prisons, barracks, airports, radio stations, secretariats, parks, marching grounds, processional routes) calculated to create the internal distinctions and divisions necessary for state ceremony, surveillance, discipline, and mobilization. These latter are also the spaces and places that create and perpetuate the distinctions between rulers and ruled, criminals and officials, crowds and leaders, actors and observers.

Through apparatuses as diverse as museums and village dispensaries, post offices and police stations, tollbooths and telephone booths, the nation-state creates a vast network of formal and informal techniques for the nationalization of all space considered to be under its sovereign authority. States vary, of course, in their ability to penetrate the nooks and crannies of everyday life. Subversion, evasion, and resistance, sometimes scatological (Mbembe 1992), sometimes ironic (Comaroff and Comaroff 1992a), sometimes covert (Scott 1990), sometimes spontaneous and sometimes planned, are very widespread. Indeed, the failures of nation-states to contain and define the lives of their citizens are writ large in the growth of shadow economies, private and quasi-private armies and constabularies, secessionary nationalisms, and a variety of nongovernmental organizations that provide alternatives to the national control of the means of subsistence and justice.

States vary as well in the nature and extent of their interest in local life and the cultural forms in which they invest their deepest paranoias of sovereignty and control. Spitting on the street is very dangerous in Singapore and Papua New Guinea; public gatherings are a problem in Haiti and Cameroon; disrespect to the emperor is not good in Japan; and inciting pro-Muslim sentiments is bad news in contemporary India. The list could be multiplied: nation-states have their special sites of sacredness, their special tests of loyalty and treachery, their special measures of compliance and disorder. These are linked to real and perceived problems of lawlessness, reigning ideologies of liberalization or its opposite, relative commitments to international respectability, variably deep revulsions about immediate predecessor regimes, and special histories of ethnic antagonism or collaboration. Whatever else is true of the world after 1989, there do not seem to be any very reliable links between state ideologies of welfare, market economics, military power, and ethnic purity. Yet whether one considers the turbulent post-Communist societies of Eastern Europe, the aggressive city-states of the Far East (such as Taiwan, Singapore, and Hong Kong), the complex postmilitary polities of Latin America, the bankrupt state economies of much of sub-Saharan Africa, or the turbulent fundamentalist states of much of the Middle East and South Asia, they appear to pose a rather similar set of challenges to the production of neighborhood by local subjects.

From the point of view of modern nationalism, neighborhoods exist principally to incubate and reproduce compliant national citizens—and not for the production of local subjects. Locality for the modern nation-state is either a site of nationally appropriated nostalgias, celebrations, and commemorations or a necessary condition of the production of nationals. Neighborhoods as social formations represent anxieties for the nation-state, as they usually contain large or residual spaces where the techniques of nationhood (birth control, linguistic uniformity, economic discipline, communications efficiency, and political loyalty) are likely to be either weak or contested. At the same time, neighborhoods are the source of political workers and party officials, teachers and soldiers, television technicians and productive farmers. Neighborhoods are not dispensable, even if they are potentially treacherous. For the project of the nation-state, neighborhoods represent a perennial source of entropy and slippage. They need to be policed almost as thoroughly as borders.

The work of producing neighborhoods—life-worlds constituted by relatively stable associations, by relatively known and shared histories, and by collectively traversed and legible spaces and places—is often at odds with the projects of the nation-state.[3] This is partly because the commitments and attachments (sometimes mislabeled "primordial") that characterize local subjectivities are more pressing, more continuous, and sometimes more distracting than the nation-state can afford. It is also because the memories and attachments that local subjects have of and to their shop signs and street names, their favorite walkways and streetscapes, their times and places for congregating and escaping are often at odds with the needs of the nation-state for regulated public life. Further, it is the nature of local life to develop partly in contrast to other neighborhoods, by producing its own contexts of alterity (spatial, social, and technical), contexts that may not meet the needs for spatial and social standardization that is prerequisite for the disciplined national citizen.

Neighborhoods are ideally stages for their own self-reproduction, a process that is fundamentally opposed to the imaginary of the nation-state, where neighborhoods are designed to be instances and exemplars of a generalizable mode of belonging to a wider territorial imaginary. The modes of localization most congenial to the nation-state have a disciplinary quality about them: in sanitation and street cleaning, in prisons and slum clearance, in refugee camps and offices of every kind, the nation-state localizes by fiat, by decree, and sometimes by the overt use of force. This sort of localization creates severe constraints, even direct obstacles, to the survival of locality as a context-generative rather than a context-driven process.

Yet the isomorphism of people, territory, and legitimate sovereignty that constitutes the normative charter of the modern nation-state is itself under threat from the forms of circulation of people characteristic of the contemporary world. It is now widely conceded that human motion is definitive of social life more often than it is exceptional in our contemporary world. Work, both of the most sophisticated intellectual sort and of the most humble proletarian sort, drives people to migrate, often more than once in their lifetimes. The policies of nation-states, particularly toward populations regarded as potentially subversive, create a perpetual motion machine, where refugees from one nation move to another, creating new instabilities there that cause further social unrest and thus further social exits. Thus, the people-production needs of one nation-state can mean ethnic and social unrest for its neighbors, creating open-ended cycles of ethnic cleansing, forced migration, xenophobia, state paranoia, and further ethnic cleansing. Eastern Europe in general and Bosnia-Herzegovina in particular are perhaps the most tragic and complex examples of such state-refugee domino processes. In many such cases, people and whole communities are turned into ghettos, refugee camps, concentration camps, or reservations, sometimes without anyone moving at all.

Other forms of human movement are created by the reality or lure of economic opportunity; this is true of much Asian migration to the oil-rich parts of the Middle East. Yet other forms of movement are created by permanently mobile groups of specialized workers (United Nations soldiers, oil technologists, development specialists, and agricultural laborers). Still other forms of movement, particularly in sub-Saharan Africa, involve major droughts and famines, often tied to disastrous alliances between corrupt states and opportunistic international and global agencies. In yet other communities, the logic of movement is provided by the leisure industries, which create tourist sites and locations around the world. The ethnography of these tourist locations is just beginning to be written in detail, but what little we do know suggests that many such locations create complex conditions for the production and reproduction of locality, in which ties of marriage, work, business, and leisure weave together various circulating populations with kinds of locals to create neighborhoods that belong in one sense to particular nation-states, but that are from another point of view what we might call *translocalities*. The challenge to producing a neighborhood in these settings derives from the inherent instability of social relationships, the powerful tendency for local subjectivity itself to be commoditized, and the tendencies for nation-states, which sometimes obtain significant revenues from such sites, to erase internal, local dynamics through externally imposed modes of regulation, credentialization, and image production.

A much darker version of the problem of producing a neighborhood can be seen in the quasi-permanent refugee camps that now characterize many embattled parts of the world, such as the Occupied Territories in Palestine, the camps on the Thailand-Cambodia border, the many United Nations organized camps in Somalia, and the Afghan refugee camps in Northwest Pakistan. Combining the worst features of urban slums, concentration camps, prisons, and ghettos, these are places where, nonetheless, marriages are contracted and celebrated, lives are begun and ended, social contracts made and honored, careers launched and broken, money made and spent, goods produced and exchanged. Such refugee camps are the starkest examples of the conditions of uncertainty, poverty, displacement, and despair under which locality can be produced. These are the extreme examples of neighborhoods that are context-produced rather than context-generative. These are neighborhoods whose life-worlds are produced in the darkest circumstances, with prisons and concentration camps being their most barbaric examples.

Yet even these brutal examples only push to an extreme the quotidian ethos of many cities. In the conditions of ethnic unrest and urban warfare that characterize cities such as Belfast and Los Angeles, Ahmedabad and Sarajevo, Mogadishu and Johannesburg, urban zones are becoming armed camps, driven wholly by *implosive* forces (chap. 7) that fold into neighborhoods the most violent and problematic repercussions of wider regional, national, and global processes. There are, of course, many important differences between these cities, their histories, their populations, and their cultural politics. Yet together they represent a new phase in the life of cities, where the concentration of ethnic populations, the availability of heavy weaponry, and the crowded conditions of civic life create futurist forms of warfare (reminiscent of films like *Road Warrior, Blade Runner,* and many others), and where a general desolation of the national and global landscape has transposed many bizarre racial, religious, and linguistic enmities into scenarios of unrelieved urban terror.

These new urban wars have become to some extent divorced from their regional and national ecologies and turned into self-propelling, implosive wars between criminal, paramilitary, and civilian militias, tied in obscure ways to transnational religious, economic, and political forces. There are, of course, many causes for these forms of urban breakdown in the First and Third Worlds, but in part they are due to the steady erosion of the capability of such cities to control the means of their own self-reproduction. It is difficult not to associate a significant part of these problems with the sheer circulation of persons, often as a result of warfare, starvation, and ethnic cleansing, that drives people into such cities in the first place. The production of locality in these urban formations faces the related problems of displaced and deterritorialized populations, of state policies that restrict neighborhoods as context producers, and of local subjects who cannot be anything other than national citizens. In the most harsh cases, such neighborhoods hardly deserve the name anymore, given that they are barely more than stages, holding companies, sites, and barracks for populations with a dangerously thin commitment to the production of locality.

Lest this seem too dark a vision, it might be noted that the very nature of these less pleasant urban dramas drives individuals and groups to more peaceful locations where they are willing to bring their wit, skills, and passion for peace. The best moments of urban life in the United States and Europe are owed to these migrants who are fleeing places far worse than Chicago, Detroit, Los Angeles, and Miami. Yet we know that the production of locality in South-Central Los Angeles, on Chicago's West Side, and in similar parts of large American cities is a highly embattled process.

The third and final factor to be addressed here is the role of mass media, especially in its electronic forms, in creating new sorts of disjuncture between spatial and virtual neighborhoods. This disjuncture has both utopian and dystopian potentials, and there is no easy way to tell how these might play themselves out in regard to the future of the production of locality. For one thing, the electronic media themselves now vary internally and constitute a complex family of technological means for producing and disseminating news and entertainment. Film tends to be dominated by major commercial interests in a few world centers (Hollywood, New York, Hong Kong, Bombay), although major secondary sites for commercial cinema are emerging in other parts of Europe, Asia, and Africa (such as Mexico City, Bangkok, and Madras). Art cinema (partly built on a growing transnational network of film festivals, exhibitions, and commercial auctions) is spread both more broadly and more thinly across the world, but crossover films (such as *Reservoir Dogs*, *The Crying Game*, as well as *Salaam Bombay* and *El Mariachi*) are on the increase.

Television, both in its conventional broadcast forms as well as through new forms of satellite hookup, increasingly leapfrogs the public spaces of cinema viewing and comes into forests of antennae, often in the poorest slums of the world, such as those of Rio de Janeiro and São Paulo. The relationship between film viewing in theaters and on videocassettes in domestic settings itself creates very important changes, which have been argued to signal the end of cinema viewing as a classical form of spectatorship (Hansen 1991). At the same time, the availability of video-production technologies to small communities, sometimes in the Fourth World, has made it possible for these communities to create more effective national and global strategies of self-representation and cultural survival (Ginsburg 1993; Turner 1992). Fax machines, electronic mail, and other forms of computer-mediated communication have created new possibilities for transnational forms of communication, often bypassing the intermediate surveillance of the nation-state and of major media conglomerates. Each of these developments, of course, interacts with the others, creating complicated new connections between producers, audiences, and publics—local and national, stable and diasporic.

It is impossible to sort through this bewildering plethora of changes in the media environments that surround the production of neighborhoods. But there are numerous new forms of community and communication that currently affect the capability of neighborhoods to be context-producing rather than largely context-driven. The much-discussed impact of news from CNN and other similar global and instantaneous forms of mediation, as well as the role of fax technologies in the democratic upheavals in China, Eastern Europe, and the Soviet Union in 1989 (and since) have made it possible both for leaders and nation-states, as well as their various oppositional forces, to communicate very rapidly across local and even national lines. The speed of such communication is further complicated by the growth of electronic billboard communities, such as those enabled by the Internet, which allow debate, dialogue, and relationship building among various territorially divided individuals, who nevertheless are forming communities of imagination and interest that are geared to their diasporic positions and voices.

These new forms of electronically mediated communication are beginning to create *virtual neighborhoods*, no longer bounded by territory, passports, taxes, elections, and other conventional political diacritics, but by access to both the software and hardware that are required to connect to these large international computer networks. Thus far, access to these virtual (electronic) neighborhoods tends to be confined to members of the transnational intelligentsia, who, through their access to computer technologies at universities, labs, and libraries, can base social and political projects on technologies constructed to solve information-flow problems. Information and opinion flow concurrently through these circuits, and while the social morphology of these electronic neighborhoods is hard to classify and their longevity difficult to predict, clearly they are communities of some sort, trading information and building links that affect many areas of life, from philanthropy to marriage.

These virtual neighborhoods seem on the face of it to represent just that absence of face-to-face links, spatial contiguity, and multiplex social interaction that the idea of a neighborhood seems centrally to imply. Yet we must not be too quick to oppose highly spatialized neighborhoods to these virtual neighborhoods of international electronic communication. The relationship between these two forms of neighborhood is considerably more complex. In the first instance, these virtual neighborhoods are able to mobilize ideas, opinions, moneys, and social linkages that often directly flow back into lived neighborhoods in the form of currency flows, arms for local nationalisms, and support for various positions in highly localized public spheres. Thus, in the context of the destruction of the Babri Masjid in Ayodhya by Hindu extremists on 6 December 1992, there was an intense mobilization of computer, fax, and related electronic networks, which created very rapid loops of debate and information exchange between interested persons in the United States, Canada, England, and various parts of India. These electronic loops have been exploited equally by Indians in the United States standing on both sides of the great debate over fundamentalism and communal harmony in contemporary India.

At the same time, continuing with the example of the Indian community overseas, both the progressive, secularist groupings and their counterparts on the Hindu revivalist side (members of the Vishwa Hindu Parishad and sympathizers of the Bharatiya Janata Party and the Bajrang Dal, sometimes referred to as the Sangh *parivar* or family) are mobilizing these virtual neighborhoods in the interest of political projects that are intensely localizing in India. The riots that shook many Indian cities after 6 December 1992 can no longer be viewed in isolation from the electronic mobilization of the Indian diaspora, whose members can now be involved directly in these developments in India through electronic means. This is not entirely a matter of long-distance nationalism of the sort that Benedict Anderson has recently bemoaned (Anderson 1994). It is part and parcel of the new and often conflicting relations among neighborhoods, translocal allegiances, and the logic of the nation-state.

These "new patriotisms" (chap. 8) are not just the extensions of nationalist and counternationalist debates by other means, although there is certainly a good deal of prosthetic nationalism and politics by nostalgia involved in the dealings of exiles with their erstwhile homelands. They also involve various rather puzzling new forms of linkage between diasporic nationalisms, delocalized political communications, and revitalized political commitments at both ends of the diasporic process.

This last factor reflects the ways in which diasporas are changing in light of new forms of electronic mediation. Indians in the United States are in direct contact with developments in India that involve ethnic violence, state legitimacy, and party politics, and these very dialogues create new forms of association, conversation, and mobilization in their "minoritarian" politics in the United States. Thus, many of those most aggressively involved through electronic means with Indian politics, are also those most committed to efforts to reorganize various kinds of diasporic politics in the cities and regions of the United States. Further, the mobilization of Indian women against domestic abuse, and the collaboration of progressive Indian groups with their counterparts involved with Palestine and South Africa, suggest that these virtual electronic neighborhoods offer new ways for Indians to take part in the production of locality in the cities and suburbs in which they reside as American teachers, cabdrivers, engineers, and entrepreneurs.

Indians in the United States are now engaged in a variety of ways in the politics of multiculturalism in the United States (Bhattacharjee 1992). This engagement is deeply inflected and affected by their involvement in the incendiary politics of their homes, cities, and relatives in India, and also in other locations where their Indian friends and relatives live and work—in England, Africa, Hong Kong, and the Middle East. Thus, the politics of diaspora, at least within the past decade, have been decisively affected by global electronic transformations. Rather than a simple opposition between spatial and virtual neighborhoods, what has emerged is a significant new element in the production of locality. The global flow of images, news, and opinion now provides part of the engaged cultural and political literacy that diasporic persons bring to their spatial neighborhoods. In some ways, these global flows add to the intense, and implosive, force under which spatial neighborhoods are produced.

Unlike the largely negative pressures that the nation-state places on the production of context by local subjects, the electronic mediation of community in the diasporic world creates a more complicated, disjunct, hybrid sense of local subjectivity. Because these electronic communities typically involve the more educated and elite members of diasporic communities, they do not directly affect the local preoccupations of less educated and privileged migrants. Less enfranchised migrants are generally preoccupied with the practicalities of livelihood and residence in their new settings, but they are not isolated from these global flows. A Sikh cabdriver in Chicago may not be able to participate in the politics of the Punjab by using the Internet, but he might listen to cassettes of fiery devotional songs and sermons delivered at the Golden Temple in the Punjab. His counterparts from Haiti, Pakistan, and Iran can use the radio and the cassette player to listen to what they choose to pick from the huge global flow of audiocassettes, especially devoted to popular and devotional music and speeches.

Different groups of Indians in the United States also hear speeches and sermons from every known variety of itinerant politician, academic, holy man, and entrepreneur from the subcontinent, while these make their American tours. They also read *India West, India Abroad,* and other major newspapers that imbricate news of American and Indian politics in the same pages. They participate, through cable television, video, and other technologies in the steady noise of home entertainment produced in and for the United States. Thus the work of the imagination (chap. 1) through which local subjectivity is produced and nurtured is a bewildering palimpsest of highly local and highly translocal considerations.

The three factors that most directly affect the production of locality in the world of the present—the nation-state, diasporic flows, and electronic and virtual communities—are themselves articulated in variable, puzzling, sometimes contradictory ways that depend on the cultural, class, historical, and ecological setting within which they come together. In part, this variability is itself a product of the way that today's ethnoscapes interact irregularly with finance, media, and technological imaginaries (chap. 2). How these forces are articulated in Port Moresby is different from their articulation in Peshawar, and this in turn from Berlin or Los Angeles. But these are all places where the battle between the imaginaries of the nation-state, of unsettled communities, and of global electronic media is in full progress.

What they add up to, with all their conjunctural variations, is an immense new set of challenges for the production of locality in all the senses suggested in this chapter. The problems of cultural reproduction in a globalized world are only partly describable in terms of problems of race and class, gender and power, although these are surely crucially involved. An even more fundamental fact is that the production of locality—always, as I have argued, a fragile and difficult achievement—is more than ever shot through with contradictions, destabilized by human motion, and displaced by the formation of new kinds of virtual neighborhoods.

Locality is thus fragile in two senses. The first sense, with which I began this chapter, follows from the fact that the material reproduction of actual neighborhoods is invariably up against the corrosion of context, if nothing else, in the tendency of the material world to resist the default designs of human agency. The second sense emerges when neighborhoods are subject to the context-producing drives of more complex hierarchical organizations, especially those of the modern nation-state. The relationship between these distinct forms of fragility is itself historical, in that it is the long-term interaction of neighborhoods that creates such complex hierarchical relations, a process we have usually discussed under such rubrics as state formation. This historical dialectic is a reminder that locality as a dimension of social life, and as an articulated value of particular neighborhoods, is not a transcendent standard from which particular societies fall or deviate. Rather, locality is always emergent from the practices of local subjects in specific neighborhoods. The possibilities for its realization as a structure of feeling are thus as variable and incomplete as the relations among the neighborhoods that constitute its practical instances.

The many displaced, deterritorialized, and transient populations that constitute today's ethnoscapes are engaged in the construction of locality, as a structure of feeling, often in the face of the erosion, dispersal, and implosion of neighborhoods as coherent social formations. This disjuncture between neighborhoods as social formations and locality as a property of social life is not without historical precedent, given that long-distance trade, forced migrations, and political exits are very widespread in the historical record. What is new is the disjuncture between these processes and the mass-mediated discourses and practices (including those of economic liberalization, multiculturalism, human rights, and refugee claims) that now surround the nation-state. This disjuncture, like every other one, points to something conjunctural. The task of theorizing the relationship between such disjunctures (chap. 2) and conjunctures that account for the globalized production of difference now seems both more pressing and more daunting. In such a theory, it is unlikely that there will be anything mere about the local.

Notes

CHAPTER 1. HERE AND NOW

1   The absence of specific citations in the text of this essay should not convey the impression that it was immaculately conceived. This introductory chapter, like the book that follows it, builds on many currents in the social and human sciences over the past two decades. Many of these debts will be apparent in the notes to the chapters that follow.

2   For a fuller treatment of this idea, see the introductory essay by Appadurai and Breckenridge on "Public Modernity in India" in *Consuming Modernity: Public Culture in a South Asian World*, ed. Carol A. Breckenridge (Minneapolis: University of Minnesota Press, 1995), 1–20. This collection of essays exemplifies one strategy for engaging the global modern in a specific site.

CHAPTER 2. DISJUNCTURE AND DIFFERENCE IN THE GLOBAL CULTURAL ECONOMY

1   One major exception is Fredric Jameson, whose work on the relationship between postmodernism and late capitalism has in many ways inspired this essay. The debate between Jameson and Aijaz Ahmad in *Social Text*, however, shows that the creation of a globalizing Marxist narrative in cultural matters is difficult territory indeed (Jameson 1986; Ahmad 1987). My own effort in this context is to begin a restructuring of the Marxist narrative (by stressing lags and disjunctures) that many Marxists might find abhorrent. Such a restructuring has to avoid the dangers of obliterating difference within the Third World, eliding the social referent (as some French postmodernists seem inclined to do), and retaining the narrative authority of the Marxist tradition, in favor of greater attention to global fragmentation, uncertainty, and difference.

2   The idea of *ethnoscape* is more fully engaged in chap. 3.

CHAPTER 3. GLOBAL ETHNOSCAPES: NOTES AND QUERIES FOR A TRANSNATIONAL ANTHROPOLOGY

1   These ideas about the cultural economy of a world in motion, as well as the logic of terms such as *ethnoscape*, are more fully developed in chap. 2.

2   This is not the place for an extended review of the emergent field of cultural studies. Its British lineages are carefully explored in Hall (1986) and Johnson (1986). But it is clear that this British tradition, associated largely with the now-diasporic Birmingham School, is taking new forms in the United States, as it comes into contact with American cultural anthropology, the new historicism, and language and media studies in the American tradition.

3   The following discussion draws heavily on Appadurai and Breckenridge (1991a).

CHAPTER 5. PLAYING WITH MODERNITY: THE DECOLONIZATION OF INDIAN CRICKET

1   These materials include the Marathi-language magazines *Chaukar, Ashtapailu, Kriket Bharati*, and *Shatkar*, which have their counterparts in Tamil, Hindi, and Bengali. These magazines provide gossip on cricket stars, reviews of cricket books in English, news and analysis of cricket in England and elsewhere in the Commonwealth, and sometimes also coverage of other sports, as well as cinema and other forms of popular entertainment. In them, therefore, both in the texts and in the advertisements, cricket is textually simultaneously vernacularized and drawn into the glamour of cosmopolitan life. A detailed analysis of these materials warrants a separate study. These magazines, along with books by cricketers such as *Shatak aani Shatkar* (ghostwritten Marathi autobiographies of Ravi Shastri and Sandip Patil), form the basis of the linguistic and readerly decolonization of cricket. I am deeply grateful to Lee Schlesinger who hunted down some of these materials for me in the bookstores and byways of Poona.

CHAPTER 6. NUMBER IN THE COLONIAL IMAGINATION

1   By *territorial*, I mean the concern of the census with boroughs, counties, and regions (Ludden 1991).

2   I owe this contrast between special and limiting cases to Dipesh Chakrabarty, to whom I also owe the reminder that this problem is critical to my argument.

CHAPTER 7. LIFE AFTER PRIMORDIALISM

1   Earlier versions of this chapter were presented at the Center for International Affairs at Harvard University, the Program in the Comparative Study of Social Transformations at the University of Michigan, and the Center for Asian Studies at the University of Amsterdam. I am grateful to the audiences on each of these occasions for their probing questions and useful criticisms.

2   Here, I am delighted to heed a call by Fredrik Barth, whose own work on ethnic groups and boundaries (1969) remains a classic study of the social context of ethnic processes, for more studies of the relationship between globalization and the mobilization of ethnic identity (Barth 1995). For an early and prescient effort to link ethnicity to the international order, see Enloe 1986.

3   In many ways, this chapter is a dialogue with the important collection edited by Clifford Geertz, *Old Societies and New States: The Quest for Modernity in Asia and Africa*

(1963). Produced under the auspices of the Committee for the Comparative Study of New Nations at the University of Chicago, this volume contains essays by sociologists, anthropologists, and political scientists and represents a major moment of cross-disciplinary interaction on the subject of modernization. Deeply influenced by the heritage of Max Weber and the subsequent efforts of Edward Shils and Talcott Parsons to interpret Weber in the United States, the essays in the collection generally represent a positive enthusiasm about modernization that I do not share. Some of the essays also subscribe to the sense of a primordialist substrate in Asian and African societies that is the direct target of my critical remarks in this chapter. Other contributions, notably the one by Clifford Geertz, are careful to note that what appear to be the primordia of social life—language, race, kinship—are just that, appearances. Geertz sees them as part of the rhetoric of nature, of history and roots to which many politicians in the new states appealed. The primordialist view still has widespread currency. One example among many, more than two decades after the appearance of the Geertz volume, is *The Primordial Challenge: Ethnicity in the Contemporary World* (1986), edited by John Stack. It shows the sturdiness of the idea of the primordial as a fact, not just an appearance or a trope, in the social life of ethnic groups.

4 This theory of the extreme violence now frequently associated with ethnic clashes is adumbrated in the most preliminary of forms here. In developing it, I have relied on a variety of sources and interpretations. Notable among these have been Benedict Anderson's specific formulations about racism and violence in *Imagined Communities* (1983). The work of Ashis Nandy and Veena Das on communal violence in South Asia in the past decade (in Das 1990) and Das's most recent work on Sikh militant discourse in India since the late 1970s (1995) have given me valuable insights into the ways in which violence is localized, narrativized, and personalized. Finally, a chilling essay by Donald Sutton (1995) on cannibalism among counterrevolutionary peasants in China in 1968 offers a powerful glimpse into the ways in which the most extreme forms of political violence can be linked to state-level politics and policies. Liisa Malkki's brilliant ethnography about Hutu refugees in Tanzania (1995) has been a painful inspiration. Taken together, these works (and many others) lend support to the idea that brutal damage to the embodied Other (as instanced in the bodies of Others) is closely tied up with the link between individual identities and extralocal labels and categories. The full development of this argument about rage, betrayal, state-sponsored categories, and intimate knowledge of persons must await another occasion. Sherry Ortner is responsible for persuading me that this chapter as well as this book needed some serious engagement with the topic of ethnic violence.

5 I should note here that my view should not be strictly identified with a statecentered perspective on contemporary ethnic violence. I am sympathetic to the general argument of Robert Desjarlais and Albert Kleinman (1994) that not all contemporary violence can be attributed to the violent disciplinary techniques of the modern nation-state. There is certainly a great deal of uncertainty and anomie that feeds the worst scenes of ethnic violence in the world. This notion of uncertainty, rather than knowledge, as characterizing the moral economy of violence certainly needs systematic exploration. For the moment, it is worth noting that even in those situations in which moral disorder, epistemological breakdown, and social uncer-

tainty are rampant, the facts of violence often show the remarkable salience of state-sponsored techniques of identification and politically staged dramas of uncertainty, scapegoating, and exposure (see, for example, de Waal 1994 on the genocide in Rwanda).

CHAPTER 8. PATRIOTISM AND ITS FUTURES

1   Earlier versions of this essay were presented at the Center for the Critical Analysis of Contemporary Culture at Rutgers University, at the Center for Transcultural Studies (Chicago), and at the University of Chicago.
2   See the convergence between this proposal and the argument from the Chicago Cultural Studies Group (1992, 537).
3   I am grateful to Philip Scher, who introduced me to the term *transnation*.

CHAPTER 9. THE PRODUCTION OF LOCALITY

1   There is no ideal way to designate localities as actual social forms. Terms such as *place, site, locale* all have their strengths and weaknesses. The term *neighborhood* (apart from its use in avoiding the confusion between locality as the singular form of localities and locality as property or dimension of social life) also has the virtue that it suggests sociality, immediacy, and reproducibility without any necessary implications for scale, specific modes of connectivity, internal homogeneity, or sharp boundaries. This sense of neighborhood can also accommodate images such as circuit and border zone, which have been argued to be preferable to such images as community and center-periphery, especially where transnational migration is involved (Rouse 1991). Nevertheless, it carries the burden of co-opting a colloquial term for technical use.
2   This critique is entirely consistent with (and partly inspired by) Johannes Fabian's critique of the denial of coevalness in ethnography and the resulting creation of a fictive time of and for the Other (1983). Yet this essay does not take up the vexed question of the relationship between the coproduction of space and time in ethnographic practice, nor the debate (see below) over whether space and time tend to cannibalize each other in modern, capitalist societies. The present argument about locality is in part intended to open up the question of time and temporality in the production of locality. I am grateful to Pieter Pels for reminding me that the production of temporality is equally relevant to how ethnography and locality have historically produced one another.
3   At this point, my view of localization converges with the general argument of Henri Lefebvre (1991), although he stresses the relationship of capitalism and modernity to this negative sense of localization. Lefebvre's own account of the nation-state is brief and cryptic, although it is clear that he also saw the links between the presuppositions of the modern nation-state and the capitalist process of localization. The question of how my argument might relate to those of Lefebvre (1991) and Harvey (1989), although important, exceeds the scope of this chapter.

Bibliography

Abu-Lughod, L. (1989) *Before European Hegemony: The World System A.D. 1250–1350*. New York: Oxford University Press.

———. (1991) Writing against Culture. In R. Fox (Ed.) *Recapturing Anthropology: Working in the Present*. Santa Fe: School of American Research.

Ahmad, A. (1987) Jameson's Rhetoric of Otherness and the "National Allegory," *Social Text* 17: 3–25.

Ali, S. M. (1981) *Cricket Delightful*. Delhi: Rupa.

Allen, D. R. (1985) *Cricket on the Air*. London: British Broadcasting Corporation.

Amin, S. (1980) *Class and Nation: Historically and in the Current Crisis*. New York and London: Monthly Review Press.

———. (1984) Gandhi as Mahatma: Gorakhpur District, Eastern UP, 1921–2. In Ranajit Guha (Ed.) *Subaltern Studies: Writings on South Asian History and Society*, vol. 3. Delhi and London: Oxford University Press.

Anderson, B. (1983) *Imagined Communities: Reflections on the Origin and Spread of Nationalism*. London: Verso.

———. (1991) Census, Map, Museum. In his *Imagined Communities* (rev. edition). New York and London: Verso.

———. (1994) Exodus, *Critical Inquiry* 20 (2): 314–27.

Appadurai, A. (1981) *Worship and Conflict under Colonial Rule*. New York: Cambridge University Press.

———. (Ed.) (1986) Commodities and the Politics of Value. In his *The Social Life of Things: Commodities in Cultural Perspective*. Cambridge: Cambridge University Press.

———. (1988) Putting Hierarchy in Its Place, *Cultural Anthropology* 3 (1, February): 37–50.

———. (1990) Topographies of the Self: Praise and Emotion in Hindu India. In C. A. Lutz and L. Abu-Lughod (Eds.) *Language and the Politics of Emotion*. Cambridge: Cambridge University Press.

Appadurai, A., and C. A. Breckenridge. (1991a) Marriage, Migration and Money: Mira Nair's Cinema of Displacement, *Visual Anthropology* 4 (1, Spring): 95–102.

———. (1991b) Museums Are Good to Think: Heritage on View in India. In I. Karp, S. Levine, and T. Ybarra-Frausto (Eds.) *Museums and Their Communities: The Politics of Public Culture.* Washington, D.C.: Smithsonian Institution Press.

———. (1995) Public Modernity in India. In C.A. Breckenridge (Ed.) *Consuming Modernity: Public Culture in a South Asian World.* Minneapolis: University of Minnesota Press.

Apter, D. E. (1965) *The Politics of Modernization.* Chicago: University of Chicago Press.

Armstrong, N. (1990) The Occidental Alice, *Differences: A Journal of Feminist Cultural Studies* 2 (2): 3–40.

Arnason, J. P. (1990) Nationalism, Globalization and Modernity, *Theory, Culture and Society* 7 (2–3, June): 207–36.

Arnold, D. (1988) Touching the Body: Perspectives on the Indian Plague. In R. Guha and G. C. Spivak (Eds.) *Selected Subaltern Studies.* New York and Oxford: Oxford University Press.

Asad, T. (1983) Notes on Body, Pain and Truth in Medieval Christian Rituals, *Economy and Society* 12: 285–327.

Balibar, E. (1991) The Nation Form: History and Ideology. In E. Balibar and I. Wallerstein (Eds.) *Race, Nation, Class: Ambiguous Identities.* London and New York: Verso.

Balibar, E., and I. Wallerstein. (Eds.) (1991) *Race, Nation, Class: Ambiguous Identities.* London and New York: Verso.

Barber, K. (1987) Popular Arts in Africa, *African Studies Review* 30 (3, September): 1–78.

Barrier, G. N. (Ed.) (1981) *The Census in British India: New Perspectives.* New Delhi: Manohar.

Barth, F. (Ed.) (1969) *Ethnic Groups and Boundaries.* Boston: Little, Brown.

———. (1995) Redefining the Domains of Anthropological Discourse. Presented at the University of Chicago, 9 October.

Baruah, S. (1986) Immigration, Ethnic Conflict and Political Turmoil, Assam 1979–1985, *Asian Survey* 26 (11, November): 1184–1206.

Basch, L., N. Glick Schiller, C. Szanton Blanc, et al. (1994) *Nations Unbound: Transnational Projects, Postcolonial Predicaments, and Deterritorialized Nation-States.* Langhorne, Pa., and Reading, U.K.: Gordon and Breach.

Baudrillard, J. (1975) *The Mirror of Production.* St. Louis: Telos Press.

Bauman, R., and C. L. Briggs. (1990) Poetics and Performance as Critical Perspectives on Language and Social Life, *Annual Review of Anthropology* 19: 59–88.

Bayly, C. A. (1986) The Origins of Swadeshi (Home Industry): Cloth and Indian Society, 1700–1930. In A. Appadurai (Ed.) *The Social Life of Things: Commodities in Cultural Perspective.* Cambridge: Cambridge University Press.

———. (1988) *Indian Society and the Making of the British Empire.* New Cambridge History of India, II, 1. Cambridge: Cambridge University Press.

———. (1989) *Imperial Meridian: The British Empire and the World, 1780–1830.* London and New York: Longman.

Benjamin, W. ([1936] 1969) The Work of Art in the Age of Mechanical Reproduction. In H. Arendt (Ed.) *Illuminations.* H. Zohn (Trans.) New York: Schocken Books.

Berlant, L. (1991) *The Anatomy of National Fantasy: Hawthorne, Utopia, and Everyday Life.* Chicago and London: University of Chicago Press.

Berlant, L., and E. Freeman (1992) Queer Nationality, *Boundary* 2 19 (1): 149–80.

Bhabha, H. K. (Ed.) (1990) *Nation and Narration.* London and New York: Routledge.

———. (1994) *The Location of Culture*. London and New York: Routledge.

Bhattacharjee, A. (1992) The Habit of Ex-nomination: Nation, Woman and the Indian Immigrant Bourgeoisie, *Public Culture* 5 (1): 19–44.

Birbalsingh, F. (1986) Indo-Caribbean Test Cricketers, *Toronto South Asian Review* 5 (1): 105–17.

Black Public Sphere Collective (1995) The Black Public Sphere: A Public Culture Book. Chicago: University of Chicago Press.

Bloch, M. (1986) *From Blessing to Violence: History and Ideology in the Circumcision Ritual of the Merina of Madagascar*. Cambridge: Cambridge University Press.

Bondurant, J. V. (1958) *Conquest of Violence: The Gandhian Philosophy of Conflict*. Princeton, N.J.: Princeton University Press.

Borneman, J. (1992) *Belonging in the Two Berlins: Kin, State, Nation*. Cambridge: Cambridge University Press.

Bourdieu, P. (1977) *Outline of a Theory of Practice*. Cambridge: Cambridge University Press.

———. (1984) *Distinction: A Social Critique of the Judgement of Taste*. Cambridge, Mass.: Harvard University Press.

Brass, P. R. (1994) *The Politics of India since Independence*. Cambridge: Cambridge University Press.

Braudel, F. (1981–1984) *Civilization and Capitalism, 15th–18th Century* (3 Vols.). London: Collins.

Breckenridge, C. A. (Ed.) (1983) Number Use in the Vijayanagara Era. Presented at the Conference on the Kingdom of Vijayanagar, the South Asia Institute, University of Heidelberg, Heidelberg, July 14–17, 1983.

———. (1989) The Aesthetics and Politics of Colonial Collecting: India at World Fairs, *Comparative Studies in Society and History* 31 (2): 195–216.

———. (1995) (Ed.) *Consuming Modernity: Public Culture in a South Asian World*. Minneapolis: University of Minnesota Press.

Breckenridge, C. A., and Peter van der Veer (Eds.). (1993) *Orientalism and the Postcolonial Predicament: Perspectives on a South Asian World*. Philadelphia: University of Pennsylvania Press.

Brewer, J. (1989) *The Sinews of Power: War, Money, and the English State, 1688–1783*. New York: Knopf.

Calhoun, C. (Ed.) (1992) *Habermas and the Public Sphere*. Cambridge, Mass., and London: MIT Press.

Campbell, C. (1987) *The Romantic Ethic and the Spirit of Modern Consumerism*. Oxford: Basil Blackwell.

Canguilheim, G. (1989) *The Normal and the Pathological*. New York: Zone Books.

Carrithers, M., S. Collins, and S. Lukes (Eds.) (1985) *The Category of the Person*. Cambridge: Cambridge University Press.

Cashman, R. (1980) *Patrons, Players and the Crowd: The Phenomenon of Indian Cricket*. New Delhi: Orient Longman.

Castoriadis, C. ([1975] 1987) *The Imaginary Institution of Society*. Cambridge, Mass.: MIT Press.

Chakrabarty, D. (1983) Conditions for Knowledge of Working-Class Conditions: Employers, Government and the Jute Workers of Calcutta, 1890–1940. In R. Guha and G. C. Spivak (Eds.) *Selected Subaltern Studies*. New York and Oxford: Oxford University Press.

Chatterjee, P. (1986) *Nationalist Thought and the Colonial World: A Derivative Discourse?* London: Zed Books.

———. (1993) *The Nation and Its Fragments: Colonial and Postcolonial Histories.* Princeton, N.J.: Princeton University Press.

Chicago Cultural Studies Group (1992) Critical Multiculturalism, *Critical Inquiry* 18 (3): 530–55.

Clarke, A., and J. Clarke (1982) "Highlights and Action Replays": Ideology, Sport and the Media. In J. Hargreaves (Ed.) *Sport, Culture and Ideology.* London: Routledge and Kegan Paul.

Clifford, J., and G. E. Marcus (Eds.) (1986) *Writing Culture: The Poetics and Politics of Ethnography.* Berkeley: University of California Press.

Cohn, B. S. (1969) Structural Change in Indian Rural Society. In R. E. Frykenberg (Ed.) *Land Control and Social Structure in Indian History.* Madison: University of Wisconsin Press.

———. (1987) The Census, Social Structure and Objectification in South Asia. In *An Anthropologist among the Historians and Other Essays.* Delhi and London: Oxford University Press.

Comaroff, J., and J. L. Comaroff (1992a) The Madman and the Migrant. In *Ethnography and the Historical Imagination.* Boulder, Colo.: Westview Press.

———. (1992b) Of Totemism and Ethnicity. In *Ethnography and the Historical Imagination.* Boulder, Colo.: Westview Press.

Cooper, F., and A. L. Stoler (1989) Tensions of Empire and Visions of Rule, *American Ethnologist* 16 (4): 609–21.

Corbin, A. (1986) *The Foul and the Fragrant: Odor and the French Social Imagination.* Cambridge, Mass.: Harvard University Press.

Cortázar, J. (1984) *A Certain Lucas.* G. Rabassa (Trans.) New York: Knopf.

Crane, D. (1972) *Invisible Colleges.* Chicago: University of Chicago Press.

Curtin, P. (1984) *Cross-Cultural Trade in World History.* Cambridge: Cambridge University Press.

Das, Veena (Ed.) (1990) *Mirrors of Violence: Communities, Riots and Survivors in South Asia.* Delhi and New York: Oxford University Press.

———. (1995) *Critical Events: An Anthropological Perspective on Contemporary India.* Delhi: Oxford University Press.

de Certeau, M. (1984) *The Practice of Everyday Life.* Berkeley and London: University of California Press.

Deleuze, G., and F. Guattari (1987) *A Thousand Plateaus: Capitalism and Schizophrenia.* B. Massumi (Trans.) Minneapolis: University of Minnesota Press.

de Mellow, M. (1979) *Reaching for Excellence: The Glory and Decay of Sport in India.* New Delhi and Ludhiana: Kalyani.

Desjarlais, R., and A. Kleinman. (1994) Violence and Demoralization in the New World Disorder, *Anthropology Today* 10 (5): 9–12.

de Waal, A. (1994) Genocide in Rwanda, *Anthropology Today* 10 (3): 1–2.

Diawara, M. (1990) Englishness and Blackness: Cricket as Discourse on Colonialism, *Callaloo* 13 (2): 830–44.

Dirks, N. B. (1987) *The Hollow Crown: Ethnohistory of an Indian Kingdom.* Cambridge: Cambridge University Press.

———. (1989) The Policing of Tradition in Colonial South India. Presented at the Ethnohistory Workshop, University of Pennsylvania, Philadelphia, 1989.

Docker, E. (1976) *History of Indian Cricket*. Delhi: Macmillan.

Douglas, M. (1967) Primitive Rationing. In R. Firth (Ed.) *Themes in Economic Anthropology*. London: Tavistock.

Douglas, M., and B. Isherwood (1981) *The World of Goods*. New York: Basic Books.

Duranti, A., and Goodwin, C. (1992) *Language as an Interactive Phenomenon*. Cambridge: Cambridge University Press.

Elias, N. ([1939] 1978) *The Civilizing Process*, vol. 1. E. Jephcott (Trans.) Oxford: Basil Blackwell.

Elias, N., and E. Dunning (1986) *Quest for Excitement: Sport and Leisure in the Civilizing Process*. Oxford: Basil Blackwell.

Enloe, C. (1986) Ethnicity, the State, and the New International Order. In J. F. Stack (Ed.) *The Primordial Challenge: Ethnicity in the Contemporary World*. New York: Greenwood Press.

Ewald, F. (1986) *L'Etat Providence*. Paris: B. Grasset.

Fabian, J. (1983) *Time and the Other: How Anthropology Makes Its Object*. New York: Columbia University Press.

Featherstone, M. (1990) *Global Culture: Nationalism, Globalization and Identity*. London and Newbury Park, Calif.: Sage.

Feld, S. (1988) Notes on World Beat, *Public Culture* 1 (1): 31–37.

Felman, S. (1989) Narrative as Testimony: Camus' *The Plague*. In J. Phelan (Ed.) *Reading Narrative: Form, Ethics, Ideology*. Columbus: Ohio State University Press.

Foster, R. J. (1991) Making National Cultures in the Global Ecumene, *Annual Review of Anthropology* 20: 235–60.

Fraser, N. (1992) Rethinking the Public Sphere: A Contribution to the Critique of Actually Existing Democracy. In C. Calhoun (Ed.) *Habermas and the Public Sphere*. Cambridge, Mass., and London: MIT Press.

Frazer, J. G. (1900) *The Golden Bough: A Study in Magic and Religion*. London: Macmillan.

Freitag, S. (1989) *Collective Action and Community: Public Arenas in the Emergence of Communalism in North India*. Berkeley: University of California Press.

———. (1990) Letter to author.

Friedman, J. (1990) Being in the World: Globalization and Localization. In M. Featherstone (Ed.) *Global Culture*. London: Sage.

Frykenberg, R. E. (1977) The Silent Settlement in South India, 1793–1853: An Analysis of the Role of Inams in the Rise of the Indian Imperial System. In R. E. Frykenberg (Ed.) *Land Tenure and Peasant in South Asia*. New Delhi: Orient Longman.

———. (1987) The Concept of "Majority" as a Devilish Force in the Politics of Modern India: A Historiographic Comment, *Journal of the Commonwealth History and Comparative Politics* 25 (3, November): 267–74.

Gans, E. (1985) *The End of a Culture: Toward a Generative Anthropology*. Berkeley: University of California Press.

Geertz, C. (1963) *Old Societies and New States: The Quest for Modernity in Asia and Africa*. New York: Free Press.

———. (1973) Ritual and Social Change: A Javanese Example. In *The Interpretation of Cultures*. New York: Basic Books.

———. (1975) Common Sense as a Cultural System, *Antioch Review* 33: 5–26.

———. (1980) Blurred Genres: The Refiguration of Social Thought, *American Scholar* 49: 125–59.

————. (1983) *Local Knowledge*. New York: Basic Books.

————. (1988) *Works and Lives: The Anthropologist as Author*. Stanford, Calif.: Stanford University Press.

Gellner, E. (1983) *Nations and Nationalism*. Ithaca, N.Y.: Cornell University Press.

Giddens, A. (1979) *Central Problems in Social Theory: Action, Structure and Contradiction in Social Analysis*. Berkeley: University of California Press.

Ginsburg, F. (1993) Aboriginal Media and the Australian Imaginary, *Public Culture* 5 (3): 557–78.

Goffman, E. (1951) Symbols of Class Status, *British Journal of Sociology* 2 (December): 294–304.

Government of Maharashtra (1975) *The Joint Report of 1847: Measurement and Classification Rules of the Deccan, Gujerat, Konkan and Kanara Surveys*. Nagpur: Government Press.

Guha, R. (1983) The Prose of Counter-Insurgency. In R. Guha (Ed.) *Subaltern Studies: Writings on South Asian History and Society*, vol. 2. New Delhi and London: Oxford University Press.

Gupta, A., and J. Ferguson (1992) Beyond "Culture": Space, Identity, and the Politics of Difference, *Cultural Anthropology* 7 (1, February): 6–23.

Habermas, J. (1989) *The Structural Transformation of the Public Sphere*. Cambridge, Mass.: MIT Press.

Habib, I. (1963) *The Agrarian System of Mughal India (1556–1707)*. Bombay and London: Asia Publishing House.

————. (1982) *An Atlas of the Mughal Empire: Political and Economic Maps*. Delhi and New York: Oxford University Press.

Hacking, I. (1975) *The Emergence of Probability: A Philosophical Study of Early Ideas about Probability, Induction and Statistical Inference*. Cambridge and New York: Cambridge University Press.

————. (1982) Biopower and the Avalanche of Printed Numbers, *Humanities in Society* 5 (3–4, Summer and Fall): 279–95.

————. (1986) Making Up People. In T. C. Heller, M. Sosna, and D. E. Willbery (Eds.) *Reconstructing Individualism: Autonomy, Individuality, and the Self in Western Thought*. Stanford, Calif.: Stanford University Press.

Halbwachs, M. ([1950] 1980) *The Collective Memory*. New York: Harper & Row.

Hall, S. (1986) Cultural Studies: Two Paradigms. In R. Collins et al. (Eds.) *Media, Culture, and Society: A Critical Reader*. London: Sage.

Hamelink, C. (1983) *Cultural Autonomy in Global Communications*. New York: Longman.

Handler, R. (1988) *Nationalism and the Politics of Culture in Quebec*. Madison: University of Wisconsin Press.

Hanif, M. (1995) City of Death, *India Today*, 15 July, 34–41.

Hanks, W. F. (1989) Text and Textuality, *Annual Review of Anthropology* 18: 95–127.

Hannerz, U. (1987) The World in Creolization, *Africa* 57 (4): 546–59.

————. (1989) Notes on the Global Ecumene, *Public Culture* 1 (2, Spring): 66–75.

————. (1992) *Cultural Complexity: Studies in the Social Organization of Meaning*. New York: Columbia University Press.

Hansen, M. (1991) *Babel and Babylon: Spectatorship in American Silent Film*. Cambridge, Mass.: Harvard University Press.

————. (1993) Unstable Mixtures, Dilated Spheres: Negt and Kluge's *The Public Sphere and Experience*, Twenty Years Later, *Public Culture* 5 (2, Winter): 179–212.

Hargreaves, J. (Ed.) (1982) *Sport, Culture and Ideology*. London: Routledge and Kegan Paul.

Harvey, D. (1989) *The Condition of Postmodernity: An Enquiry into the Origins of Cultural Change*. Cambridge, Mass.: Basil Blackwell.

Hasan, M. (1979) *Nationalism and Communal Politics in India, 1916–1928*. New Delhi: Manohar.

Hazare, V. (1976) *Cricket Replayed*. Bombay: Rupa.

——. (1981) *A Long Innings*. Bombay: Rupa.

Hebdige, D. (1979) *Subculture: The Meaning of Style*. London and New York: Routledge.

Hechter, M. (1975) *Internal Colonialism: The Celtic Fringe in British National Development, 1536–1966*. Berkeley: University of California Press.

Helms, M. W. (1988) *Ulysses' Sail: An Ethnographic Odyssey of Power, Knowledge, and Geographical Distance*. Princeton, N.J.: Princeton University Press.

Herzfeld, M. (1982) *Ours Once More: Folklore, Ideology and the Making of Modern Greece*. Austin: University of Texas Press.

Hinkson, J. (1990) Postmodernism and Structural Change, *Public Culture* 2 (2, Spring): 82–101.

Hirschman, A. O. (1970) *Exit, Voice and Loyalty: Responses to Decline in Firms, Organizations and States*. Cambridge, Mass.: Harvard University Press.

Hobsbawm, E. (1992) Ethnicity and Nationalism in Europe Today, *Anthropology Today* 8 (1): 3–8.

——. (1990) *Nations and Nationalism since 1780: Programme, Myth and Reality*. Cambridge: Cambridge University Press.

Hobsbawm, E., and T. Ranger (Eds.) (1983) *The Invention of Tradition*. New York: Columbia University Press.

Hodgson, M. (1974) *The Venture of Islam, Conscience and History in a World Civilization*. (3 vols.) Chicago: University of Chicago Press.

Huizinga, J. ([1944] 1950) *Homo Ludens: A Study of the Play-Element in Culture*. New York: Roy.

Hutchins, F. G. (1967) *The Illusion of Permanence: British Imperialism in India*. Princeton, N.J.: Princeton University Press.

Hymes, D. H. (1969) *Reinventing Anthropology*. New York: Pantheon.

——. (1974) *Foundations in Sociolinguistics: An Ethnographic Perspective*. Philadelphia: University of Pennsylvania Press.

Inden, R. B. (1990) *Imagining India*. Oxford and Cambridge, Mass.: Basil Blackwell.

Isaacs, H. (1975) *Idols of the Tribe: Group Identity and Political Change*. New York: Harper & Row.

Ivy, M. (1988) Tradition and Difference in the Japanese Mass Media, *Public Culture* 1 (1): 21–29.

——. (1989) Critical Texts, Mass Artifacts: The Consumption of Knowledge in Postmodern Japan. In M. Miyoshi and H. D. Harootunian (Eds.) *Postmodernism and Japan*. Durham, N.C.: Duke University Press.

——. (1995) *Discourses of the Vanishing: Modernity, Phantasm, Japan*. Chicago: University of Chicago Press.

Iyer, P. (1988) *Video Night in Kathmandu*. New York: Knopf.

James, C. L. R. (1963) *Beyond a Boundary*. London: Stanley Paul.

Jameson, F. (1983) Postmodernism and Consumer Society. In H. Foster (Ed.) *The Anti-Aesthetic: Essays on Postmodern Culture*. Port Townsend, Wash.: Bay Press, 111–25.

————. (1986) Third World Literature in the Era of Multi-National Capitalism, *Social Text* 15 (Fall): 65–88.

————. (1989) Nostalgia for the Present, *South Atlantic Quarterly* 88 (2, Spring): 517–37.

————. ([1979] 1990) Reification and Utopia in Mass Culture. In *Signatures of the Visible*. New York and London: Routledge.

Johnson, R. (1986) What Is Cultural Studies Anyway? *Social Text* 16: 38–80.

Kang, S.-Y., J. MacAloon, and R. DaMatta (Eds.) (1988) *The Olympics and Cultural Exchange*. Seoul: Hanyang University, Institute for Ethnological Studies.

Kapferer, B. (1988) *Legends of People, Myths of State*. Washington, D.C.: Smithsonian Institution Press.

Kaviraj, S. (1994) On the Construction of Colonial Power. In D. Engels and S. Marks (Eds.) *Contesting Colonial Hegemony: State and Society in Africa and India*. London and New York: I. B. Tauris.

Kelly, W. (1990) Japanese No-Noh: The Crosstalk of Public Culture in a Rural Festivity, *Public Culture* 2 (2): 65–81.

Keohane, R. (Ed.) (1986) *Neo-Realism and Its Critics*. New York: Columbia University Press.

King, A. (1991) *Culture, Globalization and the World-System: Contemporary Conditions for the Representation of Identity*. Basingstoke: Macmillan Education.

Kopytoff, I. (1986) The Cultural Biography of Things: Commoditization as Process. In A. Appadurai (Ed.) *The Social Life of Things*. Cambridge: Cambridge University Press.

Kothari, R. (1989a) Communalism: The New Face of Indian Democracy. In *State against Democracy: In Search of Humane Governance*. Delhi: Ajanta Publications; New York: New Horizon Press.

————. (1989b) Ethnicity. In *Rethinking Development: In Search of Humane Alternatives*. Delhi: Ajanta Publications; New York: New Horizon Press.

————. (1989c) *State against Democracy: In Search of Humane Governance*. New York: New Horizons.

Kotkin, J. (1993) *Tribes: How Race, Religion, and Identity Determine Success in the New Global Economy*. New York: Random House.

Laclau, E., and C. Mouffe (1985) *Hegemony and Socialist Strategy*. London: Verso.

Lakoff, G., and M. Johnson (1980) *Metaphors We Live By*. Chicago and London: University of Chicago Press.

Lash, S., and J. Urry (1987) *The End of Organized Capitalism*. Madison: University of Wisconsin Press.

Lawton, R. (Ed.) (1978) *The Census and Social Structure: An Interpretive Guide to Nineteenth Century Censuses for England and Wales*. London and Totowa, N.J.: F. Cass.

Lee, B. (1993) Going Public, *Public Culture* 5 (2): 165–78.

Lefebvre, H. (1991) *The Production of Space*. Cambridge, Mass., and Oxford, U.K.: Blackwell.

Lefort, C. (1986) *The Political Forms of Modern Society: Bureaucracy, Democracy, Totalitarianism*. Cambridge, Mass.: MIT Press.

Lewis, G. (1986) The Look of Magic, *Man* 21 (3): 414–37.

Ludden, D. E. (1988) Agrarian Commercialism in Eighteenth Century South India: Evidence from the 1823 Tirunelveli Census, *Indian Economic and Social History Review* 25(4): 493–519.

————. (1991) Conversation with author, Philadelphia.

————. (1993) Orientalist Empiricism: Transformations of Colonial Knowledge. In C. A. Breckenridge and P. van der Veer (Eds.) *Orientalism and the Postcolonial Predicament: Perspectives on South Asia.* Philadelphia: University of Pennsylvania Press.

Lutz, C. A., and L. Abu-Lughod (Eds.) (1990) *Language and the Politics of Emotion.* Cambridge: Cambridge University Press.

MacAloon, J. (1981) *This Great Symbol: Pierre de Coubertin and the Origins of the Modern Olympic Games.* Chicago: University of Chicago Press.

————. (1984) *Rite, Drama, Festival and Spectacle.* Philadelphia: Institute for the Study of Human Issues.

————. (1990) Steroids and the State: Dubin, Melodrama and the Accomplishment of Innocence, *Public Culture* 2 (2): 41–64.

Malinowski, B. ([1922] 1950) *Argonauts of the Western Pacific.* New York: E. P. Dutton.

Malkki, L. H. (1995) *Purity and Exile: Violence, Memory and National Cosmology among Hutu Refugees in Tanzania.* Chicago: University of Chicago Press.

Mandel, E. (1978) *Late Capitalism.* London: Verso.

Mani, L. (1990) Contentious Traditions: The Debate on *Sati* in Colonial India. In K. Sangari and S. Vaid (Eds.) *Recasting Women: Essays in Colonial History.* New Delhi: Kali for Women.

Marcus, G., and M. Fischer (1986) *Anthropology as Cultural Critique: An Experimental Moment in the Human Sciences.* Chicago: University of Chicago Press.

Marshall, T. (1987) It's Now Cricket to Play Hardball, *This World* November 22.

Martin, E. (1992) The End of the Body? *American Ethnologist* 19 (1): 121–40.

Mattelart, A. (1983) *Transnationals and the Third World: The Struggle for Culture.* South Hadley, Mass.: Bergin and Garvey.

Mauss, M. (1973) Techniques of the Body, *Economy and Society* 2 (1): 70–85.

————. ([1923] 1976) *The Gift.* New York: Norton.

Mbembe, A. (1992) The Banality of Power and the Aesthetics of Vulgarity in the Postcolony, *Public Culture* 4 (2): 1–30.

Mbembe, A., et al. (1992) Belly-up: More on the Postcolony, *Public Culture* 5 (1, Special Section): 46–145.

McCracken, G. D. (1988) *Culture and Consumption: New Approaches to the Symbolic Character of Consumer Goods and Activities.* Bloomington: Indiana University Press.

McKendrick, N., N. J. Brewer, and J. H. Plumb (1982) *The Birth of a Consumer Society: The Commercialization of Eighteenth-Century England.* Bloomington: Indiana University Press.

McLuhan M., and B. R. Powers. (1989) *The Global Village: Transformations in World, Life and Media in the 21st Century.* New York: Oxford University Press.

McQueen, H. (1988) The Australian Stamp: Image, Design and Ideology, *Arena* 84 (Spring): 78–96.

Meyrowitz, J. (1985) *No Sense of Place: The Impact of Electronic Media on Social Behavior.* New York: Oxford University Press.

Miller, D. (1987) *Material Culture and Mass Consumption.* London: Basil Blackwell.

Miller, M. (1981) *The Bon Marche: Bourgeois Culture and the Department Store, 1869–1920.* Princeton, N.J.: Princeton University Press.

Mintz, S. W. (1985) *Sweetness and Power.* New York: Viking-Penguin.

Mitra, A. (1986) Cricket Frenzy Unites a Dishevelled Subcontinent, *Far Eastern Economic Review* (July 10): 48–49.

Money, J. (1989) Teaching in the Marketplace, or Caesar Adsum Jam Forte Pompey

Aderat: The Retailing of Knowledge in Provincial England. Presented at Clark Library, UCLA, March 4.

Moore, S. F. (1993) *Moralizing States and the Ethnography of the Present*. Arlington, Va.: American Anthropological Association.

Mukerji, C. (1983) *From Graven Images: Patterns of Modern Materialism*. New York: Columbia University Press.

Mulvey, L. (1975) Visual Pleasure and Narrative Cinema, *Screen* 16 (3): 6–18.

Munn, N. D. (1986) *The Fame of Gawa: A Symbolic Study of Value Transformation in a Massim (Papua New Guinea) Society*. Cambridge: Cambridge University Press.

Nandy, A. (1983) *The Intimate Enemy: Loss and Recovery of Self under Colonialism*. Delhi: Oxford University Press.

———. (1987) *Traditions, Tyranny and Utopias*. Delhi: Oxford University Press.

———. (1989a) The Political Culture of the Indian State, *Daedalus* 118 (4): 1–26.

———. (1989b) *The Tao of Cricket: On Games of Destiny and the Destiny of Games*. New York: Viking.

Neale, W. C. (1969) Land Is to Rule. In R. E. Frykenberg (Ed.) *Land Control and Social Structure in Indian History*. Madison: University of Wisconsin Press.

Nicoll, F. (1989) My Trip to Alice, *Criticism, Heresy and Interpretation* 3: 21–32.

Nigam, S. (1990) Disciplining and Policing the "Criminals by Birth," Part 2: The Development of a Disciplinary System, 1871–1900, *Indian Economic and Social History Review* 27 (3, July–September): 257–87.

Ortner, S. B. (1991) Reading America: Preliminary Notes on Class and Culture. In R. Fox (Ed.) *Recapturing Anthropology: Working in the Present*. Santa Fe, N.M.: School of American Research.

Pandey, G. (1990) *The Construction of Communalism in Colonial North India*. New Delhi and London: Oxford University Press.

Pant, R. (1987) The Cognitive Status of Caste in Colonial Ethnography: A Review of Some Literature of the North West Provinces and Oudh, *Indian Economic and Social History Review* 24 (2): 145–62.

Parfit, D. (1986) *Reasons and Persons*. Oxford: Clarendon Press.

Parkin, D. (1978) *The Cultural Definition of Political Response*. London: Academic Press.

Perlin, F. (1983) Proto-Industrialization and Pre-Colonial South Asia, *Past and Present* 98 (30): 94.

———. (1987) Money-Use in Late Pre-Colonial India and the International Trade in Currency Media. In J. F. Richards (Ed.) *The Imperial Monetary System of Mughal India*. Delhi: Oxford University Press.

Pitkin, H. F. (1967) *The Concept of Representation*. Berkeley and Los Angeles: University of California Press.

Prakash, G. (1990) Bonded Histories: Genealogies of Labor Servitude in Colonial India. *South Asian Studies* 44. Cambridge and New York: Cambridge University Press.

Presler, F. A. (1987) *Religion under Bureaucracy: Policy and Administration for Hindu Temples in South India*. Cambridge and New York: Cambridge University Press.

Preston, L. W. (1989) *The Devs of Cincvad: A Lineage and the State in Maharashtra*. Cambridge and New York: Cambridge University Press.

Puri, N. (1982) Sports versus Cricket. *India International Centre Quarterly* 9 (2): 146–54.

Rabinow, P. (1986) Representations are Social Facts: Modernity and Post-modernity in

Anthropology. In J. Clifford and G. Marcus (Eds.) *Writing Culture: The Poetics and Politics of Ethnography*. Berkeley: University of California Press.

———. (1989) *French Modern: Norms and Forms of the Social Environment*. Cambridge, Mass.: MIT Press.

Raiji, V. (1976) *L. P. Jai: Memories of a Great Batsman*. Bombay: Tyeby.

Robbins, B. (Ed.) (1993) *The Phantom Public Sphere*. Minneapolis: University of Minnesota Press.

Roberts, M. (1985) Ethnicity in Riposte at a Cricket Match: The Past for the Present, *Comparative Studies in Society and History* 27: 401–29.

Robertson, R. (1990) Mapping the Global Condition: Globalization as the Central Concept, *Theory, Culture and Society* 7 (2–3, June): 15–30.

———. (1992) *Globalization: Social Theory and Global Culture*. Newbury Park, Calif., and London: Sage.

Robinson, F. (1974) *Separatism among Indian Muslims: The Politics of the United Provinces' Muslims, 1860–1923*. London and New York: Cambridge University Press.

Rojek, C. (1987) *Capitalism and Leisure Theory*. London: Tavistock.

Rosaldo, R. (1989) *Culture and Truth: The Remaking of Social Analysis*. Boston: Beacon Press.

Rosenau, J. (1990) *Turbulence in World Politics: A Theory of Change and Continuity*. Princeton, N.J.: Princeton University Press.

Rouse, R. (1991) Mexican Migration and the Social Space of Postmodernism, *Diaspora* 2 (2, Spring). 8–23.

Sahlins, M. (1972) *Stone Age Economics*. New York: Aldine.

———. (1981) *Historical Metaphors and Mythical Realities: Structure in the Early History of the Sandwich Islands Kingdom*. Ann Arbor: University of Michigan Press.

———. (1985) *Islands of History*. Chicago: University of Chicago Press.

———. (1992) Goodbye to Tristes Tropes: Ethnography in the Context of Modern World History, The 1992 Ryerson Lecture (April 29), University of Chicago. *The University of Chicago Record*. February 4, 1993.

Said, E. W. (1978) *Orientalism*. New York: Vintage Books.

Salve, N. K. P. (1987) *The Story of the Reliance Cup*. New Delhi: Vikas.

Saraswathi, S. (1974) *Minorities in Madras State: Group Interest in Modern Politics*. Delhi: Impex India.

Sawchuk, K. (1988) A Tale of Inscription/Fashion Statements. In A. and M. Kroker (Eds.) *Body Invaders: Panic Sex in America*. Basingstoke: Macmillan Education.

Schafer, E. (1963) *Golden Peaches of Samarkand: A Study of T'ang Exotics*. Berkeley: University of California Press.

Schieffelin, E. (1985) Performance and the Cultural Construction of Reality: Spirit Seances among a New Guinea People, *American Ethnologist* 12 (4): 707–24.

Schiller, H. (1976) *Communication and Cultural Domination*. White Plains, N.Y.: International Arts and Sciences.

Schudson, M. (1984) *Advertising, the Uneasy Persuasion*. New York: Basic Books.

Scott, J. C. (1985) *Weapons of the Weak: Everyday Forms of Peasant Resistance*. New Haven, Conn.: Yale University Press.

———. (1990) *Domination and the Arts of Resistance: Hidden Transcripts*. New Haven, Conn.: Yale University Press.

Shah, A. M. (1989) Caste and the Intelligentsia, *Hindustan Times* March 24.

Shastri, R., and S. Patil (1982) *Shatak Shatkar* (in Marathi). Bombay: Aditya Prakashan.

Shils, E. (1957) Primordial, Personal, Sacred, and Civil Ties, *British Journal of Sociology* 8 (2): 130–45.

Simmel, G. ([1904] 1957) Fashion, *American Journal of Sociology* 62 (6): 541–58.

Smith, P. (1988) Visiting the Banana Republic. In A. Ross (Ed.) *Universal Abandon? The Politics of Postmodernism*. Minneapolis: University of Minnesota Press.

Smith, R. S. (1985) Rule-By-Records and Rule-By-Reports: Complementary Aspects of the British Imperial Rule of Law, *Contributions to Indian Sociology* 19 (1): 153–76.

Stack, J. F. Jr. (Ed.) (1986) *The Primordial Challenge: Ethnicity in the Contemporary World*. New York: Greenwood Press.

Stewart, S. (1984) *On Longing: Narratives of the Miniature, the Gigantic, the Souvenir, the Collection*. Baltimore: Johns Hopkins University Press.

Sutton, D. S. (1995) Consuming Counterrevolution: The Ritual and Culture of Cannibalism in Wuxuan, Guangxi, China, May to July 1968, *Comparative Studies in Society and History* 37 (1): 136–72.

Tambiah, S. J. (1986) *Sri Lanka: Ethnic Fratricide and the Dismantling of Democracy*. Chicago: University of Chicago Press.

———. (1990) Presidential Address: Reflections on Communal Violence in South Asia, *The Journal of Asian Studies* 49 (4, November): 741–60.

Thapar, R. (1989) Imagined Religious Communities? Ancient History and the Modern Search for a Hindu Identity, *Modern Asian Studies* 23: 209–32.

Thomas, K. (1987) Numeracy in Modern England, *Transactions of the Royal Historical Society* 37 (5th Series): 103–32.

Thompson, E. P. (1967) Time, Work-Discipline and Industrial Capitalism, *Past and Present* 38: 56–97.

Thornton, R. (1988) The Rhetoric of Ethnographic Holism, *Cultural Anthropology* 3 (3, August): 285–303.

Tripathi, S. (1990) Sharjah: A Crass Carnival, *India Today* May 31: 88–91.

Trouillot, M.-R. (1991) Anthropology and the Savage Slot: The Poetics and Politics of Otherness. In R. Fox (Ed.) *Recapturing Anthropology: Working in the Present*. Santa Fe, N.M.: School of American Research.

Turner, T. (1992) Defiant Images: The Kapayo Appropriation of Video, *Anthropology Today* 8 (6): 5–16.

Urban, G., and J. Sherzer (Eds.) (1991) *Nations-States and Indians in Latin America*. Austin: University of Texas Press.

Vachani, L. (1989) Narrative, Pleasure and Ideology in the Hindi Film: An Analysis of the Outsider Formula. M. A. Thesis, Annenberg School of Communication, University of Pennsylvania.

van der Veer, P. (1989) The Power of Detachment: Disciplines of Body and Mind in the Ramanandi Order, *American Ethnologist* 16: 458–70.

———. (1994) *Religious Nationalism: Hindus and Muslims in India*. Berkeley and London: University of California Press.

van Gennep, A. ([1908] 1965) *The Rites of Passage*. London: Kegan Paul.

Veblen, T. (1912) *The Theory of the Leisure Class*. New York: Macmillan.

Wallerstein, I. (1974) *The Modern World System*. (2 Vols.) New York and London: Academic Press.

Warner, M. (1990) *The Letters of the Republic: Publication and the Public Sphere in Eighteenth-Century America*. Cambridge, Mass.: Harvard University Press.

——. (1992) The Mass Public and the Mass Subject. In C. Calhoun (Ed.) *Habermas and the Public Sphere*. Cambridge, Mass.: MIT Press.

Washbrook, D. A. (1976) *The Emergence of Provincial Politics: The Madras Presidency, 1870–1920*. Cambridge and New York: Cambridge University Press.

Williams, R. (1976) *Keywords*. New York: Oxford University Press.

Williams, R. H. (1982) *Dream Worlds: Mass Consumption in Late Nineteenth-Century France*. Berkeley: University of California Press.

Wolf, E. (1982) *Europe and the People without History*. Berkeley: University of California Press.

Yoshimoto, M. (1989) The Postmodern and Mass Images in Japan, *Public Culture* 1 (2): 8–25.

Zarilli, P. (1995) Repositioning the Body: An Indian Martial Art and its Pan-Asian Publics. In C. A. Breckenridge (Ed.) *Consuming Modernity: Public Culture in a South Asian World*. Minneapolis: University of Minnesota Press.

Zolberg, A. R., A. Suhrke, and S. Aguayo. (1989) *Escape from Violence*. New York and Oxford: Oxford University Press.

Index

Compiled by Caitrin Lynch

Balibar, E., 119, 159, 188, 189
Barber, K., 32
Barrier, G. N., 116
Barth, F., 140, 202
Baruah, S., 39
Basch, L., 188
Baudrillard, J., 30, 42, 67, 81
Bauman, R., 187
Bayly, C. A., 28, 73, 125
Bell, R., 6
Benjamin, W., 43
Berlant, L., 169, 170, 174, 176
Bhabha, H. K., 94, 159, 188
Bhattacharjee, A., 197
Birbalsingh, F., 91
Birmingham School, 145
Black Public Sphere Collective, 169
Bloch, M., 183
body: colonial control of Indian, 120, 124, 125, 130, 132; consumption and, 67–68, 74, 83–85; embodied experiences of group identity, 157; enumeration of colonial, 132, 133; in Indian cricket, 103, 104, 112, 113; inscription of locality onto, 14, 67, 112, 179; manipulation, 84, 120; revolt of the Indian, 133, 134; as site of language use and experience, 103; techniques of (*see* techniques, bodily)
Bondurant, J. V., 134
Borges, J. L., 122
Borneman, J., 188
Bosnia Fallacy, 21
Bourdieu, P., 51, 67; bodily hexis and, 111; distinction and, 75; embodiment and, 148; habitus and, 44, 55; improvisation and, 55, 68
Brass, P. R., 141
Braudel, F., 27
break, theory of (*see also* rupture), 3, 9
Breckenridge, C. A., 57, 77, 94, 103, 129, 201, 202
Brewer, J., 66, 115, 117, 125
Briggs, C. L., 187

cadastral politics, 121, 124, 125, 127, 129

Calhoun, C., 161
Campbell, C., 68, 72, 83
Canguilheim, G., 118
capitalism, 6, 27, 32, 73, 175, 204; consumption and, 67, 72, 85; disorganized, 33, 40, 52, 150; electronic, 8, 161; nostalgia and, 30–31, 85; print, 8, 28, 112, 161, 188
Carrithers, M., 52
Cashman, R., 93, 94, 100, 101
caste, 129, 132, 143, 146; classification and, 119; in Indian census, 118, 127–28, 131, 162; and politics of group representation, 114, 130
Castoriadis, C., 145
census, 18, 118, 121, 126, 130, 157, 202; All-India Census, 127–29; British vs. Indian, 117; and caste, 127, 129, 162; communal identity in India and, 98, 114, 128–29, 131; creation of identity in India and, 116, 125, 129
Chakrabarty, D., 116, 202
chaos theory, 46–47, 150, 166
Chatterjee, P., 28, 39, 132, 159, 188
cinema (*see also* film; media; media, mass; television), 4, 53, 64, 77, 153; art, 194; displacement in, 61, 63; as electronic capitalism, 161; imagination and, 53; Indian, 36, 40, 62–63, 101–2, 110, 202; mediascapes and, 40; nostalgia in, 77; as public space, 3, 101
Clarke, A., 94
Clarke, J., 94
class, 198; in censuses, 118; in Indian cricket, 91–92, 94–96, 105; in Victorian cricket, 91, 94, 96
classification, 119, 123, 162
Clifford, J., 58
Cohn, B. S., 98, 116, 120, 126
Collins, S., 52
colonialism (*see also* decolonization), 28, 188; constructed ethnicities and, 28, 98; cricket in English, 93–94, 109; exoticization in, 115, 118, 123, 128; measurement and classification in, 123, 132; nostalgia for, 78; orientalism and, 118, 119, 133–34; quantification

Mintz, S. W., 71

Mitra, A., 111

modernity (see also modernization), 1–3, 17, 142, 204; at large, 19, 23; of ethnicity, 139, 144, 157; indigenization and, 90; means of, 112, 113; migration and, 3; nation-state and, 19; reproduction of locality in, 181; as theory, 2; theory of rupture in, 2, 3, 9; as vernacular globalization, 10; work of imagination and, 3

modernization (see also modernity), 203; democracy and, 141; development and, 10, 20, 144; nation-state and, 2, 9, 10; theory, 2, 3, 6, 9, 11, 19, 31, 140

Money, J., 117

Moore, S. F., 188

Mouffe, C., 145

movements, culturalist (see also reproduction, cultural), 156, 157; culture, culturalism and, 13–16; nation-state and, 15, 146, 147

Mukerji, C., 72

multiculturalism, 15, 22, 199; in England, 143, 146; in United States, 169, 171, 197

Mulvey, L., 84

Munn, N. D., 180

Nair, M., 10, 38, 61, 63

Nandy, A., 39, 52, 90, 92, 96, 106, 141, 203

nationalism (see also ethnicity; nation-state; patriotism; tribalism), 20, 158, 171, 188, 190; cricket nationalism, 91, 99, 107, 109, 112; diasporic, 10, 40, 172, 196; as disease, 19; electronic mediation and, 9, 196; ethnicity and, 139, 162; imagined communities and, 28; long-distance, 22, 196; patriotism and, 159–60; politics of memory in, 155, 156; as primordialism, 21; territory and, 161, 165–66, 171; trojan, 165

nationality, queer, 159, 174, 176

nation-state (see also communities, imagined; nationalism): control over difference, 39, 42, 130, 177; crisis of, 19,

39, 157, 158, 160–61, 169, 179; culturalism of, 146, 147, 156, 157; diasporic public spheres and, 4; end of, 18, 19, 169, 176; global cultural economy and, 39; heritage politics and, 39, 42, 146; homogenization and, 32, 39, 42, 146, 177, 189; human motion and, 4, 156, 157, 191; hyphen in, 19, 39–40, 159, 176; imagination and, 39, 161; as locality, 42; mobilization of identity by, 155–56, 163; monopoly over modernization, 10; neighborhoods and, 190–93, 198; primordialism and, 146, 162; production of locality by, 187, 190–91; production of people and, 119, 159, 176, 189, 191; space and, 189; territory and, 161, 189, 191; transnational destabilization of, 178, 189

Neale, W. C., 125

neighborhoods (see also locality; territory), 164, 180; colonization and, 184, 186; context and, 183–88, 193, 195, 198; cultural reproduction in, 44; definition of, 178, 179; ethnic violence in, 193; ethnoscapes and, 183, 184, 186; imagination and, 7; local, 181; locality and, 179, 182, 199, 204; nation-state and, 190–93, 198; rituals of, 183–84; social, 53; spatial and virtual, 189, 194–98; as translocalities, 192; Yanomami villages as, 185–86

Nicoll, F., 32

Nigam, S., 118

nominalism, dynamic, 116, 125

nongovernmental organizations (NGOs), 168, 190

nostalgia (see also consumption; fantasy; fashion; patina), 165, 196; armchair, 78; and catalogs, 76, 78; consumption and, 85; fantasy and, 77–78, 81–82, 83; fashion and, 76, 77; without memory, 30, 77, 82; for the present, 30, 77; reruns and, 30

number (see also enumeration): in British political imagination, 117; in cadastral politics, 121, 125; in colonial imagination, 117; for colonial and social control, 117, 125, 129; dynamic nominalism of, 125, 132; as form of translation, 126; justificatory and disciplinary role of, 119–21, 125–26; in records and reports, 126

Olympic Games, 4, 8, 60, 167
orientalism (*see also* empiricism, orientalist): colonialism and, 118, 119, 133–34; critiques of area studies and, 16; enumeration in, 115, 129; imagination and, 115
Ortner, S. B., 55, 203

Pandey, G., 98, 127, 128, 130
Pant, R., 127–28
Parfit, D., 52
Parkin, D., 48
Parsons, T., 6, 203
Patil, S., 104
patina (*see also* fashion; nostalgia), 75–76, 78, 82
patriotism (see also nationalism; nation-state; tribalism; violence, ethnic), 124, 176; detached from territory, 21; links with biculturalism, 170; media and, 196; nationalism and, 159–60; social science and, 18–23
Pels, P., 204
Perlin, F., 71, 129
Pierce, C., 69
Pitkin, H. F., 131
place (*see also* displacement; locality; media): imagination and, 53, 58; media and, 29; nationalism and, 161, 166; nation-state and, 189, 191; neighborhood and, 183–86, 188; people, heritage and, 46; ritual and, 183–85
pleasure: agency and, 7, 111; agonistic sport and, 110–11; of consumption, 7, 68, 83; of cosmopolitanism, 2, 112; of ephemerality, 83–84; fashion and, 68; of the gaze, 84; mass media and, 8
Plumb, J. H., 66
political correctness, 171
postnational (*see also* transnation; transnational), 9, 158–59, 164–71,

173–77; ethnic mobilizations, 164; forms of allegiance, 166; heterogeneity and, 23; imagination, 21–22, 177; vs. multinational and international, 167–68; network of diasporas, 171; political world, 22–23; politics, 173; social forms, 158, 167; sodalities, 8
Powers, B. R., 29
Prakash, G., 98, 116, 126
Presler, F. A., 120
Preston, L. W., 126
primordialism (*see also* ethnicity), 139–42, 203; ethnic violence and, 21, 140–41, 144, 149, 153, 156–57; globalization of, 41; modernity and, 140, 144; paradox of constructed, 28; politics of affect and, 144–47, 153; tribalism and, 170
production: and consumer fetishism, 41, 42; of local subjects, 179–81, 185, 187, 190; of locality, 152, 180–82, 185, 189, 192–94; of natives, 179; of people, 119, 159, 176, 189, 191; of space, 178
Proust, M., 76
Puri, N., 90

queer nationality, 159, 174, 176
Quetelet, A., 130

Rabinow, P., 49, 118
Raiji, V., 93
Ranger, T., 41, 145
Ranji, 95–97
Ranjitsinhji. *See* Ranji
refugees, 43, 161, 166, 199; camps and, 6, 167, 191, 192–93; cultural politics of, 45; culturalism and, 15; ethnoscapes and, 33; implosion and, 149; nation-state policies on, 34, 191; in postnational order, 22, 167–68; in transnation, 172–73
religion, 7, 8, 20, 27, 143; in censuses, 118; role in nationalism, 161
reproduction, cultural (*see also* movements, culturalist), 171, 185; deterritorialization and, 37–38, 43–45, 48, 49;

globalized relations of, 51, 198; for
Hindus abroad, 38, 57; motion and,
43–44; standard, 54; tension between
local and global in, 63
resistance, 29, 63, 84, 133, 189; cultural
transactions and, 27; mass media and,
7; to modernization, 140; primordialism and, 140, 145
rites of passage, 68–70, 84, 179–80
ritual, 69; dialogue with imagination, 5,
6, 57; local subjects and, 181, 185; role
in locality, 180–84
Robbins, B., 169
Roberts, M., 91
Robertson, R., 150, 188
Robinson, F., 130
Rojek, C., 79, 83
Rosaldo, R., 58
Rosenau, J., 150, 151, 164, 166, 188
Rouse, R., 188, 204
rupture (see also break, theory of), 121;
relation to nostalgia, 76; theory of, 2,
3, 9
Rushdie, S., 8, 53, 58

Sahlins, M., 69, 72, 185, 188
Said, E., 16, 114–15
Salve, N. K. P., 99, 109
Saraswathi, S., 131
Satanic Verses, The, 8, 53, 58, 59
Saussurean linguistics, 12
Sawchuk, K., 84
Schafer, E., 27, 71
Scher, P., 204
Schieffelin, E., 180
Schiller, H., 32
Schlesinger, L., 202
Schudson, M., 53
Scott, J. C., 145, 149, 189
Shah, A. M., 114, 131
Shastri, R., 104
Sherzer, J., 188
Shils, E., 6, 139, 203
Simmel, G., 50, 75
Smith, P., 78
Smith, R. S., 117, 119, 120–21, 126,
127, 128

sociolinguistics, 187
sociology: colonial, 93, 98; culture concept in, 51; of displacement, 39
space: globalization and, 9; nation-state
and, 189; production of, 178; time
and, 180, 186, 204
Stack, J. F. Jr., 203
Stewart, S., 77
Stoler, A. L., 94
subaltern studies, 145
subjects, local: locality and, 179–80,
188; nation-state and, 190–91, 193,
197; neighborhoods and, 181, 185,
187, 190, 198; ritual and, 181, 185
superorganic, 12
Sutton, D. S., 155, 203

Tambiah, S. J., 141, 149, 150–51, 153, 188
techniques, bodily (see also body), 69, 83;
consumption and, 67–68, 74;
ephemerality and, 84; relation to discipline, 147–48
technoscapes, 33, 34, 35, 37, 40, 45
television (see also cinema; film; media;
media, electronic; media, mass): advertising and consumption, 73, 77, 84;
cinema and, 194; as electronic capitalism, 161; the gaze and, 84; in Indian
cricket, 101, 102, 104, 106, 112;
mediascapes and, 35; migration and, 6;
in postnational political order, 166;
role in imagination, 53
territory (see also deterritorialization;
nation-state; neighborhoods), 70, 98,
125, 186; as alibi for nationalism, 165;
in counternationalisms, 21; nation-
state and, 161, 189, 191; neighborhoods and, 195; politics of cultural reproduction in, 44
Thapar, R., 114
Thomas, K., 117
Thompson, E. P., 17, 79, 82, 145
Thornton, R., 46
time: commodification of, 79, 82; consumption and, 70, 76, 78–79, 85;
space and, 180, 186, 204
Toennies, F., 3, 179

ARJUN APPADURAI is professor of anthropology and of South Asian languages and civilizations at the University of Chicago, where he was previously director of the Chicago Humanities Institute. His many publications include *Worship and Conflict under Colonial Rule* (Cambridge, 1981), *The Social Life of Things* (as editor, Cambridge University Press, 1986), and *Gender, Genre and Power* (as coeditor, University of Pennsylvania Press, 1991). He is the director of the Globalization Project at the University of Chicago and is currently researching the relation between ethnic violence and images of territory in modern nation-states.